Hither Shore

Interdisciplinary Journal
on Modern Fantasy Literature

Jahrbuch der
Deutschen Tolkien Gesellschaft e. V.

Tolkien's *Philosophy of Language*

Interdisziplinäres Seminar der DTG
6. bis 8. Mai 2016, Jena

Herausgegeben von:
Thomas Fornet-Ponse (Gesamtleitung),
Thomas Honegger, Julian T.M. Eilmann

SCRIPTORIUM OXONIAE

Bibliografische Information
der Deutschen Bibliothek

Die Deutsche Bibliothek verzeichnet diese
Publikation in der Deutschen Nationalbibliografie;
detaillierte bibliografische Daten sind im
Internet über http://dnb.ddb.de abrufbar.

ISBN 978-3-9818313-1-3

Hither Shore, DTG-Jahrbuch 2016
veröffentlicht im Verlag »Scriptorium Oxoniae«

Deutsche Tolkien Gesellschaft e. V. (DTG)
E-Mail: info@tolkiengesellschaft.de

Scriptorium Oxoniae im atelier für TEXTaufgaben e. K.
Brehmstraße 50 · 40239 Düsseldorf · Germany
E-Mail: rayermann@scriptorium-oxoniae.de

Hither Shore, Gesamtleitung: Thomas Fornet-Ponse
E-Mail: hither-shore@tolkiengesellschaft.de

Vorschläge für Beiträge in deutscher oder englischer Sprache (inklusive
Exposé von ca. 100 Wörtern) werden erbeten an o.g. E-Mail-Adresse.

Abwicklung: Susanne A. Rayermann, Düsseldorf
Layout/Design: Kathrin Bondzio, Solingen
Umschlagillustration: Anke Eißmann, Herborn
Druck und Vertrieb: Books on Demand, Norderstedt

Inhalt

Additional Essay

Reviews/Rezensionen

Preface

In view of Tolkien's own assessment of the linguistic character of his oeuvre and the importance of the languages he invented for it—an act he described as the work's basis in a letter from June 1955 (cf. *Letters* 289)—and the increasing research into the field, for example by Dimitra Fimi or John Garth, the topic of "Tolkien's Philosophy of Language" was an apt choice for the 13th Tolkien Seminar of the German Tolkien Society DTG.

Attracting a high number of international participants and speakers again, the topic was analysed from diverse angles across Tolkien's whole oeuvre in May 2016 in Jena. The relatively small number of lectures can be attributed to the specificity of the topic, which did however not lessen the number of conference guests.

Starting with more introductory contributions on Tolkien's linguistic philosophy or the relationship between language and world view, moving on to the analysis of specific names and their meaning or to the narrative function of languages, the Seminar showed again—particularly in the extensive discussions after the lectures—how complex Tolkien's work is. It also confirmed that with such a conference and such a publication insights, maybe even representative ones, can be conveyed, alongside impetus for further research, without claiming to have fully exhausted the topic.

Apart from the articles on the Seminar's topic (including a contribution by an author who could not make it to the conference), this volume additionally includes an article on understanding the *Lord of the Rings* musical as a fairy story as well as the usual reviews of new secondary literature.

The tried and tested cooperation with Prof. Dr. Thomas Honegger and his team at the Friedrich-Schiller-University in Jena was again *conditio sine qua non* for a successful Tolkien Seminar. I would like to thank him as well as *Walking Tree Publishers* for their kind support. Further thanks are due to all authors, co-editors, Marie-Noëlle Biemer for translations and corrections of English texts as well as our publisher's team Susanne A. Rayermann and Kathrin Bondzio, so that the 13th volume of *Hither Shore* could be published.

Thomas Fornet-Ponse

Vorwort

Angesichts der Bedeutung, die Tolkien selbst dem linguistischen Charakter seines Werkes und den von ihm erfundenen Sprachen für dieses beimaß, wenn er beispielsweise in einem Brief vom Juni 1955 die Erfindung der Sprache als Fundament bezeichnet (vgl. Briefe 289), und der zunehmenden Erforschung dieser Fragestellung z.b. durch Dimitra Fimi oder John Garth, war es sehr angemessen, das 13. Tolkien Seminar der Deutschen Tolkien Gesellschaft Tolkiens Philosophie der Sprache zu widmen.

So wurde dieses Thema im Mai 2016 in Jena unter wieder einmal erfreulich hoher internationaler Beteiligung in einer großen Vielfalt an Themen und mit Bezug auf das gesamte Werk Tolkiens in den Blick genommen. Die im Vergleich zu einigen Vorjahren geringere Anzahl an Vorträgen dürfte auf die speziellere Thematik zurückzuführen sein, die indes nicht zu einer geringeren Teilnahme am Seminar geführt hat.

Beginnend mit eher einführenden Beiträgen zu Tolkiens Sprachphilosophie oder dem Zusammenhang von Sprache und Weltanschauung über Untersuchungen von Namen sowie ihrer Bedeutung bis hin zur narrativen Funktion der Sprachen hat sich wieder einmal – gerade auch in den ausführlichen Diskussionen im Anschluss an die Vorträge und darüber hinaus – gezeigt, wie vielschichtig das Werk Tolkiens ist und dass in einem solchen Seminar und mit einer solchen Publikation einige – vielleicht sogar repräsentative – Einsichten vermittelt und viele Anregungen für die weitere Erforschung gegeben werden können, ohne zu beanspruchen, die Thematik erschöpfend behandelt zu haben.

Neben den Beiträgen zur Seminarthematik (unter Aufnahme eines Beitrags eines beim Seminar verhinderten Autors) enthält dieser Band einen zusätzlichen Beitrag zum Verständnis des Musicals zum *Lord of the Rings* als Fairy-story und wie üblich einige Rezensionen zur neueren Sekundärliteratur.

Ein weiteres Mal war die gute und bewährte Zusammenarbeit mit Prof. Dr. Thomas Honegger und seinem Team von der Friedrich-Schiller-Universität Jena conditio sine qua non für ein erfolgreiches Seminar. Dafür danke ich ihm herzlich ebenso wie dem Verlag *Walking Tree Publishers* für die freundliche und tatkräftige Unterstützung. Darüber hinaus sei allen Beitragenden, den Mitherausgebern, Marie-Noëlle Biemer für die Übersetzungen und Korrekturen englischer Fassungen sowie schließlich der Verlegerin Susanne A. Rayermann und Kathrin Bondzio für die Gestaltung gedankt, sodass nun auch ein dreizehnter Band von *Hither Shore* erscheinen kann.

Thomas Fornet-Ponse

"A Natural Product of our Humanity": Tolkien's Philosophy of Language

Ross Smith (Madrid)

The full quotation of the words included in this title is: "Language—and more so as expression than as communication—is a natural product of our humanity" (MC 190). These words encapsulate two of Tolkien's fundamental linguistic principles, namely that the expressive, emotional, creative side of language is at least as important as its communicative function, and that language is inextricably bound to our identity as human beings.

A good starting point for a paper about a famous academic's Philosophy of Language is to define what we mean by "philosophy" in this context. The *Concise Oxford English Dictionary* offers the following as the second option under this entry: "a set of theories of a particular philosopher". It is likely that Tolkien would not be too happy with the word "philosopher", regarding himself first and foremost as a "philologist" (see Shippey on this distinction), but otherwise the definition is acceptable. The focus of this paper is therefore to analyse the distinct theories that together can be viewed as Tolkien's overall philosophy on the subject of human speech.

When we examine the separate strands of thought that can be said to make up a coherent theory of language in Tolkien, two fundamental concepts come to mind, these being the centrality of words to our sense of community, and the centrality of word-sound to meaning. In other words, the question of how language relates to the social, geographical and historical scope of a given human community, and how the sounds of a language are an essential component of the meaning of words.

Native Language

The first of these components, i.e. language as a fundamental factor in the human community, brings us to Tolkien's notion of what he called "native language". As has been noted by a number of scholars, Tolkien's idea of a "native language" did not coincide with what is ordinarily meant by this term, perhaps even more nowadays than when he wrote, with the concept of "native speaker" being an established part of our modern language-learning vocabulary. Tolkien was not referring to the language people learn as infants, the language of their parents and community, but rather to an individual, inherited linguistic identity. As he said in his much-cited paper *English and Welsh*: "We each have our own personal linguistic potential; we each have a native language" (MC 190). Elsewhere he uses the phrases "inherent linguistic predilections" and "native linguistic potential", as well as "the individual's innate linguistic taste", to try to convey what he means. In essence, when he uses the term "native language" Tolkien is trying to express, in terms understandable to the rest of us, what he himself had felt on the profoundest level at various stages of his own life, with respect to an essential identification he noted between certain languages, or dialects, and his own innermost sensations.

Two salient examples of this in Tolkien's case are the Middle-English dialect of the region of England historically known as Mercia, and the Welsh language. There are numerous references in Tolkien's papers and letters (see Hemmi) to the strong identification he felt with the West-Midlands area of England, which borders on Wales, and a commensurate identification with the language historically spoken in that part of the world. In one of his letters (to the great English poet W.H. Auden), he even goes as far as to say: "I am a West-midlander by blood (and took to early west-midland Middle English as a known tongue as soon as I set eyes on it)" (L 213). Tolkien is therefore suggesting that there was a special bond between his cultural sensitivity, his sense of his own place in the world, and the dialect of English spoken in that geographical location many centuries earlier, to such an extent that merely seeing the language written was enough to understand it, despite the intervening centuries. This, then, is the essence of "native language"; an innate empathy with a given tongue, the stirring of "deep harp-strings" when one comes into contact with its phonemes.

Better known is Tolkien's infatuation with the Welsh language, which he remarked had its origin in words written in Welsh on the sides of the coal trucks that passed along the roads of his childhood countryside en route from the mines in Wales to the rest of Britain. Tolkien's love of Welsh and how he used it in his invented languages is well documented and requires no further elaboration here; what is of particular interest for our purposes is the relation between Welsh and Tolkien's notion of native language. As mentioned above, Tolkien's childhood home was close to the Welsh border and in his philological mind the ancient roots of English and Welsh mingled in that frontier space: there was a "constant reflection, in the Welsh borrowing of older date, of the forms of West-Midland English" (MC 189). Further references are made to this linguistic melange, including Old Mercian and some ancient Norse, in his stories *The Lost Road* and *The Notion Club Papers*. As time went by, Tolkien's identification of his own "native language" pushed further back in time to the lost tongue that lay behind the Welsh that he found so attractive, this being the ancient Celtic language—British or Brittonic—spoken in England before it was obliterated by the successive conquests of Romans, Angles, Saxons and Danes. Welsh, along with Cornish and Breton, is a neo-Brittonic language; to get to the essence of his aesthetic predilections, therefore, Tolkien felt he had to go to the source. He sums up his feeling about the deep-rooted Welsh and extinct Brittonic tongue in the following terms:

> For many of us it rings a bell, or rather it stirs deep harp-strings in
> our linguistic nature. In other words: for satisfaction and therefore
> for delight—and not for imperial policy—we are still 'British' at
> heart. It is the native language to which in unexplored desire we
> would still go home.   (MC 194)

As mentioned above, in all these references to the concept of "native language",
Tolkien is trying to communicate to us exactly what he felt when he came into
contact with certain languages. He is not trying in any way to "prove" that we
all have a native language, since he knew that would be impossible, but he does
suggest that there is something in all of us that, if given the chance, will resonate
deeply with a specific tongue or dialect. And indeed, Tolkien himself wished
to give his readers that chance, by including in *The Lord of the Rings* names
of characters and sites that were "mainly composed on patterns deliberately
modelled on those of Welsh". Yet Tolkien's love of the ancient Celtic language
of southern Britain goes beyond the merely linguistic, or even aesthetic: there
is a very powerful emotional component as well, which is intimately linked
with the idea of "home". In the above quote he says that our native language is
the one to which we "would still go home" and the notion of home repeatedly
comes up in Tolkien's discussion of native language. In reality, his overarching
concept combines language, people and place. As he said of Welsh: "Welsh is
of this soil, this island, the senior language of the men of Britain" (MC 189).
Thus, British soil, the island of Britain, and especially its southern half, mingles
with the language and the folk.

   This is an essential factor of the psychological aspects that underlie Tolkien's
theory of language in this specific area. As is well known, Tolkien was not born
in the UK but in South Africa, which is where he spent his early childhood.
This fact seems to have caused him a certain amount of existentialist discomfort during his lifetime and he felt obliged, as if seeing himself as an outsider,
to make repeated affirmations in his letters and work concerning his love of
England, of the English countryside, of English culture and of Englishness
in general. He famously said that he wanted to create a new mythology "for
England; for my country" (S xii). He was even prepared to define himself by
exclusion, saying in a letter to his son Christopher (L 53): "For I love England
(not Great Britain and certainly not the British Commonwealth)". Fortunately
for his non-English admirers, Tolkien was prepared to be a bit more generous
in relation to the ideal climate for his personal mythology:

> It should possess the tone and quality that I desired, somewhat cool
> and clear, be redolent of our 'air' (the clime and soil of the North
> West, meaning Britain and the hither parts of Europe).   (S xii)

In *English and Welsh* he also refers to the "north-west of Europe" in positive terms as regards its ancient Norse and Germanic tongues, saying that with so many linguistic and cultural interconnections it can be regarded as a single philological province.

Therefore, Tolkien's native language and personal linguistic predilection was clearly delimited geographically, to Wales and the bordering zone of middle England, at its most restrictive, and north-western Europe at its most expansive, and this evidently coincides with the location where he felt especially "at home". He considered that everyone had a native language even if it is in a dormant condition, and evidently one's native language varies depending on one's ancestry. As a component of his linguistic philosophy, we can say that the idea of "native language" reflects Tolkien's belief that a people, their language, their country and their mythology form a whole which goes back to the most distant past and which, though perhaps only faintly, can still pluck at the strings of our emotions even without our knowing exactly why. As mentioned above, he hoped that these distant resonances would be felt by the readers of his fiction through the use of names derived from an ancient Celtic tongue and he was prepared to cite songs, poems and exclamations in languages that presumably none of his readers could possibly know but which he hoped would be comprehensible to them on a level deeper than that of ordinary linguistic meaning.

The use of Sindarin and Quenya in *The Lord of the Rings* is in some ways a philological experiment in linguistic perception and aesthetics, the outcome of which, on the basis of the available evidence, was very satisfactory. The reactions of the readers of the early editions of *The Lord of the Rings* in the 1950s and 1960s ranged from comments simply mentioning how nice Elvish sounded to requests for detailed explanations of the languages' grammar and phonology. Whether or not Tolkien's readers—in those days, English speakers mainly from a similar cultural background to the author—were actually tuning in to their own "native language" is hard to ascertain, but it is certainly one possible explanation of the success of Tolkien's daring decision to expose his readers to untranslated art languages.

The Elvish that is sprinkled through Tolkien's fiction provokes a reaction not only in readers, but also in the characters themselves. When Frodo, Sam and Pippin first hear the Elves singing in the woods of the Shire, the following happens:

> One clear voice rose now above the others. It was singing in the fair elven tongue, of which Frodo knew only a little, and the others knew nothing. Yet the sound blending with the melody seemed to shape itself in their thoughts into words which they only partly understood.   (LotR 79)

In other words: Even though the Hobbits had no prior knowledge of Elvish, they could partly understand the language. Quite possibly the Hobbits are having an experience which is parallel to the book's English readers; in the latter case, Tolkien's choice of phonemes evokes a distant memory of Celtic British, while for the Hobbits, the sound of Elvish evokes echoes of the origin of their own tongue. Whatever the case, Elvish has a powerful impact on the Hobbits, so powerful in fact that in moments of extreme danger both Frodo and Sam suddenly quote entire passages of Sindarin or Quenya. In Sam's case, this happens when he is confronted, alone, by the monstrous Shelob and the power to utter Sindarin seems somehow to come upon him when he seizes the shining Phial of Galadriel. For his part, and also feeling inspired by Galadriel, Frodo cries an invocation to the elvish hero Eärendil in Quenya to raise his own courage and dismay his enemy. In both cases, we are explicitly told by the narrator that neither of them knew the language they had spoken.

How, we might ask, is this possible? I think the answer is that in our world, it isn't, but in a sub-created world, these things can be allowed to happen, perhaps as a testimony to the special power of the Elves and the languages they spoke. Tolkien vaguely suggested that Sam and Frodo might be repeating Elvish phrases that had subliminally entered their memories during their sojourns among the Elves at Rivendell and Lothlórien, but he seems to accept that there really is no "logical" explanation: a case of Elvish magic, as Sam might have said.

In any event, J.R.R. Tolkien was not the only 20th century British author to include the idea of a primeval language, understandable on a purely intuitive level, in his fiction. In 1951, three years before the publication of *The Fellowship of the Ring*, the Anglo-Welsh author John Cowper Powys, who like Tolkien was deeply interested in mythology and made it a cornerstone of his literary creations, published his great novel *Porius*, which is set in Wales during the post-Roman period of British history. Cowper Powys also loved the sound of Welsh and included Welsh terms in *Porius* rather like Tolkien included Elvish words in the *Lord of the Rings*, in order to provide it with a kind of ethnic credibility and depth. He too assumed his readers would not understand any of it. But in addition to Welsh, *Porius* contains other linguistic variants, one of which is the Language of the Giants.

In *Porius*, the original inhabitants of the land are Giants, called the Cewri, and their language is both ancient and magical, and is known only to those with special powers (specifically, Merlin, known here as *Myrddin Wyllt*, and the Druid of the indigenous British people). The central character, the Brythonic prince Porius, learns a few words of the language from one of the Druid's acolytes. One phrase he memorises is *Tungerong larry ong*, which means "endure until the end" (Powys 465), and this becomes Porius's secret mantra or war cry, to fall back on for courage or clarity of mind, rather like Frodo and Sam in their use of Elvish. The language has special attributes: "certainly there did seem to be some occult power in the sound of these words" (Powys 469), and in some cases Porius finds himself "remembering" Cewri words he did not know that he knew: "Out of some lost chasm in his memory this queer word scrabbled forth, like an Avanc roused from sleep." It seems that Cowper Powys's mythological thinking had led him, in this case, down the same path as Tolkien, at much the same historical moment.

Another writer who is worth mentioning in this context is the Irish poet Seamus Heaney. In the preface to his famous translation of *Beowulf* Heaney speaks glowingly of Tolkien's Beowulfian scholarship, and tells us about his own experience of working with Old English and translating alliterative verse. There is a curious passage in which the poet tells us of his reasons for struggling on with the project to translate *Beowulf* despite the many difficulties involved:

> I had noticed, for example, that without any conscious intent on
> my part certain lines in the first poem in my first book confor-
> med to the requirements of Anglo-Saxon metrics ... Part of me,
> in other words, had been writing Anglo-Saxon from the start.
>
> (Heaney xxiii)

This is reminiscent to some extent of Tolkien's comments about his instinctive empathy with Mercian Middle-English; it is almost as if these ancient languages were there waiting to be discovered, and esteemed, by these two poets.

In fact, one of Heaney's poems, called *Bone Dreams*, deals precisely with this subject. In it, Heaney describes the powerful feelings provoked by the sound of Old English, particularly the well-known kenning *bān-hūs*, i.e. "bone house" (human body): he takes us on a philological journey back in time, through flowery Middle English, past the Churchmen's Latin, to the "scop's twang, the iron flash of consonants cleaving the line:

> In the coffered
> riches of grammar
> and declensions
> I found bān-hūs,
>
> its fire, benches,
> wattle and rafters,
> where the soul
> fluttered a while

Viewed in the context of the present essay, it seems that Heaney might be telling us that his "native language"—or at least one of his native languages—is Old English. Heaney spoke English and Irish and was emotionally connected to both languages. Tolkien does not tell us whether the same person can have more than one "native language", but perhaps this is possible in the case of people that have inherited two linguistic traditions. Or perhaps Heaney's "iron flash of consonants" goes beyond both Old English and ancient Gaelic, and back to some Celtic predecessor of both.

Whatever the case, I can understand Heaney's preferences. The question of whether one has or not a native language is evidently rather difficult to demonstrate in any analytical way, but on a personal level I share Heaney's empathy with sounds that have come down through the centuries from the days of *Beowulf*. Words of ancient Germanic origin containing long vowels, such as 'dawn', 'dale', 'brew', 'strode', 'cove', or 'cleave' make those distant "harp-stings" vibrate in my own emotional reactions, and I honestly cannot say why, unless it is due to the influence of reading *The Hobbit* as a child and *The Lord of the Rings* many times since. If that is the explanation, then in my particular case Tolkien certainly achieved his aim.

Phonetic Fitness

Another essential reason why Tolkien's stories are so well loved is his unique and brilliant use of sound-symbolism. To Tolkien, sound-symbolism was not a theory, but an absolute reality. The link between meaning and sound was the foundation of his invented languages and an essential part of his linguistic beliefs. He repeated this idea in many of his papers and letters, and with particular clarity in *A Secret Vice*, when he said, among other things: "I am personally more interested perhaps in word-form in itself, and in word-form in relation to meaning (so-called phonetic fitness) than in any other department" (MC 211). The notion that the meaning and the sound of a word should be intrinsically linked provided the basis for Tolkien's choices when creating the lexicon for his Elvish languages, but his desire that sound should reflect meaning was present in his choices of English (or Westron) words as well, particularly with regard to names, as we shall see below.

We must bear in mind that Tolkien created new words and whole languages because he really enjoyed it, and the principal element of enjoyment was the phonetic and aesthetic link between sound and meaning: "Certainly, it is the contemplation of the relation between sound and notion which is the main source of pleasure" (MC 206). Tolkien recognised that he had an "acute sensibility" in this area and the invention of aesthetically pleasing languages was a way for him to find a practical outlet for his phonosemantic gifts. And as a by-product of his hobby, the general reading public has been able to enjoy fictional creations in which the attention given to individual word sound and shape is taken to a wholly new level.

Tolkien's ideas about phonetic fitness, as they were expressed in his papers and publications during the 1930s and 1940s, were very unorthodox[1]. Tolkien knew this and felt rather embarrassed about it: he even called one of the papers which described his ideas as "absurd" (MC 203). His enthusiastic but uncertain attitude towards this subject can be seen clearly in a draft paper on sound symbolism discovered among his working papers and published in 2016 by the Cardiff University scholars Dimitra Fimi and Andrew Higgins under the title "Essay on Phonetic Symbolism" in their book *A Secret Vice: Tolkien on Invented Languages*. The "essay" dates back to the early 1930s, the same period during which *A Secret Vice* was first read to the members of the Johnson Society in Oxford. The document seems to be an initial approach to a description of what Tolkien refers to as "phonetic symbolism" (a term probably taken from Edward Sapir) and also includes an early reference to his notions about native language in the guise of what he calls "phonetic predilection". To judge by the very tentative, unpolished nature of the paper, however, he abandoned this project at an early stage and concentrated instead on the more specific and personal subject of his own linguistic inventions (eventually leading to *A Secret Vice*).

This lack of clarity is unequivocally reflected in the opening words of Tolkien's paper: "Phonetic symbolism: what is meant? I don't know. What do I mean?" It seems that Tolkien wanted to put forward a coherent theory of phonosemantics to support his own belief that sound symbolism is a reality. He states this belief firmly: "I must say that I believe there is such a thing as phonetic symbolism." However, he finds it difficult to pin down: "[I]t becomes vague and less susceptible of analysis or demonstration the more general (the more means: human) you try to make it… It is like trying to find pure water."

One reason why Tolkien found it difficult to stake out the limits of a coherent account of sound symbolism might be that he started off from the hardest angle of all, this being to identify examples of phonetic equivalence across different languages. Roman Jakobson also researched sound symbolism using multiple linguistic sources but most linguists have used the vocabulary of a single language to support their theories, which is considerably easier than taking a multilingual approach. Tolkien also seems to have been disheartened by the fact that counter-examples are almost always at hand (e.g. teeny, tiny, little; but also small, minute, etc.). Modern researchers of phonosemantics accept this lack of universality as inevitable because the lexis of a language derives from many sources, not just from phonetic suitability. However, it seemed to exasperate Tolkien ("like trying to find pure water") and probably explains why

---

[1]   See Smith for a description of Tolkien's ideas on linguistic aesthetics in a historical context.

he never published this particular essay, or any other work explicitly devoted to this topic. Instead, he chose to present his ideas on sound symbolism and phonetic predilection more surreptitiously, as mere components of the broader themes of language invention (in *A Secret Vice*) and linguistic aesthetics (in *English and Welsh*). It is also likely that he was reluctant to publicly challenge what was at the time regarded as an undeniable truth, i.e. that word-sound was entirely arbitrary, largely due to the influence of the Swiss linguist Ferdinand de Saussure.

Saussure insisted that the linguistic sign (word) was completely unrelated to the referent (what the word refers to). In his opinion, this was the first principle of linguistic study and so important that it should be regarded as "the organising principle for the whole of linguistics". In general terms, one has to agree with Saussure that many common words do not seem to bear any relation to the things they refer to (table, chair, pencil, wall, paper, etc.). However, to lay this down as an unbreakable rule is questionable and Tolkien was not the only scholar to dismiss Saussure's insistence on this matter: the great 20th century linguists Otto Jespersen, Edward Sapir and Roman Jakobson all believed in the existence of sound symbolism, and they conducted research and devised tests to support their arguments, noting how different emotional values were given by participants to words containing contrasting phonemes. In fact, over the course of the last century the weight of opinion seems to have gradually shifted from an outright rejection of any relationship between sound and meaning (the Saussure approach) to a sometimes grudging acceptance that, at least in certain cases, word-form and meaning are interdependent.

An interesting example of this change of approach is to be seen in the work of Steven Pinker. Pinker is perhaps the best-known linguist and neuroscientist of the last thirty years in the English-speaking world, and was originally a disciple of the great Noam Chomsky, who was also dismissive of the claims of phonosemantics. Steven Pinker became famous almost overnight through an extremely influential book published in 1994 called *The Language Instinct,* in which he provided, in terms understandable to the non-specialist, an extensive defence of Chomsky's notions concerning "universal grammar" and an inherent capacity for language learning in humans. Following the classic Saussurean line, Pinker actually states the following in *The Language Instinct* in relation to sound symbolism: "Since a word is a pure symbol, the relation between its sound and its meaning is utterly arbitrary" (Pinker 152). There does not seem to be any room for doubt there.

Now we should fast-forward to 2007, the year in which Pinker published another non-fiction best-seller called *The Stuff of Thought*. Astonishingly, despite his total dismissal of phonetic fitness in his first book, in his new work Pinker devoted a whole six pages to the subject! We should not expect an open admission of error from Pinker on this subject, as doing so would effectively undermine the line of argument taken in his own previous books. However, it is absolutely clear that during the 13 year period elapsing from one publication to the other, Pinker's ideas had changed fundamentally, from an outright rejection of any link between word-sound and meaning to an acceptance of a demonstrable relationship in this respect.

Thankfully, therefore, the theoretical linguistics community seems to be coming round to accepting a viewpoint which, in Tolkien's opinion, was absolutely obvious from the start. The reason for this about-turn, we can imagine, is simply the weight of evidence piled up by linguists and cognitive researchers, from Jespersen through Jakobson to modern scholars such as Margaret Magnus and Cynthia Whissel, and scientists like Vilayanur Ramachandran, who in their own way have arrived at the same conclusions as Tolkien concerning sound and meaning. One of the most famous figures in modern English language studies, Professor David Crystal, has also argued in favour of the existence of sound symbolism. In his monumental work *The Cambridge Encyclopaedia of Language*, Crystal treats phonetic fitness as being a self-evident fact, and informs us that English is actually a pretty poor language in this respect compared with, say, Korean or Japanese. The evidence in favour of The Professor continues to accumulate thanks to research such as that of the phonologist and Elvish specialist Matthew Coombes, whose investigations clearly back the idea that people's emotional responses differ according to the sound of the words they hear (see Coombes). We are inclined to agree with Jespersen, therefore, when he said: "There is no denying that there are words which we feel instinctively to be adequate to express the ideas they stand for" (397).

In this respect, a convincing example in favour of the validity of phonosemantics is the manner in which a certain insect is named in a number of languages, which brings us back to Tolkien and his intuitive sensitivity to linguistic aesthetics.

Wilwarin is Tolkien's Elvish name for the creature known in English as a butterfly. In Quenya, *wilwa* means "fluttering to and fro" and *wilwarin* is a derivative noun. The stem, therefore, is *wilwa*, which describes an action, and the suffix *rin* is added to create a noun denoting a creature that habitually moves in such a manner, just as in English we add *er* to a verb to make the corresponding noun (run-runner, drive-driver, etc.). In English, therefore, under Tolkien's system, if *wilwa* equates to "flutter", then *wilwarin* would be "flutterer". From a phonosemantic viewpoint, the phonemes in *wilwa* and *wilwarin* have evidently been chosen with care. The source verb *wilwa*, as Tolkien tells us, indicates a "fluttering to and fro" action, i.e. a repetitive up-and-down or side-to-side action. The two phonetically similar syllables (*wi* and *wa*) are used deliberately to reflect the repetitive nature of the action. This is a very clear example of sound-symbolism in action, and interestingly it is not restricted by any means to Tolkien's invented tongues.

Quite the opposite: we can observe that a duplication of similar sounding syllables is used in various languages to denote the insect in question, starting with Welsh, so dearly loved by Tolkien, in which butterfly is "pili-pala". Other instances are:

> Basque: *tximeleta*
> Catalan: *papallona*
> Filipino: *paruparo*
> Hawaiian: *lepelepe*
> Hebrew: רפרפ
> Indonesian: *kupu-kupu*
> Italian: *farfalla*
> Malay: *rama-rama*
> Portuguese: *borboleta*
> Yoruba: *labalaba*

There are more examples, but these should be sufficient to evidence that, due simply to humanity's "inherent predilections", there is a tendency to repeat identical or similar vowel sounds in the words created to designate butterflies in languages all over the world, apparently due to the way they move when they fly. To show that this is no mere coincidence, let us look at the words for "ant" in the above languages:

> Basque: *innuri*
> Catalan: *formiga*
> Filipino: *guyam*
> Hawaiian: *puamauu*
> Hebrew: הלמנ
> Indonesian: *semut*
> Italian: *formica*
> Malay: *semut*
> Portuguese: *formiga*
> Yoruba: *kokoro*

With the exception of Yoruba, no phoneme duplication is to be observed. And in case anyone is wondering, the Welsh for ant is "morgrugyn".

In his review of *The Fellowship of the Ring*, the English poet W.H. Auden remarked that Tolkien "had an amazing gift for naming" and the names given to the characters and places in Tolkien's fiction is one of its most memorable aspects for countless readers. Many of these names in fact are taken from ancient Germanic and Norse sources, as is well known, while others are invented by the author. In a very long story with a large number of characters, this facility for inventing, or "finding", memorable names happens to be very useful for readers as it makes it easier to remember who is who, and helps to make Tolkien's great works of fiction more manageable. The fact that the names seem so well suited to the characters or places they denote is evidently an example of the effectiveness of phonetic fitness.

As an example, we can look at the names given to two beings that figure in *The Hobbit* and *The Lord of the Rings*, and their descriptions by the author.

We originally meet the first character inside a tunnel in *The Hobbit*, and the narrator describes him as being "a small slimy creature… as dark as darkness, except for two big round pale eyes in his thin face." The second character is to be found early on in *The Fellowship of the Ring*, and is described thus: "He had a blue coat and a long brown beard; his eyes were blue and bright, and his face was red as a ripe apple, but creased into a hundred wrinkles of laughter."

One of these personages is called Tom Bombadil, and the other Gollum. Could be any doubt which is which, even for a person completely unfamiliar with Tolkien's work?

Aesthetic, and even ethical, considerations are of considerable importance in Tolkien's choice of names. As the Norwegian scholar Lykke Guanio-Uluru has noted with regard to *The Lord of the Rings*: "To a great extent in this text, what *sounds* good, *is* good (Lothe 233; her emphasis). Tolkien wanted his beautiful characters to sound beautiful (e.g. the elves Galadriel and Arwen) and his ugly characters to sound ugly (like the orcs Shagrat and Gorbag); but furthermore, he wanted his good people and places to sound good, and the evil creatures and places to sound bad. He achieved this through a careful selection of phonemes and syllables, as we shall see in the following examples.

From an objective standpoint, the place names "Imladris" and "Gorgoroth" are rather similar. They both contain three syllables, three vowels and five consonants. However, their impact on the aesthetic linguistic reception centres in our minds is very different. Imladris sounds like a pleasant kind of place, while Gorgoroth sounds somewhat sinister. In Tolkien's system of phonological values, which coincides with the general perception of sounds among native English speakers (in the UK and US at least), the higher sounding front vowels (/i/, /e/, /i:/, as in "bit", "bet", "beet" in standard English) are regarded as light, attractive and positive, while the back vowels, such as /o/ and /u/, are generally regarded as dark, unattractive and negative. In addition, the /l/ phoneme is positive (Tolkien specifically mentions his fondness for this consonant in the "essay on phonetic symbolism" referred to earlier), while the hard /g/ sound is negative. "Gorgoroth" contains a "negative" vowel sound repeated three times and a "negative" consonant twice, while "Imladris" contains the more airy and pleasant /l/ and the more positive sounding /i/ and /æ/. It is therefore not difficult to ascertain which word relates to a delightful wooded valley inhabited by Elves, and which to a war-scarred wasteland in the shadow of Mount Doom.

It is interesting to note here that, in Tolkien's system, it is not only the vowel that matters, but also the consonant to which it is attached. In a number of Tolkien's names and words, we can see that, for instance, the combination "g + front vowel" is good, while "g + back vowel" is bad. Thus, we have, on the good side, Galadriel, Gandalf, Gimli, and on the bad, Gollum, Morgul and Gorbag. Something similar happens with /l/: if combined with a front vowel (Elrond, Galadriel, Gimli, Legolas) it is positive, while if combined with a back vowel it is negative (Lugburz, Morgul, Nazgûl, Gollum). The elvish heroes Galadriel and Gil-galad enjoy both these positive options, leaving no doubt as to whose side they are on.

This distinction between front and back vowels and the emotional impact of certain consonants is again noteworthy in the names of the dwarves in *The Hobbit*. As Tolkien himself tells us in one of his early letters following the publication of *The Hobbit* (L 25), the dwarves' names are mostly taken from an ancient Icelandic source (the *Elder Edda*), but it was Tolkien that decided what character each of the dwarves was to have. We should not be surprised, therefore, when we confirm that Fili and Kili, whose names include high front vowels and the light /l/, are young, keen, sharp-eyed and musically talented, while Bombur, with a plosive /b/ that often relates to rather undistinguished concepts, as well as two low back vowels, is middle-aged, fat, slow and unhelpful. It is interesting to note in this connection that in Tolkien's entire legendarium, as far as I have been able to ascertain, there are only two Elves whose names contain the "bo" combination, namely Celeborn and Celebrimbor, while among the non-elvish cast the "bo" syllable appears in numerous cases (including the high-profile characters Bilbo and Boromir).

This matter can be analysed almost endlessly in Tolkien's work, but the above examples are sufficient to illustrate his method. Being especially sensitive with respect to the aesthetic aspects of language, Tolkien knew all these associations instinctively. But scientific research comes up with the same observations: numerous experiments show that the higher front vowels and the lower back vowels carry opposing connotations, while the varying types of consonant (plosive, fricative, etc.) elicit differing reactions from listeners[2]. Tolkien's genius was to weave these subconscious reactions into his narrative, enriching the experience for his readers.

Conclusion

This essay does not purport to be an all-encompassing description of Tolkien's linguistic theories, since there are other elements—such as the importance of myth—that would need to be taken into account in a full analysis (see Smith; Verlyn Flieger in Arduini). Having said that, there can be

---

2   See, for instance, tests by E. Sapir and V.S. Ramachandran described in Smith 2011, as well as a detailed account in Coombes.

no doubt that phonetic fitness and what we might call hereditary linguistic predilection were essential factors in Tolkien's philosophy of language. They were the subject of his most heart-felt writings on language, in which he was willing to communicate his theories in this regard to his fellow-scholars even at the risk of facing ridicule. It is important to note that, in his lifetime, Tolkien delivered only two papers specifically on the subject of Language (*A Secret Vice* and *English and Welsh*), and they both dealt precisely with these subjects. In addition, Tolkien's linguistic creativity added a completely original ingredient to his works of fiction in the form of his art languages and his choice of names, which explains a considerable part of his popularity as an author of fiction right up to the present day.

Bibliography

Arduini, Roberto, & Testi, Claudio (Eds.). *Tolkien and Philosophy*. Zurich & Jena: Walking Tree Publishers, 2014

Carpenter, Humphrey (Ed.). *The Letters of J.R.R. Tolkien*. London: HarperCollins, 1999

Coombes, Matthew. *Language as a Linguistic Art: The Expression of Emotion in the Spoken and Written Word (MA Thesis)*. De Montfort University, 2014

Fimi, Dimitra, & Higgins, Andrew. *A Secret Vice. Tolkien on Invented Languages*. London: HarperCollins, 2016.

Flieger, Verlyn. "Tolkien and the Philosophy of Language". In: Roberto Arduini & Claudio Testi (Eds.) *Tolkien and Philosophy*. Zurich & Jena: Walking Tree Publishers, 2014

Heaney, Seamus. *Beowulf. A New Verse Translation*. London: Norton, 2000

Hemmi, Yoko. "Tolkien's *The Lord of the Rings* and His Concept of Native Language: Sindarin and British-Welsh". In: *Tolkien Studies VII*. West Virginia University Press, 2010

Jespersen, Otto. *Language: Its Nature, Development and Origin*. London: Allen & Unwin, 1950 [originally published 1922]

Lothe, Jakob, & Hawthorn, Jeremy (Eds.). *Narrative Ethics*. New York: Editions Rodopi, 2013

Pinker, Steven. *The Language Instinct*. William Morrow. New York: 1994

---. *The Stuff of Thought*. London: Penguin, 2007

Powys, John Cowper. *Porius*. London: Duckworth, 2007 (originally published 1951)

Shippey, Tom, & Manni, Franco. "Tolkien between Philosophy and Philology". In: Roberto Arduini & Claudio Testi (Eds.) *Tolkien and Philosophy*. Zurich & Jena: Walking Tree Publishers, 2014

Smith, Ross. *Inside Language: Linguistic and Aesthetic Theory in Tolkien*. Zurich & Jena: Walking Tree Publishers, 2011

Tolkien, J.R.R. *The Monsters and the Critics and Other Essays*. London: HarperCollins, 1997

---. *The Silmarillion*. London: HarperCollins, 1992

---. *The Lord of the Rings* (50th Anniversary Ed.). London: HarperCollins, 2004

Sprache und Weltverständnis

Thomas Fornet-Ponse (Köln)

> Ich spreche Spanisch zu Gott, Italienisch zu den Frauen,
> Französisch zu den Männern und Deutsch zu meinem Pferd.
> (Karl V. zugeschrieben)

Als vor einigen Jahren Daniel Everett sein Buch *Don't sleep, there are snakes. Life and Language in the Amazonian Jungle* über sein Leben bei den Pirahã veröffentlichte und darlegte, was er dort über das Wesen der Sprache gelernt habe, wurden einige Thesen auch in überregionalen Zeitungen vorgestellt bzw. diskutiert. Denn der besondere Charakter ihrer Sprache als lediglich drei Vokale und acht Konsonanten aufweisend, ohne Wörter für Zahlen, gestern und heute führte zu einer intensiven Debatte unter Linguisten. Mit seiner Analyse unterstützt Everett die These, wonach Sprache und Lebensweise bzw. -raum eng miteinander verbunden sind – und widerspricht damit beispielsweise der oft vertretenen Theorie einer universalen sprachlichen Grundstruktur und Grammatik, wie sie besonders von Chomsky propagiert wurde. Nun ist es keine Neuheit, dass Tolkien eher der Verbundenheit von Sprache und Lebenswelt und Weltanschauung zuneigte, wie sich mit diversen Stellen aus seinem narrativen wie wissenschaftlichen Werk belegen lässt (vgl. ausführlich Smith). In diesem Beitrag soll es nach einer kurzen Einordnung in die sprachwissenschaftliche Diskussion in einem groben Überblick um die Frage gehen, ob und inwiefern sich diese Überzeugung Tolkiens auch an seinen erfundenen Sprachen (bzw. in dem, was von ihnen bekannt ist) verifizieren lässt.

Sprachwissenschaftliche Diskussion

Ausgehend von der beobachtbaren Vielfalt menschlicher Sprachen mit zum Teil erheblichen Unterschieden sowie den wohl allen hier bekannten Problemen bzw. Herausforderungen, einen Gedankengang in eine andere Sprache möglichst exakt zu übersetzen, liegt es nahe, einen Zusammenhang von Sprache und Denken bzw. Weltanschauung oder Lebenswelt, d.h. einen linguistischen Relativismus zu vermuten. Die Gegenposition ist die These der Universalgrammatik.

Gemäß dem linguistischen Relativismus verwundert es nicht, wenn ein im Amazonas-Gebiet lebendes Volk wie die Pirahã keine Wörter für Abstrakta kennen, sondern alles möglichst konkret ausdrücken, weil dies ihrer Lebenswelt und -weise entspricht. Vielmehr gilt dies als ein Paradebeispiel dafür, dass Umwelt und Lebensbedingungen eine maßgebliche Wirkung auf das Denken zeitigen und sich dies dann in Grammatik, Struktur, Vokabular etc. der Sprache, die sich in diesem Kontext entwickelt, ausdrückt. Ein anderes Beispiel ist der von Josef Estermann anhand der Topographie deutlich herausgestellte Unterschied zwischen andinem Denken und semitisch bzw. hellenistischem Denken, da im andinen Raum aufgrund der primär von Bergen und Tälern geprägten Lebenswelt die Vertikale vorherrscht, wohingegen in der abendländischen Philosophie, die sich u.a. im »fruchtbaren Halbmond« konstituierte, die Horizontale und die Dialektik zwischen Festland und Meer prägend ist (vgl. Estermann 64f).

Eine solche Korrespondenz von Landschaft und Sprache des Volkes, das in dieser lebt, findet im *Herrn der Ringe* einen klaren Niederschlag:

> »That, I guess, is the language of the Rohirrim,« said Legolas; »for it is like to this land itself; rich and rolling in part, and else hard and stern as the mountains. But I cannot guess what it means, save that it is laden with the sadness of Mortal Men.«   (LotR 497)

In diesem Zitat wird auch das von Tolkien vertretene Konzept der Phono-semantik angesprochen, d.h. der Beziehung zwischen Laut und Bedeutung, worauf in diesem Kontext allerdings nicht weiter eingegangen werden braucht (vgl. dazu Smith).

Während sich die genannten Beispiele vor allem auf die Prägung einer Sprache durch ihren Kontext, ihre Umwelt und ihre Kultur beziehen, ist für die Frage nach Sprache und Weltanschauung auch der Zusammenhang von Sprache und Denken in den Blick zu nehmen. Everett sieht diesen deutlich z.B. im Fehlen von Zahlwörtern oder Abstrakta ausgedrückt, sodass sich in der Sprache und der Unfähigkeit der Pirahã, Zählen zu lernen oder überlieferten, aber nicht selbst erlebten Geschichten Glauben zu schenken, ihr auf die Unmittelbarkeit des Erlebens und »objektive« Belege konzentriertes Weltverständnis und ihre Wertmaßstäbe niederschlagen (vgl. Everett 177-259).

Während Everett somit für eine klare Beeinflussung der Sprache durch die sie tragende Kultur plädiert und sich in den Unterschieden der Sprache die verschiedenen Lebensräume und Wertmaßstäbe widerspiegeln, kann auch ge-fragt werden, ob und inwiefern die Sprache das Denken beeinflusst. Eindeutig mit ja beantwortet wird diese Frage von Edward Sapir und Benjamin Whorf:

> The Sapir-Whorf hypothesis is commonly regarded as holding that the structure of a language places restrictions on the perception and understanding of its speakers, i.e. a given language actually determines the cognitive scope of its community. Taking this to an extreme, it can be postulated that different language communities have different mind-sets, and that certain cognitive processes may simply be unavailable to the speakers of certain languages because of the limits on thought those languages impose.   (Smith 87)

Pelz unterscheidet dabei zwei Thesen: zum einen das Prinzip der sprachlichen Relativität, wonach sich Sprachen auf unterschiedliche Weise auf die außersprachliche Wirklichkeit beziehen (Beispiele dafür sind Unterschiede bei den Farbbezeichnungen sowie lexikalische Inkongruität), und zum anderen ein sprachlicher Determinismus, d.h. die Abhängigkeit der Begriffsbildung von der Sprache (Pelz 35ff). In der strikten Deutung der Hypothese geht es nicht bloß um eine Beeinflussung des Denkens durch die Sprache, sondern um eine kausal zwingende Determination durch die Sprache, weshalb eine Sprache nicht in eine andere übersetzt werden kann (vgl. Stolze, *Übersetzungstheorien* 30). Ein solcher linguistischer Determinismus ist aber von Sapir und Whorf selbst nie vertreten worden – ebenso wenig wie die ihnen zugeschriebene Hypothese, die eine spätere Konstruktion vonseiten derer, die sie widerlegen wollte, darstellt. Vielmehr schrieb Whorf selbst:

> Users of markedly different grammars are pointed by their grammars toward different types of observations and different evaluations of externally similar acts of observation, and hence are not equivalent as observers but must arrive at somewhat different views of the world.   (zitiert nach Evans 196)

Abgesehen von der begründeten Kritik an Whorfs empirischer Basis, seinen Untersuchungen über die Sprache der Hopi, gibt es gute Argumente für einen linguistischen Relativismus, sofern damit kein Determinismus vertreten wird. Wichtig ist, bei den entsprechenden Forschungen auf den Unterschied zwischen Korrelation und Kausalität zu achten, da die angeblich so vielen Wörter für Schnee in Inuit-Sprachen auch einfach mit der Bedeutung im Alltagsleben zu tun haben, was dann zur Notwendigkeit der Differenzierung geführt hat. (Vgl. Pinker, *Stuff* 124ff.) Zudem bedeuten Differenzierungen, die in einer Sprache in der Struktur angelegt sind – wie die Bedeutung des Tempus im Englischen sowie der Notwendigkeit im Türkischen, zwischen eigener Erfahrung oder des Kennens durch Hörensagen zu unterscheiden –, nicht, solche Unterscheidungen seien den Sprechern_innen anderer Sprachen nicht möglich. Wenn Everett die begrenzte Fähigkeit der Pirahã, numerisch zu denken, auf allgemeine Charakteristika ihrer Kultur zurückführt, nicht aber auf das Fehlen von Zahlwörtern, ist er nicht notwendigerweise ein Anhänger der (Neo-)Whorf-These.[1] Allerdings zeigen neuere Experimente eine enge Beziehung von Sprache und vorbewusster

---

1   »The reason the non-Whorfian interpretation is plausible is that we don't find modern urbanized societies that lack an elaborate system of number words, nor do we find hunter-gatherer societies that have them. Granted, a people could hardly have developed into an urban civilization without number words and number concepts, so we wouldn't expect a modern society to lack number words and still be modern. But that's just the point—when the need arises, both number words and numerical reasoning are soon developed from existing cognitive resources.« (Pinker 139)

Perzeption, beispielsweise aufgrund der im Griechischen vorhandenen Unterscheidung zwischen zwei Blautönen, die mit einem Unterschied in der Gehirnaktivität zwischen Griechischsprachigen und Englischsprachigen einhergeht: »Different languages, which label physical objects in different ways, give rise to a restructuring effect on cognition: speakers of different languages perceive those objects in language-specific ways« (Evans 217).

Auch Tolkien dürfte mit dieser schwächeren Position sympathisiert haben. Der linguistische Relativismus geht weit über die allgemein geteilte Annahme hinaus, mit Sprache könne Denken beeinflusst werden, was in der Rhetorik geschieht. Er richtet sich deutlich gegen die These der Universalgrammatik[2]:

> In the final analysis, linguistic relativity seems not to relate to how we influence the thoughts of others—no one disputes this as a significant function of language: we aim to persuade, prevaricate, request, seduce, all using language. Rather, linguistic relativity is, ultimately, a phenomenon that impacts on the cognitive apparatus of the language user—a consequence of the language one uses: by virtue of using English, rather than, say, Greek, my habitual patterns of thought, in terms of the colour domain, are structured—or restructured—in a relativistic way. I perceive colours in somewhat different terms, whether I like it or not... The language I speak does this to me: we have slightly different minds as a consequence of the language(s) we use. Linguistic relativity concerns, then, not what we convince others to do by virtue of our word play; rather, it relates to what happens to our minds because of the language(s) we happen to grow up speaking. And, as such, linguistic relativity is, ultimately, a usage-based phenomenon. (Evans 227)

Für unsere Fragestellung für den Zusammenhang von Sprache und Weltanschauung bei Tolkien muss nicht geklärt werden, ob die These des linguistischen

---

2   Evans kritisiert an Chomsky, seine Überlegungen basierten nicht auf Fakten, sondern resultierten aus der Annahme, die genetische Ausstattung sei entscheidend für die Sprache. Schon die Diversität der Sprachen spreche gegen die Annahme, gewisse Uni-versalien – seien es verschiedene Wörterklassen oder Regeln – seien in allen Sprachen vorhanden und könnten über das Studium der englischen Sprache erkannt werden. Vgl. Evans 90ff, dazu auch Evans und Levinson. Problematisch sei auch die Annahme des »Mentalese«: »The language-as-instinct thesis proposes that we are born with a mental operating system—Mentalese—that allows us to represent ideas and mental states. As we proceed though our life journey, from birth onwards, experience is filtered, allowing us to build up ideas based on experience. But the architecture and ›grammatical‹ principles that allow us to manipulate mental representations—to produce complex thought—are present at birth: we enter the world pre-equipped with Mentalese« (Evans 162). Problematisch daran sei, dass Konzepte angeboren sein müssten und vor allem das Verständnis des menschlichen Geistes als Computer. Die Empirie spreche dagegen für einen »embodied mind« (mit Verweis auf Lakoff und Johnson, 191).

Relativismus nun alle Phänomene besser erklärt als konkurrierende Theorien; es muss auch nicht abschließend geklärt werden, ob tatsächlich sprachliche Eigenheiten die Kausalursache unterschiedlicher Weltsichten sind. Relevant sind primär der deutlich gewordene enge Zusammenhang von Sprache, Denken und Lebenswelt und die Korrespondenz verschiedener Denkweisen mit sprachlichen Eigenheiten. Bevor wir uns nun Tolkien zuwenden, nenne ich einige sprachliche Besonderheiten, die zuweilen in der philosophischen Diskussion aufgegriffen werden:

Beispiele für die philosophische Relevanz sprachlicher Eigenheiten

Ein erstes Beispiel aus afrikanischer Perspektive richtet sich gegen den Geltungsanspruch des cartesianischen Denkens, da zwar viele europäische Sprachen grammatisch das »cogito ergo sum« zulassen und sich daher die Vorstellung eines absolut autonomen Selbst entwickeln kann. In vielen afrikanischen Sprachen gibt es aber kein Äquivalent für dieses »sein«, sondern ist der Seinsbegriff immer schon relational verstanden. In der Sprache der Akan beispielsweise ist Existenz immer örtlich bestimmt und Existenz ein Attribut der Dinge bezogen auf andere Dinge oder einen Ort. (Wiredu 49; vgl. auch Kimmerle) Dies entspricht einer wesentlich höheren Bedeutung der kollektiven Dimension im afrikanischen Denken im Vergleich zur individuellen im europäischen Raum.

Ein anderes Beispiel wird vom baskischen Philosophen Xavier Zubiri mit dem in semitischen Sprachen vorhandenen status constructus angeführt, da damit eine ganz andere Konzeption der Beziehung verschiedener Dinge ausgedrückt würde. Denn während in indoeuropäischen Sprachen der Zusammenhang zwischen einem Sohn und seinem Vater als »Sohn von Peter« (hijo de pedro) ausgedrückt wird und somit zwei Namen und zwei Realitäten, von denen eine von der anderen abhängt, vorhanden sind (bei einer Genetiv-Konstruktion wird interessanterweise der Vater verändert, nicht der Sohn), liegt beim status constructus eine untrennbare, aus zwei Momenten bestehende, Einheit vor: »hijo-de-pedro«, wobei der Sohn im status constructus und der Vater im status absolutus steht. (Zubiri 220)

Im Swahili kann beispielsweise auf die Differenzierung nach Nominalklassen hingewiesen werden:

> Das Swahili ist eine Sprache mit Nominalklassen, d.h. mit einer Klassifizierung von Substantiven nach gewissen Aspekten wie belebt/unbelebt, konkret/abstrakt, örtlicher Dimension, Dimension des Handelns (wie Infinitiv) und ähnlichem, im Gegensatz zur deutschen Sprache mit der Klassifizierung nach männlich/weiblich/sächlich. (Wandeler 4)

Konkret bedeutet dies, dass ein Verb anders gebildet wird, wenn es sich auf einen Menschen oder einen Baum bezieht: So heißt mtu anapendeza der Mensch gefällt und mit unapendeza der Baum gefällt (Wandeler 20, 33). Darüber hinaus nenne ich nur einen weiteren Unterschied, der m.E. aber viel über das Verständnis von Beziehungen aussagt: Während wir mit dem Verb »haben« nicht nur Besitzverhältnisse ausdrücken, sondern auch Beziehungen beschreiben (ich habe einen Freund, eine Frau etc.), gibt es im Swahili kein eigenes Wort für »haben«, sondern ist das entsprechende »wa na« mit »sein mit« zu übersetzen, d.h. auch Besitzverhältnisse werden eher als Beziehungsverhältnisse ausgedrückt (ich hatte eine Zahnbürste – nilikuwa na mswaki).

Zuletzt seien noch Forschungen erwähnt, die auf die Bedeutung des grammatischen Geschlechts abheben. So wurde ein Experiment durchgeführt mit Spanisch als einer Sprache, in der das grammatische Geschlecht eine große Rolle spielt, und Englisch als einer Sprache ohne Substantivgenus, bei dem bei verschiedenen Objekten angegeben werden sollte, ob sie semantisch zueinander passen oder nicht. Dabei konnte per Messung der Gehirnaktivität bei den Spanischsprachigen eine Beeinflussung durch das Genus nachgewiesen werden, bei den Englischsprachigen hingegen nicht.

> This finding provides incontrovertible evidence that language has an impact on a non-linguistic categorisation task in a relativistic way: Spanish-speakers cannot help but use grammatical gender in the task even though the task does not relate to language. In contrast, English-speakers, who have no such thing as grammatical gender, are unable to deploy this information in making categorisation judgements. (Evans 221)

Vor diesem Hintergrund der Argumente für einen linguistischen Relativismus bzw. zumindest für einen engen Zusammenhang von Sprache, Denken und Lebenswelt können wir uns nun der Frage zuwenden, wie der Zusammenhang von Sprache und Weltverständnis von Tolkien in seinen erfundenen Sprachen ausgedrückt wird.

Der Zusammenhang von Sprache und Weltanschauung bei Tolkiens Sprachen

Ohne dies ausführlich untersuchen zu können, zeigt sich insbesondere anhand der sprachphilosophischen Parallelen zwischen Owen Barfield und Tolkien, dass Tolkien selber vom Zusammenhang von Sprache und Weltanschauung bzw. Weltsicht überzeugt war. Zudem entspricht besonders die Tolkien'sche Lichtmetaphorik Barfields Theorie der semantischen Einheit. »Both words and light are agents of perception, enabling us to see phenomena. The word for a thing, the name, governs the way it is perceived and can be said to make us 'see' it« (Flieger 44). Darin fügt sich nicht nur die Ansicht ein, durch das Wort geschehe die Schöpfung, sondern auch Tolkiens eigene Aussage, er habe seine Welt als Hintergrund für seine Sprachen geschaffen. Die Sprache ging somit der Erschaffung der Welt voraus und führte dazu, die Völker, ihre Kulturen und Mythen zu entwickeln – durch die Sprache. »And so it comes full circle, and the ›inner consistency of reality‹ is one in which myth, language, and culture reflect one another and shape the world that gives them life« (Flieger 61).

Die hohe Bedeutung der Sprache schlägt sich nicht nur in diesem großen Maßstab nieder, sondern zeigt sich auch individuell, da Tolkien die Sprechweise jedes Charakters sorgfältig gestaltete. »Tolkien wanted his characters' way of talking to reflect not only their social standing, learning, ethnicity, etc., but to mirror their very way of thinking« (Smith 29). Wie Turner beispielsweise an Tolkiens Verwendung von Archaismen erläutert, ist eine »constant awareness in the text of *The Lord of the Rings* that there is a difference between ancient and modern conceptions of the world and mankind's relationship to it« (*Translating* 34) zu konstatieren. Denn mit ihrer Hilfe vermittelt Tolkien oft eher implizit als explizit die Weltsichten vormoderner Gesellschaften, indem er beispielsweise mit Gedichten und Liedern eine auf mündlicher Überlieferung basierende Gesellschaft charakterisiert, Alliterationen und Sprichwörter verwendet werden oder die unbelebte Welt wie ein lebender Organismus beschrieben wird (vgl. Turner, *Landscapes*). »[T]he presentation of pre-modern societies through the mind of a philologist encourages the thoughtful reader to engage constructively with modes of thought and expression which are different from the ones with which he or she has grown up, but which are not necessarily any the less valid for that« (Turner, *Translating* 176). Die von Tolkien in der fiktiven Geschichte als Übersetzung (meist aus dem Westron) gekennzeichnete englische Fassung illustriert somit deutliche Unterschiede z.B. zwischen Hobbits, Rohirrim und Gondorianern – und erst recht zu Elben oder Zwergen – und unterstützt damit die Annahme, in Tolkiens Welt gebe es einen deutlichen Zusammenhang zwischen Sprache und Weltanschauung.

Fragt man vor diesem sprachphilosophischen Hintergrund, ob sich auch bei Tolkiens Sprachen anhand bestimmter sprachlicher Spezifika ein solcher Zusammenhang von Sprache und Weltanschauung feststellen lässt, können dazu zwei unterschiedliche Wege begangen werden: Zum einen kann von den uns bekannten Unterschieden zwischen den verschiedenen Sprachen ausgegangen und gefragt werden, ob diese aus philosophischer Sicht signifikant bzw. aussagekräftig genug sind, um als klare Hinweise auf ihnen zugrundeliegende unterschiedliche Weltanschauungen dienen zu können. Zum anderen können bekannte weltanschauliche Unterschiede zwischen Menschen, Elben, Zwergen oder Orks – beispielsweise hinsichtlich ihrer Sicht des Todes – den Ausgangspunkt bilden, um zu untersuchen, ob sich diese Unterschiede in den entsprechenden Sprachen ausdrücken.

Dabei stellt uns die für einige Sprachen doch eher dürftige Quellenlage zum Teil vor erhebliche Probleme, weswegen sich einige Überlegungen vor allem auf der phonetischen Ebene bewegen müssen, da hierzu schon wenige bekannte Beispiele für generalisierende Aussagen ausreichen. Im Bereich der Grammatik dagegen ist zwar eine tiefergehende Untersuchung primär für die elbischen Sprachen Quenya und Sindarin möglich, gewisse Indizien gibt es aber auch für die verschiedenen Sprachen.[3] Wenn ich diese im Folgenden darstelle, gehe ich nicht auf einen anderen Aspekt ein, in dem sich der Zusammenhang von Sprache und Weltanschauung durchaus zeigt, nämlich den Namen der Könige von Númenor und Gondor, die viel über die Geschichte dieser Reiche und der jeweils vorherrschenden Einstellung gegenüber den Valar aussagen.

> Die Könige von Númenor hatten zunächst Namen wie **Amandil** (›Freund von Aman‹) oder **Meneldur** (›Diener des Himmels‹), dann aber gewannen sie an Stolz und nannten sich **Atanamir** (›Juwel der Menschen‹) oder **Ardamin** (›Pfeiler der Erde‹). Schließlich nahmen sie ihre Namen ganz in der númenórischen Sprache an – auch wenn sie nach wie vor, sei es aus Tradition oder aus Aberglauben, auf Quenya in die Rolle der Könige eingetragen wurden –, um damit ihre Abkehr von den göttlichen Mächten und ihre eigene Macht zu betonen. (Pesch 24)

Im Hintergrund dieser veränderten Praxis steht dann die Überzeugung, die Verwendung der Quenya-Namen sei ein Ausdruck der Fremdherrschaft der Valar. Wird dagegen die eigene Sprache verwendet, zeigt sich darin nicht nur ein gestiegenes Autonomiebewusstsein, sondern mit diesem verbunden möglicherweise auch der Zusammenhang von Sprache und Weltanschauung, insofern die Verwendung der eigenen Sprache als Ausdruck der eigenen Identität gelten kann, was nur unzureichend der Fall ist, wenn eine andere Sprache gesprochen wird. Über diese Motivation kann angesichts der Quellenlage indes nur spekuliert werden, weshalb nun zunächst die gut erforschten Unterschiede zwischen den einzelnen Sprachen in den Blick genommen werden sollen.

Die Sprachen Tolkiens und ihre Eigenheiten[4]

Wie Carl Hostetter in seiner Übersicht über die von Tolkien erfundenen Sprachen ausführt, lässt sich eine klare Entwicklungslinie von den ersten Versuchen in seiner Kindheit bis zu den letzten Bemühungen nachzeichnen:

---

3   Vgl. zur Quellenlage Pesch 34-39, 55-74 sowie Hostetter.
4   Vgl. Pesch, Hostetter.

> In short, we see a movement from language creation as a utilitar-
> ian and thus shared endeavor toward glossopoeia that is at once
> strongly abstract and artistic in pursuing and expressing a private
> and personal linguistic aesthetic and that is rigorously historical and
> systematic, susceptible within the fictive construct to the scientific
> tools of historical philology: an aspect of language creation nearly
> if not entirely unique to Tolkien.   (Hostetter 332)

Zu den Besonderheiten der erfundenen Sprachen Tolkiens gehört ihre doppelte Geschichte, d.h. ihre jahrzehntelange Konstruktion und Veränderung durch Tolkien, in der sich seine linguistischen Vorlieben niederschlagen[5], sowie ihre fiktive Geschichte der phonologischen und lexikalischen Entwicklung. Aus dieser folgt auch ihre Verwandtschaft untereinander aufgrund ihrer Abstammung von einer Ursprache – mit den Ausnahmen der Zwergensprache, die von Aule konstruiert wurde, und der Schwarzen Sprache, die von Sauron entwickelt, aber selbst von den Orks nicht vollständig übernommen wurde. Fragt man nach den Einflüssen realer Sprachen auf die erfundenen Sprachen, so liegt dieser nach Hostetter selten auf der lexikalischen Ebene und ist zumeist strukturell, phonologisch und phonetisch.[6]

Die Bedeutung der Sprachfähigkeit in Tolkiens Werk schlägt sich schon in der Selbstbezeichnung der ersten Elben nieder, die sich Quendi, d.h. »die mit Stimmen reden« nannten; während sie nach den frühen Entwürfen der Mythologie (Lhammas, Etymologies, frühes *Silmarillion*) ihre Sprache durch Oromë erhalten, erfinden sie nach den späten Entwürfen (Quendi and Eldar) ihre Sprache von Beginn an selbst.

> Like all language, whether that be of a Primary or a Secondary
> World, Elven languages must derive from and be expressive of the
> perception of their speakers, and so must both reflect and create
> their world.   (Flieger 73)

Einen Ausdruck davon sieht Flieger im ersten primitiven Ausruf *ele* (»behold«), den die Elben tätigten, als sie bei ihrem Aufwachen die Sterne sahen (vgl. S 358), wobei mit dem Akt des Sehens auch die Trennung zwischen ihnen als den

---

5   »That is, rather than indicating flaws or deficiencies in the earlier forms of the languages as compared with later forms, this succession of conceptual forms of Tolkien's invented languages reflects, and arose to *express*, his changing linguistic ideas and aesthetic over time.« (Hostetter 335)

6   »We thus find languages that have a structurally Semitic character (e.g., Khuzdul and Adûnaic) against those that are structurally Indo-European (e.g., the Eldarin tongues), and we find languages phonologically and phonetically similar not just to Finnish (Quenya) and to Welsh (Sindarin) but also to various members of the Germanic language family, such as Old English (Danian/Nandorin) and Gothic (Taliska).« (Hostetter 335)

Sehenden und dem Gesehenen etabliert wird.[7] Weitere Unterscheidungen bzw. Trennungen der Elben untereinander erfolgen dann im Laufe der Geschichte und führen zur Auseinanderentwicklung verschiedener Sprachen, die auch einer steigenden Individualisierung entspricht. »Elves of the Light and Elves of the Dark, by their conflicting perceptions and what will come to be related yet different modes of speech, build in Tolkien's world that inner consistency of reality that it is the function of language to give to any world« (Flieger 83). Weitere Unterscheidungen korreliert Flieger mit der Bereitschaft verschiedener Elben, dem Rufen der Valar zu folgen, was sich dann jeweils in ihrer Bezeichnung sowie im Bewusstsein der Sprache für unterschiedliche Helligkeitsarten niederschlägt. Die sich entwickelnden unterschiedlichen elbischen Sprachen werden mithin phonologisch, morphologisch und semantisch vom Grad der Nähe zum Licht Amans beeinflusst, was am ehesten an den beiden gut entwickelten Sprachen Quenya und Sindarin deutlich gemacht werden kann.[8]

Die allen gemeinsame Ursprache hieß primitives Quendisch (Primitive Quendian) und aus ihr entwickelte sich allmählich zunächst das »Gemeine Eldarin« (Common Eldarin) – beide Rekonstruktionen gemäß der fiktiven Geschichte – und später in Aman die Dialekte Quendya und Quenya mit weiterer Entwicklung insbesondere nach der Erfindung des Alphabets sowie in Beleriand vor allem Sindarin.[9]

Entsprechend ihrer Herkunft besitzen alle Elbensprachen strukturell und phonetisch einen stark indoeuropäischen Charakter (zumindest entsprechend dem Forschungsstand zu Tolkiens Zeiten), d.h. die Wörter werden meist von einer Wurzel mit zwei, drei Konsonanten und einem charakteristischen Vokal gebildet; eine Ausnahme ist die Abwesenheit des grammatischen Geschlechts. Ein bemerkenswerter Unterschied zwischen Quenya und Sindarin besteht darin, dass die Sprachen von Mittelerde natürlich gewachsen sind und eine radikale Veränderung in Klang und Struktur erfahren haben, während »die Noldor die Veränderungen ihrer Sprache selbst gesteuert hatten« (Pesch 45). Gerade in einer solchen bewussten Veränderung der eigenen Sprache dürfte sich der Zusammenhang von Sprache und Weltanschauung niederschlagen, wie beispielsweise die Bemühungen um genderfaire Sprache zeigen. Das die

---

7   Hierin zeigt sich die Nähe zwischen Tolkiens und Barfields Auffassungen. Vgl. dazu Flieger und Smith 121ff.

8   Flieger nennt als Beispiel den Unterschied zwischen der Bedeutung von Elentári (Quenya) »Star-Queen« und Elbereth (Sindarin) »Star-spouse«, womit sich eine Verkleinerung verbindet. »The Quenya name recognizes Varda as Queen in her own right, suggesting the elevated feminine principle as bringer of light, while the Sindarin name emphasizes her position first as wife and only second as queen« (Flieger 90).

9   Vgl. die Grafik bei Pesch 53 und die unterschiedlichen Stufen in LR 169f, 196f.

Noldor bei ihren Veränderungen leitende Motiv war indes das der Schönheit, insofern weichere und harmonischere Formen gewählt wurden (vgl. WJ 20).[10]

Wenngleich für unsere Fragestellung nicht direkt ertragreich, ist bei Quenya zunächst auf den Charakter als eine alte Sprache hinzuweisen, den Tolkien z.B. durch die Existenz zahlreicher Endungen – für Possessivpronomen wie für die Kennzeichnung der Numeri und dergleichen mehr – deutlich macht. Diese vielen Endungen ermöglichen eine freie Wortstellung, was Gesang und Poesie sehr erleichtert. Dieser Eignung für Kunst entspricht die in der Regel als sehr ästhetisch wahrgenommene Phonetik: »Quenya ist eine wohlklingende, offene Sprache, deren Wörter nur auf Vokale oder die zentralen Konsonanten *l, n, r, s* und *t* enden. Das heißt, wenn man ein Wort auf Quenya spricht, beendet man es mit geöffnetem Mund – oder einem Lächeln« (Pesch 28). Darüber hinaus gibt es mehr Vorderzungenvokale als Hinterzungenvokale; Konsonantencluster und gutturale Phoneme fehlen, weshalb die Silben sehr gleichmäßig gebildet werden. Dies begründet den leichten und melodischen Klang sowie den fließenden Eindruck, den Quenya macht (vgl. Smith 60f).

Während Quenya phonologisch von Latein und weniger stark von Griechisch sowie phonetisch stark von Finnisch beeinflusst ist, zeigt sich der Einfluss des Finnischen in der Grammatik an den vielen Inflexionen (die es auch im Lateinischen gibt), aber auch am Fehlen eines grammatischen Geschlechts, am adverbialen Kasus für Position oder Bewegung und an dem Unterschied zwischen einem generellen und partitiven Substantiv (vgl. Hostetter 337f). Insbesondere das Fehlen eines grammatischen Geschlechts könnte für unsere Fragestellung relevant sein, als sich darin die unter den Elben in Aman deutlich geringere Bedeutung des biologischen Geschlechts im Vergleich zu den Menschen ausdrücken könnte (Vgl. MR 213f). Ebenfalls aufschlussreich ist die fiktive Geschichte von Quenya in Mittelerde, da es zu einer toten Sprache wird, die lediglich für Poesie, Gesang oder gelehrte bzw. zeremonielle Texte verwendet wird und in dieser Beziehung von Tolkien als »Elf-latin« bezeichnet wird (vgl. Hostetter 340).

Zu den Besonderheiten des Sindarin – gerade im Vergleich zu Deutsch oder Englisch – gehören vor allem die auf die Schwächung bzw. das Verschwinden

---

10 Gilson macht auf einen bemerkenswerten Unterschied zwischen der externen und der internen (fiktiven) Geschichte der Sprachen aufmerksam, insofern Sindarin auf Gnomisch basiert, das in *Book of Lost Tales* die ursprüngliche Sprache der Noldor war und nicht wie in den späteren Entwürfen die Sprache der Sindar war und von den Noldor erst im Exil angenommen wurde. »It is because Gnomish continued to be conceived of by Tolkien as the same language that his alterations of it could actually achieve the refinement of art. And it is perhaps paradoxical that the greatest refinement in word form, nicety of notional range, and skillfulness of grammar, gave such a clear identity to *Noldorin* ›Gnomish‹ as an actual language, that Tolkien could completely alter its fictional origins and rename it *Sindarin* ›Grey-elven‹, with little or no change require to the language itself, though naturally he continued its refinement till the end of his life.« (Gilson, *Gnomish* 104)

ursprünglicher Endvokale zurückzuführende deutliche Reduktion der Inflexionen im Vergleich zum Quenya, die Bildung von Pluralformen durch Vokaländerungen (was es zuweilen auch im Deutschen gibt) und stärker noch die »Tatsache, dass sich bei Wörtern im Sindarin nicht das Wortende, sondern der Wortanfang verändern kann« (Pesch 29f), was vor allem aus keltischen Sprachen bekannt und ein Beispiel dafür ist, wie Walisisch Sindarin in Phonologie und Grammatik beeinflusst hat. Damit verbunden wird die Wortstellung im Sindarin wichtiger als im Quenya, was zu einer etwas geringeren Eignung für Gesang oder Poesie führt.

Der oben erwähnte Unterschied beider Sprachen vor dem Hintergrund der Beziehung zum Licht (der Sterne bzw. Amans) zeigt sich nach Flieger auch schon im Namen der Sprache, da Quenya direkt auf die durch Licht inspirierte Sprache referiert, während Sindarin von Quenya »grau« gebildet wird. Dem korrespondiert die Zwischenstellung der Sindar, bei denen es aber nicht nur darum geht, das Licht zu suchen oder abzulehnen. »Theirs is a world in which even those who have not seen the light can, if they wish, be aware of it and of its power« (Flieger 92). Darüber hinaus betont sie, alle lichtbezogenen Wörter im Sindarin seien weicher als ihre Äquivalente im Quenya, was aber nicht wertend gedeutet werden solle – Sindarin sei zwar vom Licht weiter entfernt, aber näher an den Sorgen Mittelerdes.[11]

Während dies dem vermuteten Zusammenhang von Sprache und Weltsicht entspricht, ist es eher zweifelhaft, ob Tolkiens grammatische Entscheidungen z.B. zugunsten vieler Inflexionen im Unterschied zu einer isolierenden Sprache sich ähnlich wie die Auswahl des Vokabulars primär ästhetischen Überlegungen im Sinne ihrer »phonetic fitness« verdanken; vielmehr »we may suppose that his grammatical choices, as mentioned above, derived essentially from his wish to create languages for Middle-earth that mirrored, respectively, the ancient classical languages and the Celtic tongues in our world« (Smith 92).

Anders als die Elbensprachen nach den letzten Entwürfen erschufen bzw. entwickelten die Zwerge ihre Sprache nicht selbst, sondern erhielten diese von Aula, der auch sie gemacht hatte. Daher verwundern die möglichen Anklänge an das (kaum bekannte) Valarin nicht. Trotz der wenig ausführlichen Quellenlage lässt sich deutlich der semitische Einfluss auf Struktur und Phonetik feststellen, der sich insbesondere in den aus drei Konsonanten bestehenden Wurzeln niederschlägt. Ob es ein Äquivalent zum status constructus mit seiner philosophischen Bedeutung gibt, ist indes unbekannt. Aussagekräftig ist allerdings

---

11   Yoko Hemmi charakterisiert den Unterschied zwischen Quenya und Sindarin als denjenigen zwischen Hochsprache und allgemeiner Sprache, was sich auch an den Anrufungen der Hobbits zeige, da Frodos auf Quenya und Sams auf Sindarin seien. »The difference of speech between Frodo and Sam may be explained by a difference in their ›native linguistic potential‹ (*Letters* 375), which they shared ›in proportion‹ as they shared other elements in their ›make-up‹ (*MC* 190).« (Hemmi 165)

der Umgang der Zwerge mit ihrer Sprache, da sie sie sorgfältig bewahrt haben, »both from change and from the eyes and ears of the other races of Middle-earth« (Hostetter 341), worin sich ihr zurückgezogener und wenig geselliger bzw. nach Smith (18) ihr harter, erdnaher Charakter niederschlägt. Entsprechend ist auch ihr Dialekt der Gemeinsamen Sprache eher altertümlich.

Über die Sprachen der Menschen ist unterschiedlich viel bekannt: Während bei Taliska noch nicht einmal sicher ist, ob Tolkien es noch zur fiktiven Geschichte rechnete, aber immerhin bekannt ist, dass es in den früheren Konzepten als erste Sprache der Menschen entstand, indoeuropäischen Charakters ist, anschließend zunächst von Khuzdul sowie später von Nandorin beeinflusst wurde[12] und sowohl gotische bzw. germanische als auch elbische Charakteristika aufweist, existiert von der Nachfolgesprache Adûnaisch sogar eine Grammatik. Dieser sind zum einen eine deutliche semitische Struktur wie Wurzeln als drei Konsonanten und die Ableitung grammatischer Formen durch Variation der Vokale zu entnehmen, die sich dem engen Kontakt mit Khuzdul verdankt, sowie zum anderen andere Elemente wie Basen aus zwei Konsonanten, einem charakteristischen Vokal oder vielen phonetisch adaptierten Wörtern, die aus dem alten Quendisch stammen. In der Verbindung zentraler Charakteristika sowohl der Zwergen- als auch der Elbensprache(n) kann die Bedeutung der Menschen als zwischen diesen beiden stehend gesehen werden.[13]

Nach dem Untergang Númenors verändert sich Adûnaisch ungesteuert, da die Gebildeten in Arnor und Gondor Sindarin auch im Alltag verwendeten und es teilweise sogar zur Muttersprache wurde, während Adûnaisch die Volkssprache war (vgl. PM 315). Dies erklärt auch den Einfluss des Sindarin auf die Gemeinsame Sprache (Sôval Phâre/Adûni/Westron). Über diese ist wegen der konsequenten Übersetzung ins Englische fast nichts bekannt, »save that it was clearly intended to resemble Adûnaic in structure and phonetics« (Hostetter 343).

Zuletzt ist die von Sauron entwickelte Schwarze Sprache der Orks zu erwähnen, die als »harsh and guttural language, characterized by such sounds as *sh*, *gh*, *zg*« (Hostetter 343) konstruiert wurde und der Tolkien nur den für diesen Eindruck nötigen Aufwand gewidmet zu haben scheint. Wenngleich aufgrund der Quellenlage nicht abschließend zu bestätigen, liegt es nahe, Korrespondenzen in Grammatik und Vokabular zu anderen Sprachen anzunehmen, die zu der Vermutung Anlass geben könnten, Sauron habe keine eigene Sprache schaffen,

---

12 Dies kann als Ausdruck der Brückenfunktion innerhalb der Fiktion zwischen den Sprachen Mittelerdes und den geschichtlichen indoeuropäischen Sprachen gesehen werden.
13 Darüber hinaus mögen auch Tolkiens Überlegungen zur Verbindung Mittelerdes mit der Primärwelt eine Rolle gespielt haben, insofern diese ihren Ausdruck in der Sprachgeschichte darin fände, dass die elbischen Sprachen ein hypothetischer Vorläufer des Proto-Indoeuropäischen wären. Vgl. dazu Gilson, *Elvish*.

sondern lediglich eine neue auf der Basis anderer zusammenstellen können. Dies bleibt zwar spekulativ, entspräche aber Tolkiens Überzeugung, wonach das Böse nicht erschaffen kann, sondern lediglich Bestehendes verändern (vgl. Fornet-Ponse, *Verständnis*).

Helmut Pesch fasst die Charakteristika einiger der Sprachen Tolkiens mit Verweis auf ihren weltanschaulichen Hintergrund prägnant zusammen:[14]

> Khuzdul, die Sprache der Zwerge, hat etwas Konstruiertes, so wie auch die Zwerge im Anfang ›gemacht‹ und nicht wie die Elben ›erweckt‹ wurden. Sie ist gekennzeichnet durch geschlossene Silben, passend für ein verschlossenes Volk. Dagegen besteht die Sprache der Ents aus endlos sich verzweigenden Aneinanderreihungen von Worten, wachsend wie sie selbst. Die Sprache der Orks ist so lebensfeindlich wie ihr dunkler Herr; sie schneidet einem beim Sprechen regelrecht die Luft ab.
>
> Und die Sprache der Elben ist wie ein Lied. (Pesch 39)

Auf der lexikalischen Ebene sei lediglich ein Beispiel angeführt, in dem deutlich eine Korrespondenz zwischen elbischer Weltsicht und Vokabular besteht. So erläutert Tolkien in seinen Notizen zur eldarinischen Wurzel MBAR die Bedeutung des Sindarin *amarth*, was bedeutet: »›Fate‹ especially (when applied to the future): sc. the order and conditions of the *physical* world (or of Eä in general) as far as established and preordained at Creation, and that part of this ordained order which affected an individual with a *will*, as being immutable by his personal will« (Tolkien, *Fate* 184). Im Hintergrund steht die Bindung der Elben an Eä, d.h. der für sie bestehende enge Zusammenhang ihres (langen) Lebenslaufes mit dem Lauf der Welt, sodass die Ordnung der physischen Welt entsprechend zu dem gesehen werden kann, was sie am Lauf der Geschichte nicht beeinflussen können. Daher kann auch Quenya *ambar* sowohl »Welt« als auch »Schicksal« bedeuten, da Schicksal viel stärker als physisches Hindernis für den Willen aufgefasst wurde (vgl. dazu auch Fornet-Ponse, *Strange* 82ff). Mangels Kenntnis des menschlichen Äquivalents kann leider nicht überprüft werden, ob sich hierin der zentrale Unterschied zwischen Elben und Menschen, also die Gebundenheit an die Welt bzw. die Freiheit von ihr, niederschlägt.

---

14 »Elven language is musical and euphonious; elven diction (even in the Common Speech) is formal and archaic. Orc speech is harsh and guttural; orc diction is slang and argot. Strider's language is plainer and more direct than the epic high speech and diction of Aragorn-a particularly nice touch, since they are the same man, and the change in language signals the shift from Ranger to King.« (Flieger 6f)

Zusammenfassung

Es gibt somit auf den verschiedenen Ebenen viele Hinweise für einen engen Zusammenhang von Sprache und Weltanschauung in Tolkiens Werk, seien es der strukturelle und phonetische indoeuropäische Charakter der Elbensprachen im Unterschied zu stärker semitischem Einschlag bei den Zwergen und Menschen, die enormen phonologischen Unterschiede zwischen Quenya und der Schwarzen Sprache oder auch das lexikalische Beispiel der gleichen Wurzel für *Welt* und *Schicksal*. Indes ist der Befund nicht zu überbewerten, da die methodischen Grenzen nicht übersehen werden sollten. Die Sprachen sind in sehr unterschiedlichem Maße bekannt, sie haben eine komplexe doppelte Entwicklungsgeschichte und die jeweiligen Weltverständnisse können nur annäherungsweise bestimmt werden. Gleichwohl entsprechen die phonologischen Unterschiede sehr gut zentralen Charakteristika der Völker und lassen somit zumindest Rückschlüsse auf deren Wesen zu (und damit mittelbar auf ihre Weltsicht), auch wenn sich gerade bei der Phonologie Tolkiens ästhetische Ansichten niedergeschlagen haben dürften und sich in ihr die von Hostetter diagnostizierte Bewegung zu einer stark abstrakten und künstlerischen Sprachenschöpfung niederschlägt. Auch die gut erforschbaren Unterschiede zwischen Quenya und Sindarin sind vor allem hinsichtlich der Stellung ihrer Sprecher zum Licht in Valinor aussagekräftig.

Spricht mithin einiges für einen engen Zusammenhang von Sprache und Weltsicht in Tolkiens Werk, ist damit kein linguistischer Determinismus verbunden – eine Übersetzung von einer Sprache in die andere ist grundsätzlich möglich –, wohl aber ist ein linguistischer Relativismus sehr plausibel, während die These einer Universalgrammatik in Mittelerde kaum erfolgreich zu verteidigen wäre.

Bibliographie

Estermann, Josef. *Apu Taytayku. Religion und Theologie im andinen Kontext Lateinamerikas.* Ostfildern: Grünewald, 2012

Everett, Daniel L. *Don't Sleep, There Are Snakes. Life and Language in the Amazonian Jungle.* New York, 2008

Evans, Nicholas & Levinson, Stephen C. "The myth of language universal: language diversity and its importance for cognitive science". *Behavorial and Brain Sciences 32* (2009): 429-448

Evans, Vyvyan. *The Language Myth. Why Language is not an Instinct.* Cambridge: Cambridge University Press, 2014

Flieger, Verlyn. *Splintered Light. Logos and Language in Tolkien's World. Revised Edition.* Kent: Kent State University Press, 2002

Fornet-Ponse, Thomas. »Tolkiens Verständnis des Bösen«. *Inklings-Jahrbuch für Literatur und Ästhetik 20* (2002): 199-228

---. "Strange and free. On some Aspects of the Nature of Elves and Men". *Tolkien Studies VII* (2011), 67-89

Gilson, Christopher. "Elvish and Mannish". *Vinyar Tengwar 33* (1994): 10-26

---. "Gnomish is Sindarin. The Conceptual Evolution of an Elvish Language". *Tolkien's Legendarium. Essays on* The History of Middle-earth. Eds. Verlyn Flieger & Carl. F. Hostetter. Westport, Connecticut: Greenwood Press, 2000, 95-104

Hemmi, Yoko. "Tolkien's *The Lord of the Rings* and his Concept of *Native Language*: Sindarin and British-Welsh". *Tolkien Studies VII* (2010): 147-174

Hostetter, Carl F. "Languages Invented by Tolkien". *J.R.R. Tolkien Encyclopedia. Scholarship and Critical Assessment.* Ed. Michael D.C. Drout. New York: Routledge, 2007, 332-344

Kimmerle, Heinz. »Afrikanische Philosophie in westlichen Sprachen. Eine postkoloniale Problemkonstellation«. *Polylog 15* (2006), 47-63

Pelz, Heidrun. *Linguistik.* Hamburg: Hoffmann und Campe, 1996

Pesch, Helmut W. *Elbisch. Grammatik, Schrift und Wörterbuch der Elben-Sprache von J.R.R. Tolkien.* Bergisch Gladbach: Bastei Lübbe, 2003

Pinker, Steven. *The Stuff of Thought. Language as a Window into Human Nature.* New York: Penguin, 2008

Smith, Ross. *Inside Language. Linguistic and Aesthetic Theory in Tolkien.* Zurich & Jena: Walking Tree Publishers, 2007

Stolze, Radegundis. *Übersetzungstheorien. Eine Einführung.* Tübingen: Narr, 2011

Tolkien, John R.R. *The Lord of the Rings.* HarperCollins: London, 1995

---. *The Silmarillion.* HarperCollins: London, 1999

---. *The Lost Road and other Writings. HoME V.* Ed. Christopher Tolkien. London: HarperCollins, 2002

---. *Morgoth's Ring. HoME X.* Ed. Christopher Tolkien. London: HarperCollins, 2002

---. *Peoples of Middle-earth. HoME XII.* Ed. Christopher Tolkien. London: HarperCollins, 2002

---. "Fate and Free Will". *Tolkien Studies VI* (2010): 183-188

Turner, Allan. "Tolkien's Living Landscapes". *Hither Shore 11* (2014): 8-17

---. *Translating Tolkien.* Frankfurt: Peter Lang, 2005

Wandeler, Beat. *Lehrbuch des Swahili für Anfänger.* Mit Illustrationen von Jan Leiser. Hamburg: Helmut Buske Verlag, 2008

Wiredu, Kwasi. *Cultural Universals and Particulars. An African Perspective.* Bloomington: Indiana University Press, 1996

Zubiri, Xavier. *Vom Wesen.* München: Hueber, 1968

Tolkien's Linguistic World-Building Examined

Patrick Schmitz (Alsdorf) & David Graziano (Zweibrücken)

Before highlighting the basic principles of world-building theory, we would like to highlight the **relevance** of this art form as a literary technique. For us, the motivation of examining world-building theory in the context of fantasy literature lies in the **opportunity to refute certain concepts associated with fantasy literature**. Generally speaking, literature, including fiction, is relevant in the academic world whenever phenomena like literary discourse are applicable and works of art have an outreach into the "real" world. Tolkien himself faced literary criticism in connection to fantasy literature [BMC]. The following statement by Rosemary Jackson serves as an example for the kind of criticism often made in connection with fantasy literature: "Fantasy violates the real, contravenes it, denies it, and insists on this denial throughout" (Jackson 22). In the past, academics like Brian Attebery have stated that literary discourse in the sense of Gérard Genette typically does not occur on the level of narrative discourse but on the level of the story itself" (Attebery, 88). Consequently, we believe that the narrative itself is the fictional discourse in contemporary fantasy literature. This is also supported by James DiGiovanna, who highlights that fictional discourse is always context-bound (DiGiovanna 122). DiGiovanna states "…here [in fiction] the context is world, understood as the complete set of relevant objects and events surrounding the utterance" (DiGiovanna 122). This is the foundation for our interest in world-building theory. The **ways fictional worlds are "built"** can be analysed by using the literary techniques of world-building and **allow** many possibilities of interpretation and consequently **literary discourse**. In the following, we will examine the basic principles of world-building theory.

We understand world-building theory as subject to an ongoing **evolutional process**. Prof. Mark J.P. Wolf's *Building Imaginary Worlds* has to be mentioned as a referential work in the current development of world-building theory because it enables important conclusions and can be seen as a continuation of Tolkien's theory of sub-creation. Therefore, Tolkien's thesis on sub-creation serves as a starting point for this brief introduction. It is based on the idea of a "story-maker" creating a fictional world which can be entered with one's mind. Tolkien explains his thesis by referring to the reading experience of fictional worlds. The sub-creator "…makes a Secondary World which your mind can enter" (FS 132). He becomes even more specific by stating:

> Inside it, what he [the sub-creator] relates is 'true': it accords with the laws of that world. You therefore believe it, while you are, as it were, inside. The moment disbelief arises, the spell is broken; the

magic, or rather art, has failed. You are then out in the Primary World again, looking at the little abortive Secondary World from outside.   (FS 132)

Two consequences have to be drawn from this statement. First, the author, what Tolkien refers to as the sub-creator, lays out the **truth conditions** of a given world by sub-creating them. By doing so, Tolkien unshackles the "fairy-story" from attributes like "impossible". Many theorists define fantasy literature by its nature of "unlikeliness" and "impossibility" (Mendlesohn & James 1). However, by relying on the sub-creator's own truth conditions, say making magic possible in a world, this characterisation becomes irrelevant, since it has its complete focus on the primary world while ignoring the secondary world which it is trying to comment upon. The second consequence that follows Tolkien's statement is that the **reader has to actively participate in the creation of the secondary world**. One has to "enter" with one's mind (FS, 132). This contribution by the reader is called "[s]econdary belief" (Wolf, 25): "Secondary belief is a state of mind which is a necessary element of successful world-building" (Wolf, 25).

In order to display this theory more closely, we chose the metaphor of crossing a threshold. The **key** for crossing the passage from the "real", primary world into the sub-created, secondary world **is a belief in the truth conditions of the secondary world**. The moment the reader questions the possibility of such truth conditions, such as supernatural powers, the art has failed. For example: The moment a reader attributes traits like immortality as supernatural, his perspective has switched to a primary world viewpoint of the secondary world. Although Tolkien's theory introduces the concept of sub-creation clearly, there are no clear benchmarks for a literary technique.

Mark J.P. Wolf offers the "*tools*" for a literary analysis of a sub-creation by clarifying that sub-creation can be understood as the creation of something new **under the impression of pre-existing concepts**. Sub-creation thereby differs greatly from an ex-nihilo approach (e.g. *Genesis*) because the "strangeness" or "secondariness" of a fictional world can be understood as the **sum of its differences in comparison to the primary-world default**. We believe this development of world-building theory is highly important for the entire evolutional process of this concept, due to the conclusions which can be drawn upon this idea of **comparability** between primary and secondary world. The **measurement** of these differences is essentially the literary technique which was needed in order to classify a sub-created world's degree of secondariness. Wolf further concludes that fictional worlds can be **placed along a spectrum**, based on the amount of sub-creation present, thereby signifying the attribute "secondariness" and "invention" as technical terms for this literary practice. (Wolf 24). Wolf further categorises the relations between primary and secondary worlds into so called "**realms**": "We can divide Primary World default changes (in which invention occurs) into four distinct realms [nomina, cultural, natural and ontological], each of which affects the design of a world on a "different level" (Wolf pos. 972/11248). The first realm Wolf mentions is the *nominal* realm, "in which new names are given for existing things" (Wolf pos. 972/11248). We believe that the purpose of this categorisation of degrees of secondariness is to clarify the relation between the sub-created and its primary world default. Consequently, we suggest to **refrain from restricting** the **number of realms** of "invention" or "sub-creation" to four and instead use the concept of realms more flexibly. For our purposes, we will therefore focus on linguistic significancies of world-building and reference to a **linguistic realm** of sub-creation.

Before focusing on a selected corpus of work, we would like to briefly return to the **concept of crossing a threshold into a secondary world**. Current theories of world-building mention the importance of an active reader participating in the process of "entering" a secondary world with her or his mind. Furthermore, it has been spoken of "primary world defaults". We believe these two notions are correlated and require a deeper examination. The following theoretical example shall display the untackled issues in this matter:

A reader of LotR I who is familiar with the common custom of naming a house instead of assigning a number in the United Kingdom (for official addressing purposes) may find it very close to the primary world default when learning that Mr. Baggins resides in Bag End, Hobbiton. However, for readers unfamiliar with this custom, the absence of numbers in addressing may seem as an element with increased secondariness. Following this train of thought, we would like to suggest the usage of the concept of **primary world spheres**. Due to the individuality of every reader, we suggest considering individual thresholds for every fictional world-reader-relation. This disposition may be influenced by factors like native culture of the reader, native language of the reader, experience with other fictional worlds [e.g. familiarity with the term "Orc"] and many other factors. Consequently, when applying Wolf's spectrum of secondariness, the reader's primary sphere must be taken into consideration in order to allow accurate conclusions about a world's secondariness.

After having examined the basic principles of the world-building theory, we can use the methodology presented in order to examine the relations of certain works within the linguistic realm of sub-creation, i.e. on every aspect of language employed in fantastic literature.

Before that, we have to recall those assumptions found in Wolf's referential work that seem to be of particular importance for the language used by authors and presented to the readership. Readers should first of all be able to accept the language they are confronted with as true. This means that the language has to be acceptable enough to make reading and understanding as such possible, while—at the same time—the language has to be 'fantastic', whatever this means. This leads us to the second assumption. Fantastic literature should be characterised by a certain otherness of language. The design of the language at hand has to be unfamiliar enough to guarantee a fantastic quality. A quality that emphasises the threshold between the Primary World mentioned above and the secondary world the readership is about to emerge in. A piece of fantastic literature containing language that is not different enough from the Primary World the reader is accustomed to, may prove to be an obstacle to the readers' wish to enter the world created by the respective author. Thus, Tolkien's "moment of disbelief" (FS 132) would build up and the fantasy, the "magic" (ibid) fail. The escapism[1] (cf. Weinreich 72f), one of the targets many readers aim at by indulging in fantastic literature, would be doomed to fail due to a great resemblance between both worlds as described by Wolf.

Finally, it needs to be highlighted that both concepts, those of **trueness** and **otherness**, reciprocally determine and affect each other. If the language used in a fantastic work e.g. proves to be too different to enable the reader to enter the world and identify with characters, landmarks and entities, it is inacceptable as well. Hence, trueness and otherness have to take both the reader and his or her background into consideration, while at the same time catering to the secondary world the author wants to bring into being.

Having outlined the basic concepts taken from Wolf's world-building theory a next step is to cast further light on these. The first principle—the **trueness** of language—stands for the acceptability or the believability of a language that should facilitate the readers' step into a secondary world, the importance of which Tolkien already stressed by saying that "it is essential to a genuine fairy-story… that it should be presented as 'true' (FS 117). Still one has to keep in mind that the Primary World is part of each language (and culture) to a certain degree. The reader brings about his or her own understanding and background and makes use of the linguistic molds[2] to be found in the respective individual mind. Fittingly, the renowned German literary scholar Wolfgang Iser proposed in his theory of "Rezeptionsästhetik" or reader-response criticism that understanding literature "arises from a meeting between the **written text** and the **individual mind** of **each** reader" (Iser 59, our emphasis).

According to this, an author of fantasy literature has to form every aspect of language in a way that is acceptable to as many members of his readership as possible. The reader has to be able to admit that the name or the term used by the author is 'true' in this case, i.e. that he or she can accept that the character bears a fitting name or that an aspect of the literary work is described by dint of the very words the author decided to use—and that this choice of words can be accepted as part of the secondary world. Applied to fantastic language

---

1   Cf. L. 85. Whether fantasy literature is meant to enable readers to escape from reality remains a matter of debate.
2   Wolf calls this "Primary World defaults" (ibid 24).

this means that for instance a name chosen by an author has to agree with the reader as well as the role of the character in the secondary world. Some examples might serve as an explanation of this circumstance.

In many pieces of fantastic literature, the readership is confronted with the existence of imaginary races enriching the particular secondary world, one of which is that of the orcs. In the course of reading Tolkien's works the reader recognises this race as an evil one, a race that the author himself described in one of his letters to Forrest J. Ackerman in 1958 as "squat, broad, flat-nosed, sallow-skinned, with wide mouths and slant eyes… degraded and repulsive" (L 210). The term orc itself is very short coinciding with its' 'squat, broad' bearer, an observation already pointed out for the race of dwarves by Burelbach (ibid 136). The spelling (or pronunciation) of the word itself contributes to this very observation. The iconic association (Hough 306f) creating an idea in the mind of every reader that is based on the similarity between the characteristics of the word and the signified is underlined by the /r/ standing for "rough, strong, violent" (Jakobson & Waugh 191) characters, whereas the guttural /k/ at the very end of the term alludes to the barbarism and brutality of this race as described in many works of fantasy. In this context, Elsen proposes that the phoneme /k/ can be linked to "Potenz, Kraft und Stärke" (Elsen 46) and that antagonists often have dark vowels such as /o/ in their names (cf. 42). To sum up, many members of e.g. Tolkien's readership might be able to accept the name orcs as fitting a brutal, evil race of antagonists depicted in a very negative way.

Ross Smith has put forward similar results of his examination of Elvish and Dwarvish names, the first e.g. characterised by light vowels such as /e/ or /i/ in combination with smooth consonants as for instance /l/ or /m/ (cf. Smith 17). To underline his examination, Smith emphasises that "the phonetic quality of each term was of essential importance to Tolkien" (ibid 85)—if so, then most likely not only from an aesthetic, but also from a world-building point of view. On a semantic level, readers, who have a classical background and some knowledge of Latin or Roman mythology, might connect the name of the race to the Roman god of the underworld, *Orcus*, another element that supports the negative impression of the word orc itself, as well as that of the fictional race. Thus, Tolkien, as one of the authors to be taken into consideration, strikes in providing his readership with names that are acceptable to most of them. To turn these results around, a reader might easily accept orcs by the name of *Gorbag* and *Shagrat* (LotR II, 429) or even *Grishnákh* (LotR II, 49), but a barbaric, sinister orc called *Ildinis* would likely be harder to accept for many readers, since one connects the sound and the spelling of the term to characteristics unfitting to the Orcish race.

In addition to that, Elvish names such as *Galadriel*, *Celeborn* (LotR I, 21) or *Celebrimbor* (LotR I, 397) and their phonetic fitness (MC 211), as Tolkien calls it, could be called (more or less) true, but names as *Tuftuf*, the elven prince, are highly unacceptable due to certain expectations members of the readership might have towards members of the Elvish race. This means that authors (should) pay attention to their intended readership and have to keep in mind their possible backgrounds and expectations towards elements of the Secondary World when using fantastic language, something that many authors of fantastic literature successfully do. However, one should admit that it is highly unlikely that phonetic or semantic characteristics of fantastic language can always meet the wishes and expectations of each reader. Many readers might think that names such as *Elrond* (LotR I 17, our emphasis) or the aforementioned *Celebrimbor* are slightly less light or smooth than other Elvish names, hence losing some of their trueness. This is meant to say that there doubtlessly is no absolute trueness with respect to the literary realm when creating a secondary world. Also, it is important to underline that the image of a Primary World as described by Wolff is hardly to be agreed with an international, global readership.

Again, one has to give thought to separating the Primary World into different cultural spheres. Anglophone readers may regard the world *Gollum* (LotR I 62) as true, as fitting a "small slimy creature... as dark as darkness" (H 118f) making a "horrible swallowing noise in his throat" (120), which is "how he got his name" (ibid), a guttural name with a negative, animal connotation pronounced as /gɒləm/. On the other hand, a reader capable of speaking Turkish might be reminded of the Turkish word *oğlum* meaning 'my son', something that does not fit the creature *Gollum* as described above. There is no denying the fact that an author can only try to reach as much trueness as possible when creating his world and writing for his intended readership. The trueness of his work cannot be guaranteed for every cultural sphere among his readers and maintaining this principle might fall—if at all—into the duty of a translator.

An example of the latter circumstance might be the differences among the German translations of Tolkien's *Lord of the Rings*. The relation between Samwise and Frodo are a well-known example of the—in the eyes of some of the readers—successive and failed translation. While Tolkien himself writes "'Mr. Frodo, sir!'" (LotR I 83), the first translator, Margaret Carroux, uses the words "Herr, Herr Frodo" (HdR I (1969) 87), whereas the second translator, Wolfgang Krege, more recently resorted to "Herr Frodo, Chef" (HdR I (2003) 92). While the use of the word 'Chef', i.e. 'boss', in Krege's translation is not exactly factually incorrect—Frodo and Sam are not only friends, but also maintain a business relationship, if you might call it like that—the somewhat awkward term Krege uses nevertheless does not quite seem to agree with the reader's knowledge about Hobbits and the language of Tolkien's secondary world. For some German members of Tolkien's readership, the term 'Chef' cannot be considered true, in this case.

The second principle developed from Wolff's theory, the one of **otherness**, can similarly be elaborated on by means of examples taken from different works of fantasy literature. First, it remains to be said that Tolkien himself demands a "quality of strangeness ... in the expression" (FS 139), viz. that the language of fantasy has to set itself apart from that of everyday language used in a "mundane reality" (Butler 234). Gilman goes so far as to call the use of fantastic language "a ritual disguise" (ibid 138) and Burelbach claims that ordinary language, in this case names, can only be used as an "ironic counterpoint" (Burelbach 131)[3]. In order to set apart the fantastic language from the "vernacular" (Gilman 136), many authors employ invented languages as well as archaic languages such as Welsh, Old English, Old Norse or Latin meant to "impart a flavor of otherness and romance" (Butler 234).

The choice of archaic languages as a tool to convey a "perfect distance" (Le Guin 90) can be explained by the connotations e.g. British readers might connect to Welsh, Old English or even Old Norse, languages that are linked to a past full of legends, fighting and even magic, as it were. Thus, readers of Tolkien come across terms such as *Gorhendad* (LotR I 128) meaning 'great-grandfather' in Welsh, *Déagol* (ibid 69), an Old English word standing for 'dark, hidden, secret' or the word *Warg* (ibid 389) being a slight alteration of the Old Norse word *vargr* for 'wolf'.

But not only Tolkien, being "fascinated by the languages of the past" (James 63), uses archaic words and his own particular stock of languages to transport this feeling of otherness. In Rowling's successful works of *Harry Potter*, we find Greek mythological names such as *Argus* (Rowling 139) or quasi-Latin spells as for example *Petrificus Totalus* (ibid 294). The fact that Latin seems to be a common choice for magic spells is further underlined by its use in other works of fantasy as in Alan Garner's *Weirdstone of Brisingamen*, in which we find dark spells such as "coniuro et confirm super vos potentes in nomi fortis, metuendissimi, infandi" (ibid 111). In addition to these examples derived from languages such as Welsh or Latin, authors might also use terms that can be considered obsolete in the first language of the intended readership. While Tolkien named one of the families living in Bree *Appledore* (LotR I 203) and not Appletree, Tad Williams does not call a week simply that, but uses the archaic term *sennight* (Williams 484). In Terry Brook's works, "creatures ... **ceased** to exist" (Brooks 641) and things "**wither** and turn to dust, falling from his shuddering form" (ibid). Although these latter examples might not be called archaic or obsolete, they still differ from the language the readership is accustomed to from their everyday experience. Comparable to this even more so is Anne McCaffrey's choice of words in first novel about the Dragonriders of Pern: *Dragonflight*. In

---

3   Further below, we will try to prove that a missing otherness of a name e.g. at the very beginning of a work is often meant to ease the reader into the respective secondary world.

here, her characters do not simply *reject* something they see, but they "surveyed with mounting aversion" (McCaffrey 5), while their fear is not *pitiful, miserable* or *pathetic*, but "abject" (ibid 6). Hence, many authors of fantastic literature deliberately form their language in a way that distinguishes it from that (currently) used in the Primary World[4]. However, the language remains on a level of otherness that still enables the work to be read. If not, authors of fantastic literature could write their pieces of work in a language that is completely made up—and thus fulfilling Tolkien's wish for strangeness—without giving further help in form of a context explaining strange words or even a translation.

In this context, it is again important to underline that the otherness depends on the author as well as on the intended readers and their cultural sphere. Brennan Croft for example remarks that "Rowling's approach to naming ... is far more obvious, as befits a story aimed at younger and less experienced audience" (Brennan Croft 157). If we put fantastic literature under scrutiny, concentrating on the names we come across while reading, we might even be able to differentiate between names that are less strange and names that are highly different from the ones in the Primary World, which might induce further insight into the linguistic realm of world-building.

If we suppose a continuum to describe the otherness of names and terms, we should put creations such as *Harry Potter* from Rowling's works or *Richard Cypher* (Goodkind 18) from "The Wizard's first rule" at the lower end of this construction. Both names are very close to the Anglophone readers' background and thus the otherness from the viewpoint of the Primary World not exceedingly strong. The same holds true for some of the terms one comes across when reading Tolkien's works. When Bilbo Baggins treats the Hobbits to his "eleven**ty**-first birthday" (LotR I 27, our emphasis), the Anglophone reader can easily decipher the host's actual age by referring to similar numbers such as twen**ty** or thir**ty**. Tolkien's number is peculiar, but not all too strange from what the readership is accustomed to.

While the continuum progresses, we might examine names and creations such as *Seoman Mooncalf* (Williams 30) or *Ebekah* (ibid 12) with slight alterations such as additional or omitted letters and names such as *Severus Snape* (Rowling 139) partly based English words combined with Latin endings, which can be understood, but have a stranger flavor to them than those names mentioned before. At the opposite end of the continuum one comes across such names as *!Xabbu* (Williams, *Otherland* 82), *Binbiniqegabenik* (Williams 253) or *Angband* (LotR I, 253). Taken out of context, the reader might not be able to

---

4   In addition to that archaic terms, the use of languages such as Welsh or Old English as well as the invention of languages are meant to "enrichen the background history and consistency of tales" (Smith 81). This means that the secondary world created by the author gains deepness and proves to be more true, meeting Tolkien's demand (FS 117).

understand the meaning of those words or the whole character represented by this name, which is why he or she has to rely on further description or certain assumptions based on the phonological characteristics as already described in case of the term *orcs* further above.

Interestingly many of the authors of fantasy literature tend to play with the concept of otherness especially when it comes to the names of their characters or places. Having a look at Williams work titled *Dragonbone Throne*, we accompany his protagonist, who was named *Seoman* by his mother on her deathbed (Williams 30). The inhabitants of the Hayholt, a castle in which the first part of the plot takes place all bear names from the *Bible*, a pool of names that is well-known in many of cultures in the Primary World. It is only natural that people such as *Caleb the horse-boy* (ibid 114), *Isaak* (ibid 115), *Jakob the chandler* (ibid 15), *Jeremias* (ibid) or *Rachel* (ibid 5), who are reigned by monarchs such as *King John* (ibid) and his sons, *Prince Elias* (ibid 12) and *Prince Josua* (ibid), change Seoman's name into a more familiar *Simon* (ibid 4). On the other hand, the Sithi prince Jiriki, whom Seoman gets to know during his adventure, mostly resorts to *Seoman* (ibid 633) when talking to the protagonist. Similar to this, Seoman's troll friend Binbiniqegabenik bears a very long name with strange and unusual combinations of morphemes that the readership is not familiar with when it comes to names. Upon their first meeting, the troll asks Seoman to call him *Binabik* (ibid 253), which is much easier for the reader (as well as for the author, one might suppose). In some cases, Williams goes so far as to translate names featuring a high level of otherness in the same sentence. He presents the reader with "the huge **Circoille**, the **Combwood** of Hernystir" (ibid 65, our emphasis). While *Circoille* is an Irish word, which is not to be understood by many of his American readers, Williams translates the term into the English equivalent, *Combwood*. In doing so, the otherness is again both presented and diminished at the same time, thus supporting trueness, readability as well as a classification of the term. When Seoman first gets to know the name of his friend, the Sithi prince *Jiriki*, Williams provides the reader with its correct pronunciation by letting Seoman say "Jereekee, if that was his name" (ibid. 631). Williams makes clear that Jiriki is as strange to both the protagonist in the secondary world and the readership as other Sitha names such as *Iyu'unigato* (ibid 531) or *Shima'onari* (537).

However, by underlining the phonetic quality of the name, the reader is not completely left in the dark and can resort to his or her assumptions about the character by working with the sound of it. Finally, the reader of fantasy literature could also have a look at the compendium of names at the end of some works such as those of Tolkien or Williams.

An additional aspect of the works of fantasy that is concerned with the linguistic realm and the cultural realm at the same time is the field of referring to time, a small side note worth to be examined. While e.g. the Anglophone readership is familiar with such specifications as week, year, day as well as Monday, Tuesday, 150 BC and so on, some of the authors of fantastic literature confront their readership with slightly different systems. While Tolkien resorts to "September 22ⁿᵈ" (LotR I 28) and gives years in Shire reckoning (cf. ibid 18), Williams *November* is "Novander" (Williams 3), his *Saturday* "Satrinsday" (ibid 50) and the first of May as a holiday coinciding with the practice in many cultures is called "Belthainn" (ibid 173), the latter reminding of holidays such as *Beltane, Bealtaine* or *Beltaine*. McCaffrey in turn gives years as "turns" (Mc Caffrey 1). This again shows that the threshold between Primary and secondary world is maintained by language, which also influences the cultural background of the fictional world as such. Still, the readership has to be enabled to understand the underlying principle of the time elapsing within the novel, i.e. a year, be it turn or not, remains a year, **Nov**ander is still recognizable as **Nov**ember and **Sat**rinsday is still the sixth day of a week. Yet, we won't find a Christian chronology[5], since this would require the existence of the whole Christian culture in the secondary world, something that would hinder or diminish the otherness of this construct. Whether Williams strikes in finding an agreement between trueness and otherness by introducing the Son of God, Usires Aedon, who was executed by being nailed upside-down to a tree, into his work of fantasy, can be left to the approval or disapproval of the individual reader.

Concludingly, it can be said that the otherness or strangeness already demanded by Tolkien plays a similarly significant role as the concept of trueness mentioned above, which is intertwined with it. While the authors are obviously aware of the necessity of strangeness with regard to their language, the readership expects this quality in a way that signals them that they are entering another world. However, this threshold has to remain traversable enough.

Analysing the Trueness and Otherness of Fantastic Language

With the concepts presented above kept in mind, the analysis took three different major works of fantastic literature into consideration in order to examine the influence of the principles of the linguistic realm of worldbuilding onto the language used by the respective author. The works we chose are J.R.R. Tolkien's *The Fellowship of the Ring*, J.K. Rowling's *Harry Potter and the Philosopher's Stone* as well as Tad William's *The Dragonbone Chair*. Every work was ultimately intended for a slightly different readership—Rowling's work for instance is well-known for being aimed at a younger audience—and

---

5   "Much 'high' fantasy operates in pagan, unredeemed world" (Hunt & Lenz 34).

moreover, each piece of literature is part of a series of works and owing to his, also part of a gradually growing secondary world.

Examining the material, one might assume that names of characters, entities and landmarks play a huge role in the linguistic realm, since these are the terms a reader employs to identify with the plot and the world and to orientate himself or herself within the said world. Tolkien stresses in this matter that, to him, "a name comes first and the story follows" (L 165) revealing the huge importance of names in the linguistic realm. The author moreover fittingly rejects "any tinkering with the personal nomenclature" (L 190) in case of a translation of his oeuvre. This again underlines that the choice of names in many works is not one by accident or chance, but a well-planned part of the work offering "invaluable keys for interpreting literature" (Hough 309). Hilken is certainly right in stating that "die Wahl des Namens, besonders für wichtige Charaktere … mit besonderer Sorgfalt geschehen [muss]" (74). Else the reader would be stripped of further points of contact in the literary world providing chances to identify with and understand characters such as *Willy Loman*, *Mustapha Mond* or *Ebenezer Scrooge*.

Analysing the names one comes across in the course of reading the three works of fantasy, a categorisation of questions that need to be answered in doing so comes in handy. We decided to form two groups of aspects up for analysis. The first part, the **semantic layer**, is for example concerned with the spatiotemporal position or context every word assumes with regard to the readership. While *Harry Potter* is very close to an English reader both in a spatial and temporal sense and thus coinciding with the fact that the protagonist is part of the 'muggle' society formed after that of the Primary World, we find many terms that are further away in a spatiotemporal sense. The use of archaic languages such as Celtic, which are "extremely and surprisingly rare in English" (Meyer 199) or languages that are not well-known in the readers' culture, such as Japanese or Inuktitut in case of William's works move the marker of otherness considerably. In terms of remoteness, Burelbach differentiates between historical names from myths or fictions, places or terms from geographically remote languages and times that are historically remote (cf. 137). While in places incomplete and too narrow, Burelbach's position puts further emphasis on the significance of the sources the author uses to create otherness.

The question, which etymology lies at the basis of a term and the very effect of its origin is closely related to this, as already pointed out above. There is an obvious reason why Tad Williams resorts to Old Norse, Norwegian and Swedish terms to name aspects of his Rimmersgard culture in his work. The reader links places such as "Ijsgard" (Williams 553), characters as for example "Jarnauga" (ibid 105) or entities such as "Dror" (ibid 50) to parts of Northern cultures he or she is aware of and thus the trueness and otherness fits William's race mostly modelled after the Viking culture. On the other hand, we find many terms that are much closer to the intended readership in terms of spatio-temporal position and etymology right at the beginning of many works of fantasy literature. While Tolkien's English readership is eased over the threshold into the secondary world while experiencing "names … which are not 'meaning-less', but are English in form" (Hammond & Scull 752) such as **Baggins**, **Boffin**, **Fredegar** or **Longbottom**, Williams uses a pool of names from the *Bible*. Yet, the otherness rises with the progression of the plot. While James claims that in portal-quests, "heroes… move from familiar worlds into unfamiliar ones" (James 64), this is seemingly realised by means of the language as well. Tolkien's reader is gradually confronted with stranger names "freed from the drab blur of triteness or familiarity" (FS 146) with a stronger spatiotemporal remoteness such as *Archet* (LotR I 195) up to *Carn Dûm* (ibid 187).

It is however important to say that the remoteness does not increase with the number of pages, but with the distance from the starting point of the plot within the secondary world. Hence, the reader experiences his or her own indi-vidual thresholds by entering the secondary world as well as by accompanying Frodo Baggins through the world and away from the character's homeland. Another aspect that needs to be considered when analysing fantastic language is whether a term has its own lexical meaning that is known or unknown to the reader. Severus Snape as one of the characters to be found in *Harry Potter* clearly provides the reader with information about some of his character traits, i.e. his first name presents him as a **severe**, a strict, harsh, cold person, while his surname lets the reader think of words such as *sneap*, *snap* or *snaipen* with a meaning of 'injure' or 'rebuke'. While lexical meaning of the first part of the name is obvious to many of Rowling's readers the latter one can e.g. be deciphered on a semantic or lexical level with the help of a knowledge about Middle English or by identifying it as archaic in a way strengthening Bauer's statement that Tolkien considered language as "Rätsel, das es zu entschlüsseln gilt" (Bauer 106). This resembles the observation Wolfgang Iser described in his reader-response criticism, viz. that the "reader and author participate in a game of imagination" (Iser 51), something that the reader has to work out "for himself" (ibid). The last aspect the analysis needs to take into consideration is, whether there are similar names or words in the readers' culture, which again calls for the separation of the Primary World into cultural spheres. While English readers might not recognise names such as *Nisses* (Williams 412) in *Dragonbone Throne* as part of their familiar pool of names, a reader living in Northern Europe might accept the name as the Nordic version of Nils. A similar case would be the Danish name *Hoder* as part of "Saint Hoderund" (ibid 406) to be found in the same novel.

The second and final layer, one needs to examine, is that of the spelling or rather phonology of the terms in fantastic literature, the **phonetic layer**. While this area is admittedly difficult to analyse due to a lack of information in many cases, it is nonetheless "of essential importance" (Smith 85) e.g. to Tolkien favouring the "demotic ... a spoken language ... [that] must be read aloud" (Gilman 141) as one author puts it. The cases that were presented above, those of terms such as Orcs or the Elvish and Dwarvish names, suggest that sounds might carry additional meaning helping to raise trueness and otherness. While the reader might not be able to work with parts of the lexical meaning of the name *Severus Snape*, he or she can easily refer to his or her expectations towards a character, whose name contains sharp fricatives calling forth images that fit the character of the bearer of the name. Hough stresses in this case that "the sounds of names ... reinforce the lexical meanings and morphological forms" (Hough 307). The same holds true for examples taken from other works. The name of William's sword *Jingizu* (Williams 201) seems adequate due to its sharp sounds, while Tolkien's place *Cirith Gorgor* (LotR I 487) with its harsh and rough sounds creates a very negative connotation in the mind of his audience.

There is no denying the fact that the reader can resort to the phonetic form of a word in a work in fantasy literature in order to find support in categorising the term into different drawers e.g. labelled [STRONG], [SMALL], [GOOD] or [BAD] etc. To maintain trueness, Sauron is Sauron and not *Sari*, while Samwise is Samwise and not *Sarmwos*. As the relation between the sound and the underlying idea it stands for is the first aspect, a second one refers to the common or strange combination of sounds and the overall form of a word. While Binbiniqegabenik is very hard to pronounce due to the unfamiliar length of the term and combination of sounds or letters, we even find additional letters, signs and markers that provide additional information about the pronunciation of terms, but are—at the same time—not a significant part of the first languages of many of the readers e.g. in Anglophone countries. In Tolkien, we find "Crébain" (LotR I, 371) or "Udûn" (ibid 344) in Williams "Lluth" (Williams 49) and "Enki Annukhai Shi'Iago" (ibid 187) as well as "F'lar" (McCaffrey 5) and "F'nor" (ibid 6) in McCaffrey further emphasising the otherness between Primary World, or in this case cultural sphere, and secondary world and at the same time improving the trueness for a reader, who realises that he or she is emerging in a "very distinct" (Wolf 63) environment.

So as to further elucidate the different layers which are admittedly and unquestionably intertwined and hard to set apart from each other, one needs to examine examples taken from some of the works of fantasy mentioned above.

The first one is that of "Folco Boffin" (LotR I 56), a minor Hobbit character in Tolkien's first book of *The Lord of the Rings*. Starting off with the first name, one can recognise that *Folco* is a slightly altered form of the Germanic name *Falco* still in use in many European cultures. At the same time, *Folco* is a French name and has Latin roots linked to current words such as *falcon*. The stylistic coherence with other Hobbit names such as *Bilbo, Frodo, Lotho* or *Hugo* is obvious, all of which contain similar vowels and display a shortness fitting the very build of the race[6]. To switch over to the surname, the reader recognizes *Boffin* as an existing name in England that—at the same time—gains further deepness by having the lexical meaning of scientist in derogatory way, perhaps an ironic description of the down-to-earth-mentality of the Shire-folk. The phonetic layer of the analysis reveals further insight. While the shortness of the name reflects the well-known solidity and slowness of the Hobbits, the smoothness of the consonants /b/ and /f/ especially in the surname coincide with the description of the inhabitants of the Shire, who are "inclined to be fat and do not hurry unnecessarily" (ibid 1). Moreover, the /l/ conveys a light and weak quality (cf. Jakobson & Waugh 191). However, the harsher /k/ in the first name slightly disagrees with the smoothness of the pronunciation.

A similar example would be that of Lobelia[7] Sackville-Baggins (LotR I 27), with a rather female, short and rural first name and a surname that sets the branch of the family apart from that of Bilbo's Bagginses. The often mentioned French roots of *Sackville* Tolkien used in his "Gallophobie" (Bauer 105)[8] create further images in the mind of the readers, although Sackville is a known English name (Hammond & Scull 762) nevertheless alluding to English words such as vile or Old English words such as *sæcc* meaning 'fighting' or English verbs such as *sack*, something Lobelia obviously did during Bilbo's adventure in *The Hobbit* (H 361). The phonetic quality of the fricative /s/ further contrasts the name Sackville with smoother Hobbit names. To sum up, the name itself agrees with the cultural background of the Hobbits, while simultaneously transporting further information about the bearer and her position in the framework of Tolkien's secondary world.

An example of a term that features a higher amount of otherness and a different value of trueness can be found in William's oeuvre. The reader comes across a dragon named by the mysterious Sithi, which are close to Tolkien's elvish characters in culture and appearance, which was apparently slain by King John the Presbyter decades before the actual plot of the novel (cf. Williams 5). Going hand in hand with this circumstance, the name of the dragon, "Shurakai" (ibid 10), conveys a spatiotemporal position far away from an Anglophone readership.

---

6   This might also be the reason why names such as "Meriadoc" (LotR I, 20) or "Peregrin" (ibid) are shortened to more Hobbit-like forms as *Merry* (ibid 56) or *Pippin* (ibid) (or even Pip).

7   Interestingly, using names of flowers for female characters is a predominant way in literature in general and fantasy literature in particular. In Rowling's *Harry Potter*, one stumbles upon names such as "**Lavender** Brown" (Rowling 131) or Ginny, i.e. **Ginevra**, Weasley (cf. ibid 103).

8   We do not quite agree with the image of Tolkien using French sounding terms to stress a negative connotation. The positively connoted plant, partly French *Kingsfoil* (Hammond & Scull 781), also called *Athelas* (ibid 259) does not fit this absolute statement. Yet we find French words in *Harry Potter* as well and in there especially in negative contexts such as "Malfoy" (Rowling 120) or "Voldemort" (ibid 17).

At first glance, the reader cannot work with the lexical meaning of the name and has to resort to the information at hand. Only a second look (in this case, into a Japanese dictionary) reveals that the name is actually a compound made up of the Japanese borrowings *Shura*, meaning 'blood bath' and 'carnage' and *kai* standing for 'world' or 'sea', the latter word being even harder to pinpoint than the first one.

While the lexical meaning of the name is indeed adequate, it is nonetheless almost doomed to fail at being understood by the ordinary Anglophone reader due to its high amount of otherness. Yet the phonetic layer sheds further light on the very creature by means of hard sounds such as /k/ underlining the brutality of the creature and a fricative calling forth images of a snake or even wind and fire breath as already in the case of such syllables as –sau and –sly (cf. Brennan Croft 162). So the reader has to engage in "working things out for himself" (Iser 51) while tackling the "Rätsel" (Bauer 106). However, the otherness is prevailing due to the spatial position of the loanword and the trueness is supported by the phonetic quality of the word and—if deciphered—by the lexical meaning of the two parts of the name.

Similar to the example of *Shurakai*, Williams confronts the reader with a character by the name of *Jarnauga* (Williams 105), an old, stern eremite watching the enemy as a frontier-guard and scholarly member of the race of Rimmersmen resembling Vikings or other Nordic folks to be found in the Primary World. If we examine the semantic layer, we again are left more or less in the dark as an Anglophone reader. In terms of cultural spheres, a German reader recognises the part *auga* resembling the German *Auge* and itself taken from Old Norse, while an English reader, who is not capable of speaking languages spatiotemporally closer to *Jarnauga* has to work with the description and profession of the character, who looks around with "bright, **steely** eyes" (ibid 525, our emphasis). The first part of the name is even more unfamiliar to the intended readership. *Jarn* is an Old Norse word for 'iron', thus coinciding with the sternness and the lebensraum of the character. The etymology and origin of the name further agrees with the overall impression of the Rimmersmen as fictional Vikings. The phonetic characteristics of the name are predominated by the guttural /r/ and the long, dark vowels (Jakobson & Waugh 192) describing the bearer according to his background and manner or appearance. All in all, both otherness and trueness are maintained accordingly and combining the aspects described above.

Conclusion

Taking the examination within the linguistic realm into consideration, we can conclude the following: Although readers need to encounter a certain "otherness" in order to notice the foreignness of a sub-created world, an amount of familiarity is also critical when thinking of the notion of creating "under a certain impression" of pre-existing primary world defaults. We believe that the elements which resemble primary world defaults within a successfully sub-created [in the sense of Tolkien's FS] world are the key for literary discourse in fantasy literature. Questions like "why and how do anachronistic items help us emerge with a sub-created world?" and "what does the appreciation of obsolete elements within a readership tell us on a sociological level?" can now be analysed with the help of empirical evidence provided when using the methodology briefly introduced in the example of the linguistic realm above. Therefore we highly encourage the usage and development of this methodology and of this inter-medial field of studies. Larger corpora may enable an even deeper possibility of interpretation and understanding of the discourse between secondary and primary worlds and can ultimately lead to a higher appreciation of fantasy literature in the academic world.

Bibliography

Attebery, Brian: "Structuralism." *The Cambridge Companion to Fantasy Literature.* Eds.: Edward James & Farah Mendlesohn. Cambrige: Cambridge University Press, 2012, 81-90

Bauer, Hannspeter. "Zu Tolkiens Wortschatz". *Inklings* 10 (1992): 103-110

Brennan Croft, Janet. "Naming the Evil One: Onomastic Strategies in Tolkien and Rowling." *Mythlore* 28 (2009): 149-163

Brooks, Terry. *The Sword of Shannara. Book One of the Shannara Trilogy.* London: Orbit, 2006

Burelbach, Frederick. "An Introduction to Naming in the Literature of Fantasy". *Literary Onomastic Studies* 9 (1982): 131-148

Butler, Catherine. "Modern Children's Fantasy". *The Cambridge Companion to Fantasy Literature.* Eds.: Edward James & Farah Mendlesohn. Cambridge: CUP, 2012, 224-235

Carpenter, Humphrey (Ed.). *The Letters of J.R.R. Tolkien.* London: HarperCollins, 2006

DiGiovanna, James. "Worldmaking as Art Form". *The International Journal of the Arts in Society* Vol. 2, No. 1. Melbourne: Common Ground Publishing, 2007, 115-123

Elsen, Hilke. *Phantastische Namen – Die Namen in Science-Fiction und Fantasy zwischen Arbitrarität und Wortbildung.* Tübingen: Narr Francke Attempto, 2008

Genesis. In The Norton Anthology of World Masterpieces, Vol. I. 6th Edition. NY: W.W. Norton and Co., 1992, 49-69

Gilman, Greer. "The Languages of the Fantastic". *The Cambridge Companion to Fantasy Literature.* Eds. Edward James & Farah Mendlesohn. Cambridge: CUP, 2012, 134-146

Goodkind, Terry. *Wizard's First Rule.* New York: Tor Books, 1995

Hammond, Wayne G., & Christina Scull. *The Lord of the Rings. A Reader's Companion.* London: HarperCollins, 2014

Hough, Carole. *The Oxford Handbook of Names and Naming.* Oxford: OUP, 2016

Hunt, Peter, & Millicent Lenz. *Alternative Worlds in Fantasy Fiction.* New York: Continuum, 2001

Iser, Wolfgang. "The Reading Process: A Phenomenological Approach". *Reader-Response Criticism. From Formalism to Post-Structuralism.* Ed.: Jane Tompkins. Baltimore/ London: JHU Press, 1980, 50-69

Jackson, Rosemary. *Fantasy: The Literature of Subversion.* London: Methuen, 1981

Jakobson, Roman, & Linda R. Waugh. *The Sound Shape of Language.* Berlin/New York: Mouton de Gruyter: 2002

James, Edward. "Tolkien, Lewis and the Explosion of Genre Fantasy". *The Cambridge Companion to Fantasy Literature*. Eds.: Edward James & Farah Mendlesohn. Cambridge: CUP, 2012, 62-78

Le Guin, Ursula. "From Elfland to Poughkeepsie". *The Language of the Night. Essays on Fantasy and Science Fiction*. Ed.: Susan Wood. New York: Ultramarine Publishing, 1979, 83-96

McCaffrey, Anne. *Dragonflight*. New York: Del Rey Books, 1986

Meyer, Paul Georg, et al. *Descriptive English Linguistics. An Introduction*. Tübingen: Narr Francke Attempto, 2008

Rowling, J.K. *Harry Potter and the Philosopher's Stone*. London, Berlin, New York: Bloomsbury, 2000

Smith, Ross. *Inside Language. Linguistic and Aesthetic Theory in Tolkien*. Zürich/Jena: Walking Tree Publishers, 2011

Tolkien, John Ronald Reuel. *Der Herr der Ringe. Band 1: Die Gefährten*. Stuttgart: Klett, 1969.

---. "Beowulf: The Monsters and the Critics." *The Monsters and the Critics and Other Essays*. Ed.: Christopher Tolkien. London: Harper Collins Publishers, 2006, 5-48

---. *Der Herr der Ringe. Ausgabe in neuer Übersetzung und Rechtschreibung: Die Gefährten*. Stuttgart: Klett-Cotta, 2003

---. "On Fairy-Stories". *The Monsters and the Critics and Other Essays*. Ed.: Christopher Tolkien. London: HarperCollins, 1997, 109-161

---. *The Annotated Hobbit*. London: HarperCollins, 2003

---. *The Fellowship of the Ring. Being the First Part of The Lord of the Rings*. London: HarperCollins, 2005

---. *The Two Towers. Being the Second Part of The Lord of the Rings*. London: HarperCollins, 1999

Weinreich, Frank. *Fantasy – Einführung*. Essen: Oldib Verlag, 2007

Williams, Tad. *Otherland. City of Golden Shadow*. New York: DAW Books, 1996

---. *The Dragonbone Chair. Book One of Memory, Sorrow and Thorn*. New York: DAW Books, 1989

Wolf, Mark J.P. *Building Imaginary Worlds. The Theory and History of Subcreation*. New York: Taylor & Francis Ltd, 2012 (also: Kindle e-book edition when referenced with position)

Behind the Names of Torhthelm and Tídwald: Tolkien's Onomastic Imagination in "The Homecoming of Beorhtnoth Beorhthelm's Son"

Łukasz Neubauer (Koszalin)

Despite the practically infinite selection of all sorts of anthroponyms (both real and invented), "christening" a literary character is not always a matter of a straightforward and inconsequential assignment of names to the *dramatis personae* of a novel, short story, play or film. The authorial attitudes obviously vary considerably from absolutely indifferent ones, such as that of Woody Allen, who once claimed that his sole consideration in choosing the characters' names is their shortness (Lax 86-7), to the far more methodical approaches that may be observed in, for instance, the works of Charles Dickens, where the typically abundant *nomina propria* often reveal their bearers' personality and/or social standing (Hawes 2-4). To a certain degree, the latter also seems to be the attitude favoured by J.R.R. Tolkien, for whom names very often played a formative role in the development of a character, generating stories in his immensely imaginative mind (Carpenter 230). This naturally applies to the overwhelming majority of his writings, including the less serious stories, which he, at least initially, intended for his own children (e.g. *Roverandom* or *Farmer Giles of Ham*), the more "adult" works that constitute the Middle-earth canon (*The Hobbit*, *The Lord of the Rings* and *The Silmarillion*) and, last but not least, all sorts of quasi-academic publications of argumentative persuasion (e.g. *Mythopoeia* or "The Homecoming of Beorhtnoth Beorhthelm's Son").[1]

It is in fact the last of the aforementioned texts that is of particular interest here, since it is perhaps the only known (quasi-)literary work penned by the author of *The Lord of the Rings* that is not in any way connected with the world of fantasy (either in terms of its setting, or the characters it focuses upon), and so its small cast is almost automatically deprived of the numerous linguistic peculiarities that may so often be found in Tolkien's sub-created world (e.g. numerous alternative names or descriptive bynames in various invented languages). "The Homecoming of Beorhtnoth Beorhthelm's Son" is an alliterative dialogue directly inspired by the somewhat ambiguous heroic considerations

---

1   Although there are essentially no "characters" to be found in *Mythopoeia* (apart from the more or less explicit references to God), this spirited defence of myth-making begins with a rather unambiguous dedication from Philomythus ("myth-lover") to Misomythus ("myth-hater"), i.e., respectively, Tolkien himself and his still hesitant friend C.S. Lewis. Needless to say, both "names" were coined by the author of the poem.

examined by the anonymous late-tenth- or early-eleventh-century poet in what ultimately came to be known as *The Battle of Maldon*, perhaps "the only purely heroic poem in Old English" (Gordon 25).[2] Tolkien's work which, despite its quasi-literary form, was originally published, with two accompanying short essays ("The Death of Beorhtnoth" and "Ofermod"), in 1953, in the sixth volume of the scholarly journal *Essays and Studies by the Members of the English Association*, constitutes an extended commentary on the bearing of the English warriors who, in the summer of 991, faced their seafaring adversaries by the mouth of the river Pant. Reading *The Battle of Maldon* chiefly in line with the assumed intentions and purpose in composition, Tolkien explicitly eulogises all those who chose to stay on the battlefield after their leader had been slain and does not in the least try to exculpate those who decide to save their lives by fleeing for the safety of the nearby woods. Most importantly, however, he expresses his overt criticism (but not thorough condemnation) of the battle tactics employed by the poem's only historical (or, at least, historically-verifiable) figure, the aged Ealdorman Byrhtnoth (here referred to as "Beorhtnoth"), who, it seems, decided to seek vainglorious fame in an uneven confrontation with the vikings.[3]

The varying opinions of literary critics, whose focus hitherto had been mainly upon the heroic considerations so lavishly expressed in the poem, were here put in the mouths of practically the only two characters in "The Homecoming of Beorhtnoth",[4] his faithful retainers Torhthelm and Tídwald.[5] Although they are naturally full-scale literary figures (as much as the brevity of the text allows for it), each with a history of his own, it seems that they may—and, in all likelihood, should—be treated principally as the fictionalised projections of the critical views expressed by the contemporary academics including Tolkien's friend and colleague E.V. Gordon, E.D. Laborde, and, of course, the author himself. Alter-

---

2 Although it is known to have been originally conceived (albeit in a different form) in the early 1930s (Anderson 21), "The Homecoming of Beorhtnoth" may sometimes look as a direct response to Gordon's 1937 edition of *The Battle of Maldon*.

3 The almost universal opinion that the ealdorman's decision to allow the vikings safe passage across the water that separated them from the English defenders (*The Battle of Maldon* 84-95) was dictated by his selfless imitation of the legendary "heroic ideal" has been recently challenged by a number of scholars including, for instance, Donald G. Scragg and Stephen Pollington. This, however, is a highly complex issue which lays beyond the scope of the present work.

4 The only other (living) characters that appear in "The Homecoming of Beorhtnoth" are not assigned names of their own. These include the corpse-strippers (8-9), chanting monks from Ely (12-13) and the mysterious "Voice in the dark" (13).

5 Interestingly, the characters' full names are only listed next to their speaking parts in order to identify the speaker – as in a play. Throughout the text, both characters use hypocoristic forms of Totta (Torhthelm) and Tída (Tídwald). It is also interesting to note that in the earliest versions of "The Homecoming" Tolkien calls them 'Totta'/'Tudda' and 'Pudda'/'Tibba', without ever providing their full original names (Honegger 190).

natively, they may also stand for the two conflicting—though not necessarily mutually exclusive—sides of Tolkien's own inner dialogue, the youthful, and so rather heroic-minded approach represented by Torhthelm, versus the mature, and thus considerably more level-headed one personalised in the character of Tídwald.[6] Finally, Byrhtnoth's retainers sometimes seem to emblematise the opposite poles of the still quite syncretic conception of man's principal duties in early medieval warfare: the fundamentally, if not always overtly, Christian virtues of prudence and temperance (Tídwald) and the traditional Germanic merits of courage, boldness and thirst for fame (Torhthelm). If such indeed were Tolkien's intentions, both the interpretative scope and the depth of his work, particularly with regard to its onomastic content, should become all the more challenging to the critically-minded readers, especially that in this very case it was in all likelihood not the characters' names that "generated [the] story" (Carpenter 230), but the other way round.

Seen in the purely historical context, it comes as no surprise that the names given to the two characters that appear in "The Homecoming of Beorhtnoth" should be genuine anthroponyms found in some of the surviving records from the pre-Norman period of English history. This does not only lend authenticity to the onomastic stratum of Tolkien's dialogue, but it also, just as importantly, provides a further, extranarrative, commentary on the nature of their attitudes to Byrhtnoth's conduct prior to and, in particular, during the battle of Maldon. After all, unlike their real-life counterparts, whose birth names may at best only reflect their parents' wishful desires, literary characters are usually "born" with full bags of life experiences, values and beliefs. In other words, a real person may not always live up to the naming expectations,[7] but a fictional character is an entirely different matter. Here the possibilities to match one's onomastic potentials are literarily boundless.[8]

There are of course certain names in the world of literary imagination whose meaning needs no further clarification. Everyone who has ever read Charles

---

6   Seth Lerer, for instance, maintains that the characters of Torhthelm and Tídwald "present a vision of the two sides of Tolkien himself: the poet and philologist, the imagist and the empiricist" (86).

7   Cf., for instance, Henry VII's eldest son Arthur who died in 1502, more than five months short of his sixteenth birthday, and so never became the King Arthur his father indubitably wished him to be.

8   This may in some way call to the mind Plato's theory of forms, in particular the idea of the correctness of names which the Athenian examines in his dialogue *Cratylus*. Seen in this context, it appears that in real life people are assigned with the names that are almost purely conventional, i.e. they have little or no intrinsic relation to their bearers' character, looks or intelligence. In contrast, the names of some literary characters (e.g. Miss Murdstone in Charles Dickens's *David Copperfield* or Rick Deckard (a pun on René Descartes) in Philip K. Dick's *Do Androids Dream of Electric Sheep?*) are natural in the sense that they express the characters' essence with regard to the features that are vital to the development of the plot and, most importantly, the said work's interpretation.

Dickens's *Oliver Twist* should be aware of the fact that the novel is full of often unexpected twists and turns of the plot in which the title protagonist plays no small part. Reading the works of Tolkien, one must not, however, expect such perspicuities. Even his children's books, like the aforesaid stories of *Roverandom* and *Farmer Giles of Ham*, are abundant in various philological nuances whose subtleties may not always be so transparent to those of lesser awareness of their cultural foundations. Needless to say, the level of difficulty further increases in the case of his more serious writings, both literary and academic, where the cultural awareness of the reader should (at least in theory) go hand in hand with the knowledge of languages, real as well as invented.

Before taking a closer look at what the author of "The Homecoming of Beorhtnoth" could have had in mind in assigning his characters with the names of Torhthelm and Tídwald, we shall first try to examine their primary significance, i.e. what these two anthroponyms might have originally meant to the inhabitants of Anglo-Saxon England. Much as the bulk of English (or, in fact, all Germanic) *nomina propria*, the names of Torhthelm and Tídwald are dithematic, i.e. they constitute two-element compounds in which one of the components (in both cases the second) forms the semantic backbone and the other (here the first) acts as its adjectival or nominal modifier. In the first instance, the meaning of the Old English noun *helm* "helmet, protection, protector" is enhanced by the adjective *torht* "bright, radiant, noble, illustrious", while in the latter, the antecedent noun *tid* "time" evidently specifies what exactly the *wald* "authority, might, control" is supposed to be in command of.[9] The former, therefore, appears to denote a "bright" or "shining helmet", whereas the latter a "ruler", "wielder", "protector" or "controller of time".

It could hardly be argued that in Anglo-Saxon England both names were given by parents in good faith, trusting that they would constitute a good omen for their newly born sons. That of Torhthelm evidently invokes the heroic values of early medieval world. The helmet was, after all, an indispensable attribute of an illustrious warrior, perhaps—given its shining quality—one in command of a larger troop of *heorþgeneatas*.[10] The name of Tídwald is a bit more problematic in its interpretative dimensions, as it does not contain any of the fairly common, and thus easily identifiable components of military or

---

9   Tom Shippey points out that the meaning of Tídwald's name has also been rather obscurely
    rendered as "time forest". It is, however, far more likely, he observes, that Tolkien's *wald*
    is the Mercian form of West Saxon *weald*, the formative element in the verb *wealdan* "to
    wield" (Shippey 326).

10 There are, of course, countless male anthroponyms of indubitable Germanic provenance
    that incorporate the word *helm*. Some of them—like Diethelm, Helmut or Wilhelm—are
    still relatively popular, both in and outside the Germanic-speaking world.

mythological association.[11] Instead, the "ruler of time", if such be its accurate rendering into Modern English, appears to evoke connotations of a somewhat different nature—those of a more lordly and, above all, experienced man whose wisdom derives from both his position and age.

Not surprisingly, some of these character traits find discernible semantic expression in the Torhthelm and Tídwald of Tolkien's "Homecoming". It should be noted, however, that the names of the characters that were first brought to life in the early or mid-1930s by the author of *The Lord of the Rings* do not necessarily have to be perfectly consistent with the meanings which were assigned to their sons by the inhabitants of Anglo-Saxon England. For instance, it is more than just probable that what Tolkien seems to have envisioned in the name of Torhthelm was not quite as positive in its numerous semantic undertones as the hopes and expectations of the English parents a thousand years ago or so. Indeed, it often seems that the very idea of "christening" the younger retainer "bright helmet" was, at least in some measure, dictated by a certain degree of irony which stemmed not only from the writer's overt criticism of Byrhtnoth's battle tactics, but also his evident discontent with the eulogising views of some twentieth-century critics.

Tolkien's Torhthelm is the son of a minstrel—and, evidently, an aspiring poet himself—whose head is said to be "full of old lays concerning the heroes of northern antiquity" (HB 4). Accordingly, he often tries to cast "the hard facts of war and sorrow" (Lerer 86) into the conventional forms of early Germanic verse. He also repeatedly mouths words in praise and honour of his fallen ealdorman, calling him "a prince peerless in peace and war" (HB 6) and imagining a "high ... barrow his bones to keep" (7). Being brought up on songs and legends of the heroic and thus, predominantly pre-Christian, past, Torhthelm is therefore evidently incapable of seeing any major ethical flaws in the character of his lord and distinguishing between the acts of Byrhtnoth's self-centred heroism and the regrettably unrealised employment of more pragmatic battle tactics. What is more, instead of focusing upon the more Christian dimensions of the ealdorman's death in combat (as is the case with his older companion), the suddenly pensive Torhthelm almost fails to acknowledge any transcendental-like conclusion to Byrhtnoth's life, save for the elusive (and therefore antithetical to the Christian worldview) glory that shall live on for as long as "word or woe in the world lasteth" (7).

There could be little doubt that, just as some Anglo-Saxon parents, by "christening" him "Torhthelm", Tolkien wished to accentuate the military and

---

11 What is more, it is probable that the name Tídwald was not particularly popular in Anglo-Saxon England. The PASE (Prosopography of Anglo-Saxon England) database, which currently consists of almost 13,000 personal entries, lists only a single bearer of that name, a ninth-century priest who is known to have signed at least two charters.

heroic-minded aspects of the younger man's stance (after all, notwithstanding his absence in the battle, he does not hesitate to use Byrhtnoth's sword against one of the skulking corpse-strippers). However, given his clearly observable narrow-mindedness with respect to the more objective evaluation of the ealdorman's military endeavours and the inability to tell the difference between some imaginary "troll-shapes ... or hell-walkers" (8) and the "hungry folk and masterless men, miserable skulkers" (9) that came to collect whatever of value was left on the field of battle, the name of Torhthelm should also invoke in the readers other, far less favourable associations.

In an endocentric compound like this (much as in Æþelhelm, Winehelm or Wulfhelm), the noun *helm* constitutes the basic lexical component which is further modified by the adjective *torhth* (also found in the names like Torhtgyð, Torhtmund or Torthwald), and so is of prime significance to comprehend the semantic peculiarities of the "bright" + "helmet" combination and, consequently, rationalise Tolkien's wordplay in "The Homecoming of Beorhtnoth". One immediate association with this piece of war-gear might be, of course, with the part of the body that it actually protects. Needless to say, a helmet is invariably connected with its owner's head, which, in turn, is the very organ where certain hubristic tendencies (such as overconfidence or the wish to outdo other men in whatever the harsh reality of early medieval world would require) could sometimes be conceived.[12] It is also the head where all sorts of nightmarish dreams and fancies flourish and intermingle with one's perception and understanding of reality, as is evidently the case with the romanticising and fantasy-filled mind of the teeth-rattling (3) and night-dreaming (6, 8, 9, 12) Torhthelm.

This critical symbolism behind the name of Torhthelm (and its evident capital associations) should become even more thought-provoking when we take into consideration the amount and character of Tolkien's allusions to Byrhtnoth's head, which, as we learn from the twelfth-century *Liber Eliensis*, was hacked off by the surging vikings.[13] Upon finding the body of Byrhtnoth, the younger man sentimentally conceives his fallen lord being merely "asleep", with his head laid "upon a hard pillow" (4). In contrast, his older companion (and a downright realist) somewhat crudely swears upon the head of Saint Edmund,[14]

---

12 Note the existence of numerous semantically-related expressions (not only in English) —such as being "big-headedness" or having "a head in the clouds"—where the head is the invariably central lexical element.

13 *Adversari paucitate sociorum eius animati, facto cuneo, conglobati unanimiter in eum irruerunt et caput pungnantis vix cum magno labore secuerunt, quod inde fugientes secum in patriam portaverunt* "The enemy, heartened by their small number, formed a wedge and, grouped together, rushed with a sole resolve in mind to cut off his head; this done, they took it with them as they fled to their native land" (book II, ch. 62).

14 Interestingly (and quite fittingly, given the condition of Byrhtnoth's corpse), Tolkien makes Tídwald swear upon the head of the ninth-century East Anglian king Edmund the Martyr, who was himself slain and beheaded by the vikings during their campaign

before remarking upon the heaviness of the ealdorman's headless corpse (9). Most importantly, however, it is Byrhtnoth's head that Torhthelm—still unaware of its absence—first focuses upon when he begins to chant a sorrowful dirge in memory of the beloved leader ("His head was higher than the helm of kings with heathen crowns", 6). For the young man, fascinated by the gripping tales of some great figures of the past, headless or not, his lord clearly appears to be some sort of a role-model whose military deeds he wishes not only to eulogise in his own poetic endeavours (6-7), but also emulate as a somewhat belated avenger. However, much as his cruelly decapitated heroic exemplar, the "bright-helmeted" youth ends up losing his head (albeit figuratively) when he is suddenly confronted with the creeping shades he initially takes for some Grendel-like demons emerging from Hell (8). The somewhat parodic battle rage he then almost instantly succumbs to is without doubt a knock-on effect of his vivid imagination whose curious projections evidently eclipse some of his reasoning faculties.

Another interesting aspect to Torhthelm's name is, of course, its "brightness". In pre-Norman England it would have probably laid more emphasis upon the presumed superiority of the person, feudal, moral or both. In Tolkien's viewpoint, though, formed in some part by his personal experience of the Great War, the intensity of the *helm's* luminance could have also invoked further negative connotations, such as the accentuation of the young man's heroic illusions and the romantic falsification—or at least some sort of idiosyncratic deformation—of the true essence of warfare in general. It is a characteristic feature of any brightness—real or imagined—that it is never permanent, and so might be dimmed easily by even a small and seemingly insignificant imperfection of its form or matter, for instance a dent on the helmet's hitherto smooth surface. Evidently fascinated by the heroic image and deeds of his dear ealdorman, Torhthelm in some degree personifies all these symbolic projections. He is, of course, superficially flawless in his dedication to the good cause, cherishing the traditional heroic dimensions of Byrhtnoth's character (courage, magnanimity, endurance etc.). At the same time, however, his appreciation of these undeniable virtues are badly marred by the sheer fact that, in his romanticised vision of war, the young man practically fails to understand that the ealdorman unfortunately opted for placing his own interests (personal glory, immortalisation in poetry etc.) above those of his people (safety, advantageous positioning etc.). Torhthelm's "helmet" is, therefore, one whose brightness, to use Tolkien's words from the second accompanying essay of his 1953 publication ("Ofermod"), "is never quite pure; it is of gold and an alloy" (14).[15]

---

of conquest in 869 (Smith 21). Much as the ealdorman of Essex, Edmund is also known to have unsuccessfully negotiated with the enemy (Bale 3).

15 Although the above words originally refer to the oft-idealised "heroic ideal", or what Tolkien calls "northern heroic spirit" (13-14), it is difficult not to notice the symbol-laden analogy between the components of Byrhtnoth's flawed conduct prior to and during the

The other of the two characters that appear in "The Homecoming of Beorhtnoth" is described by Tolkien as a *ceorl*, "a farmer who had seen much fighting in the English defence-levies" (2). Despite that fact that his attitude to Byrhtnoth's heroics (and warfare in general) is by and large negative, Tídwald never openly condemns his lord, criticising, instead, the underlying principles of the "heroic ideal" (10), rather than cursing the man who ought to be held responsible for the disastrous defeat at Maldon. He is also far more pragmatic of the two, often spurring his companion to a more sensible reflection whenever Torhthelm feels like declaiming poetry (4, 6, 7, 10-12) or pursuing dubious glory in a one-sided fight against the corpse-strippers (8-9).

As has already been observed, the interpretative dimensions of Tídwald's name are perhaps not as tangible as those of Torhthelm. Nonetheless, certain conclusions can be made by juxtaposing the attitudes of the two men. Whereas the younger one pays much more attention to the glorious side of warfare, the older one remains rather sceptical, focusing chiefly upon the often shocking realism of human experience at the time of military conflicts. His name, therefore, argues Jane Chance, "intimates his awareness of time and his earthbound values" (137). There is, in other words, a great deal of Christian-inspired universalism in both the name and the words of Tídwald, which, it appears, was meant to direct the reader's attention to the timelessness of certain values, attitudes and norms and their attainability in the context of warfare, regardless of the actual time and place of the conflict.

The elder of the two men is clearly a no-nonsense realist who constantly reminds his companion (and the readers) that, notwithstanding its cause, war must never be idealised. As a "ruler of time", he seems to be in some way outside the temporal constraints of our reality, evidently suggesting that a military conflict is an invariably "wicked business" (HB 7), both in the distant past and in the more recent times. For the Anglo-Saxon retainers Torhthelm and Tídwald this would mean, on the one hand, the deceptively glorious times of Beowulf (7), Fróda, Finn (6) as well as Hengest and Horsa (10), and, on the other, the often harsh and painful reality of contemporary warfare AD 991. Analogically, for the contemporary readers of *The Battle of Maldon* and "The Homecoming of Beorhtnoth" the glorious past may be epitomised by the courageous deeds of the ealdorman of Essex and those who chose to stay on the battlefield after their leader had been slain, while the harsh reality of modern warfare is to be found in the not-too-distant recollections of the two World Wars.

There are, it appears, two entirely different ways of looking at warfare. As a rule, the further back in time, the more glorious it seems to be. Over the years, the indisputable sufferings of some, often anonymous, individuals (or

---

battle of Maldon and the somewhat dimmed "brightness" personified in the name of Torhthelm.

even entire nations) are typically forgotten or at least cease to be of any major concern to the readers. Perhaps the only two things that continuously attract the attention of the more historically-minded people are, first and foremost, the heroism of those who took part in some military conflict and, somewhat less frequently, the short- and/or long-term political effects of the campaign. Tolkien's Tídwald, however, reminds us that, despite the passage of time, the sufferings of those who died and the sorrows of those who came to bury them are in fact the only two things that never really change, regardless of the circumstances, the weapons used and the numbers of the fallen.

Being, as a "ruler of time", figuratively outside these temporal constraints, Tídwald is therefore in a perfect position to warn his inexperienced companion against the pitfalls of excessive poetic eulogy and his evidently antiquarian (and so thoroughly idealised) vision of warfare (5) which is regularly (and quite deservedly) associated with young age. At the same time, this curious extratemporal status allows him to formulate some more universal theories concerning the nature of war, theories being just as much applicable in the tenth as in the twentieth centuries (4-7, 10). Consequently, much as is the case with Torhthelm, Tídwald's role as a quasi-literary character in "The Homecoming of Beorhtnoth" ought to be seen as being both particular (his critical evaluation of the youthful poet) and universal (criticism of war in general) in its interpretative essence.

Yet, whatever the interpretative glosses one may wish to place on the issue of Tolkien's onomastic puns in "The Homecoming of Beorhtnoth", it seems that on the purely argumentative level the words of Torhthelm and Tídwald speak considerably louder than their Anglo-Saxon names. Not surprisingly, to many an average reader, often with little or no knowledge of the Old English language, its onomastic stratum is not quite intelligible. One must not forget, though, that the alliterative dialogue (along with the two accompanying essays) was originally published in an academic journal and was not at the time probably intended to be available for the general readership. Hence, the names of Torhthelm and, in particular, Tídwald are comprehensible only to a small group of specialists, and even there the consensus seems to be hardly unanimous. In fact, it is usually easier to understand and interpret the names of some characters that appear in Tolkien's fantasy works, especially when their meaning is sometimes explicitly clarified, as is, for instance, the case with the various names of Gandalf.

In any case, despite the numerous ambiguities and interpretative difficulties, it seems a shame that the names of Torhthelm and Tídwald (as well as other characters from the vast realms of Tolkien's vivid imagination) should be left undiscussed. Indeed, they often provide a noteworthy, if sometimes overlooked or even totally ignored, extranarrative commentary upon the characters' history and significance for the plot development which, despite its secondary role, should never be regarded as being in any way irrelevant.[16] True enough, they may not always be as transparent as the names of certain figures in the novels of Charles Dickens or the allegorical characters in John Bunyan's *Pilgrim's Progress* (e.g. Christian, Giant Despair, Lord Hate-Good etc.). Indeed, one must sometimes make a considerable effort—philological, cultural or both—in order to appreciate the fact that the perfectionistic painter in one of Tolkien's stories is called Niggle[17] or that most of the names borne by the dwarves that embark on the perilous quest to reclaim the Lonely Mountain and its fabulous treasures are originally to be found in the Old Norse eddic poem *Vǫluspá*.[18] It is, however, an effort which is certainly worth making, particularly if one seeks to profit from a much broader understanding of the rich tapestry of Tolkien's universe.

Perhaps a fitting commentary on the onomastic approach regularly taken by the author of *The Lord of the Rings*, one which may be successfully applied to practically every publication of his (save, of course, Tolkien's translations of various medieval poems and his genuinely academic and lexicographic work), is the astonishingly metatextual statement of one of Middle-earth's most emblematic figures, Gandalf the White. Having responded to the King of Rohan's inquiry about the inhabitants of the Entwood, the wizard curiously remarks: "Did you think that the name [of the forest] was given only in idle fancy? Nay Théoden; it is otherwise" (LotR II 549).

Bibliography

Anderson, Douglas A. "'An industrious little devil': E.V. Gordon as Friend and Collaborator with Tolkien." *Tolkien the Medievalist*. Ed. Jane Chance. New York: Routledge, 2008, 15-25.

Bale, Anthony. "Introduction. St Edmund's Medieval Lives." *St Edmund, King and Martyr: Changing Images of a Medieval Saint*. Ed. Anthony Bale. York: York medieval Press, 2009, 1-25

Blake, Ernest Oscar (Ed.). *Liber Eliensis*. London: Royal Historical Society, 1962

Carpenter, Humphrey. *J.R.R. Tolkien: A Biography*. London: HarperCollins, 2002

---

16 This is, of course, particularly important in quasi-literary works like "The Homecoming of Beorhtnoth" where the numerous argumentative underpinnings may be found practically everywhere.

17 Cf. the verb *niggle* in the sense of devoting too much time on some less important or even utterly insignificant details.

18 In point of fact, the so-called Dvergatal or "Catalogue of Dwarves" is often considered to be an interpolation. Nonetheless, most editors and translators decide to include it in their publications.

Chance, Jane. *Tolkien's Art: A Mythology for England*. Lexington: The University Press of Kentucky, 2001

Gordon, Eric Valentine (Ed.). *The Battle of Maldon*. London: Methuen, 1954

Honegger, Thomas. "The Homecoming of Beorhtnoth: Philology and the Literary Muse." *Tolkien Studies* 4 (2007): 189-199

Howes, Donald. *Who's Who in Dickens*. Abingdon: Routledge, 2002

Lax, Eric. *Conversations with Woody Allen*. New York: Knopf Publishing Group, 2009

Lerer, Seth. *Error and the Academic Self: The Scholarly Imagination, Medieval to Modern*. New York: Columbia University Press, 2002

Prosopography of Anglo-Saxon England. 2016
http://www.pase.ac.uk/jsp/pdb?dosp=VIEW_RECORDS&st=PERSON_NAME&value=6880&level=1&lbl=Tidwald (09/08/2016)

Shippey, Tom. "Tolkien and 'The Homecoming of Beorhtnoth'". *Roots and Branches: Selected Papers on Tolkien by Tom Shippey*. Zürich/Jena: Walking Tree Publishers, 2007. 323-339

Smith, Alan. *Sixty Saxon Saints*. Frithgarth: Anglo-Saxon Books, 2003

Tolkien, John Ronald Reuel. "The Homecoming of Beorhtnoth Beorhthelm's Son." *Essays and Studies* 6 (1953): 1-18

---. *The Lord of the Rings II. The Two Towers*. London: HarperCollins, 2014

Nomen est Omen

Funktion und Bedeutung von Namen in Tolkiens Werk

Helmut W. Pesch (Bergisch Gladbach)

> *The Naming of Cats is a difficult matter,*
> *It isn't just one of your holiday games;*
> *You may think at first I'm as mad as a hatter*
> *When I tell you, a cat must have THREE DIFFERENT NAMES.*

So wusste der Dichter T.S. Eliot in *Old Possum's Book of Practical Cats* zu berichten. Der erste dieser Namen ist ein Allerweltsname, der gut klingen soll: »Such as Plato, Admetus, Electra, Demeter«, der zweite ein Eigenname, der nur auf eine einzelne Katze zutrifft, wobei Eliot hier selbst sprachschöpferisch tätig wird: »Such as Munkustrap, Quaxo, or Coricopat, / Such as Bombalurina, or else Jellylorum«. Der dritte hingegen ist ein geheimer, nicht in Worte fassbarer Name, den allein die Katze kennt und über den sie meditiert, wenn sie daliegt und besonders mysteriös dreinschaut. (Eliot 11)

Eliot gilt als einer der bedeutenden Vertreter der literarischen Moderne, und dennoch verbindet ihn in diesem Gedicht aus den 1930er-Jahren mehr mit Tolkien, als man auf den ersten Blick vermuten sollte. Denn das Spiel mit Sprache, die Loslösung von Form und Sinn wie im Dadaismus, war ein wesentliches Element der Moderne in der Zeit nach dem Ersten Weltkrieg.

In diesem Sinne ist auch ein Autor wie Lord Dunsany, der Eliots Gedichte als »*frightful* nonsense« (De Camp 51; Herv. im Original) ansah, ein Kind der Moderne. Seine amoralischen Fabeln, die in einem Akt spontanen Schreibens entstanden, versteigen sich bis zu sinnfreien Namenskatalogen wie »Welleran, Soorenad, Mommolek, Rollory, Akanax, and young Iraine« (Dunsany 2). Wir finden darin Reflexe von klassischen Sprachen über die *Bibel* bis zum Orientalischen, aber kein erkennbares System.

Die amerikanische Pulp-Fantasy tat sich dagegen von Anfang an schwerer. Robert E. Howards »Hyborian Age«, die Welt von »Conan«, ist eindeutig eine Kalkierung der mittelalterlichen Welt aus europäischer Sicht, auch wenn sie in einer fiktiven prähistorischen Epoche angesiedelt ist. Dementsprechend sind auch die Bezeichnungen: Cimmeria, Asgard, Hyperborea bis hin zu Ophir und Turan. Auch die Kulturen dahinter haben einen hohen Wiedererkennungswert, von den blonden Barbaren von Vanaheim über die Ritter von Aquilonia bis hin zu den Piraten von Zingara, das geografisch der iberischen Halbinsel entspricht. Versucht Howard dagegen, eigene Namen zu kreieren, kommt er, ähnlich wie Edgar Rice Burroughs, über eine Aneinanderreihung einfacher Silben selten hinaus.

Das a-posteriorische Prinzip der Namengebung bleibt bis heute noch produktiv. Dies zeigt sich an Beispielen wie der Serie *Game of Thrones*, die zumindest in ihren Anfängen irdische Geografie und historische Machtverhältnisse widerspiegelt. Westeros von der großen Mauer im Norden über die Inseln des Nordwestens bis zur Königsstadt an der Südostküste entspricht weitgehend der britischen Hauptinsel. Auch bei den Namen und Figuren lassen sich leicht Parallelen finden; dass »Stark« und »Lannister« die Häuser von York und Lancaster der mittelalterlichen Rosenkriege anklingen lassen, ist ebenso offensichtlich wie gewollt.

Daneben gibt es in der Fantasy jedoch auch eine a-priorische Namengebung. Ursula K. Le Guin, die später in *Always Coming Home* (1985) selbst eine Kunstsprache entwerfen sollte – »what an illustrious predecessor referred to as A Secret Vice« (509) –, schreibt in ihrem Essay »Dreams Must Explain Themselves« (1975) über die Nomenklatur der *Earthsea*-Romane:

> People often ask how I think of names in fantasies, and again I have to answer that I find them, that I hear them... This all sounds very mystical, and indeed there are aspects of it I do not understand, but it is a pragmatic business, too, since if the name had been wrong the character would have been wrong—misbegotten, misunderstood.   (51f.)

Tolkien gibt den Figuren und Dingen, die er liebt, nicht nur einen Namen, sondern gleich mehrere, und er schöpft dabei aus dem Vollen:

> ... *Many are my names in many countries*, he said. *Mithrandir among the Elves, Tharkûn to the Dwarves; Olórin I was in my youth in the West that is forgotten, in the South Incánus, in the North Gandalf; to the East I go not.*   (LotR 670)
> Taniquetil the Elves name that holy mountain, and Oiolossë Everlasting Whiteness, and Elerrína Crowned with Stars, and many names beside; but the Sindar spoke of it in their later tongue as Amon Uilos.   (S 37)

Diese Namen sind aus Tolkiens Kunstsprachen hervorgegangen. Erstaunlich ist dabei, wie wenige externe Bezüge sie insgesamt aufweisen. Tolkien verweist selbst in einem seiner Briefe darauf, wo er schreibt:

> It is... idle to compare chance-similarities between names made from 'Elvish tongues' and words in exterior 'real' languages, especially if this is supposed to have any bearing on the meaning or ideas in my story. To take a frequent case: there is no linguistic

connection, and therefore no connection in significance, between *Sauron* a contemporary form of an older *Ϸ*aurond-derivative of an adjectival *Ϸ*aurā (from a base √THAW), 'detestable' and the Greek σαύρα, 'a lizard'.   (L 380)

Und an einer anderen Stelle im selben Brief verwehrt er sich gegen eine Assoziation der Zwergenminen von Moria in *The Lord of the Rings* mit dem Land Morīah, der Heimat Abrahams, in der *Bibel* und meint:

> I utterly repudiate any such significances and symbolisms. My mind does not work that way.   (L 383)

Tolkiens Briefe sind eine wichtige Informationsquelle, aber es sind subjektive Äußerungen des Autors, die zudem häufig eine rhetorische Haltung widerspiegeln. Tatsächlich ist jedoch der Anteil von nachweisbaren Bedeutungen und Symbolismen in Tolkiens Elbensprachen minimal.

Selbst im frühen »Qenya Lexicon« (entstanden 1915-1918) findet man nicht mehr als eine Handvoll Glossen mit realweltlichen Bezügen. Diese sind teilweise geografisch wie der Zusatz ›(Warwickshire.)‹ beim Stichwort *Alalminóre* (Tolkien, *Qenyaqetsa* 29), was dem Stand der Mythologie von 1915 entspricht, wo der imaginäre Ort Kortirion mit dem englischen Warwick gleichgesetzt wird. Zum Teil wirken sie der Zeit geschuldet wie die Gleichsetzung von *Kalimban* ›"Barbary"‹, abgeleitet von *kalimbo* ›a savage, uncivilized man, barbarian. — giant, monster, troll‹, mit ›Germany‹ (in einer beigefügten, schwer lesbaren Glosse auch *Ogresse* [?] ›Land der Oger‹) (44).

Es gibt nur eine echte mythologische Gleichsetzung, nämlich *Turambar* (95), später Beiname Túrins im *Silmarillion*, als Lehnübersetzung von *Sigurðr* – nach damaliger Auffassung gedeutet als Verbindung von *sig* ›Sieg‹ und *urðr* ›Schicksal‹. Im Übrigen scheint es sich hier mehr um Erklärungen in Kurzform für den Autor selbst zu handeln, wie bei ›"Asgard"‹ als Erläuterung von *Valinor* (99) oder ›Hilary‹ (lat. *Hilarius* ›der Fröhliche‹, sowohl der Vorname von Tolkiens Bruder als auch als *Hilary Term* ein Begriff aus dem akademischen Leben von Oxford) für *Amillo* ›One of the Happy Folk (the Valar)‹ (30).

Darüber hinaus gibt es Bezeichnungen für die drei Personen der Dreifaltigkeit (35, 43, 81) und jeweils verwandte Begriffe für ›Mönch‹ und ›Kloster‹ (31) und für einen christlichen Missionar und das Evangelium (36). Dies ist freilich eher Tolkiens Interessen geschuldet, der später auch Texte wie das »Vaterunser« ins Elbische übersetzt hat, als Grund zu der Annahme, dass dies Teil seiner mythologischen Schöpfung sei.

In einer Kunstsprache, die sich phonotaktisch an das Finnische anlehnt, sind auch Begriffe nicht zu vermeiden, bei denen sich Lautgestalt und Inhalt in beiden Sprachen ähneln. Wiederum sind aber die Beispiele verschwindend gering an Zahl, und es ist mitunter kaum zu entscheiden, wo es sich um wirkliche Parallelen oder um bloße Amplifikation handelt. Das Gleiche gilt auch für den Versuch, die sprachlichen Wurzeln, nach denen das Wörterbuch geordnet ist, mit den indogermanischen abzugleichen. So entspricht etwa die Wurzel √BEL ›strong‹ bei Tolkien (LR 352), die nur im Sindarin aufscheint, von der Bedeutung her dem indogermanischen *bel- ›stark‹, einer der seltenen und darum auffälligen Wurzeln mit /b/. Aus dem damit verwandten √BAL ist das Wort *Valar* ›Mächte‹ abgeleitet (350). Im »Qenya Lexicon« wird jedoch *Valar* als ›the happy folk‹ interpretiert, im Sinne von »having good "hap" or fortune... (OED)« (99).

So bezeichnend die genannten Einzelbeispiele sind, so ist es doch nur eine Handvoll von über sechstausend Vokabeln im »Qenya Lexicon«. Sucht man Vorbilder, so wird man sie eher in einer Klassifikation wie *Flowers of the Field* von C.A. Johns finden, das Tolkien als Jugendlicher gelesen und besonders geschätzt hat (Scull/Hammond 69). Bezeichnenderweise sind die Wortfelder zu Pflanzen und natürlichen Phänomenen, einschließlich Sinneseindrücken, auch besonders extensiv.

Dennoch sind die Namen *Earend[e]l* und *Turambar* insofern bemerkenswert, als sie für zwei Prinzipien der Aneignung stehen. Typisch für Tolkiens linguistische Fiktion ist die Übernahme von sprachlichen Mustern, die von ihm nicht in derselben Art und Weise eingesetzt werden wie in der Vorlage, sondern so wie es ihm schön erscheint. Dies findet sich ähnlich bei grammatischen Elementen in Tolkiens Kunstsprachen, die Vorbildern im Griechischen, Finnischen oder Walisischen ähneln, aber nach anderen Prinzipien operieren.[1]

Earendel, der personifizierte Abendstern als Präfiguration des Heils, und Turambar, der Drachentöter, sind mythologische Typen, die gleichfalls in Tolkiens Mythologie eine modifizierte Funktion haben:

Earendel, übernommen aus dem altenglischen Gedicht *Crist*, dort mit der ursprünglichen Wortbedeutung ›leuchtender Wanderer‹, ist in Tolkiens Welt der Bote der Elben und Menschen gegenüber den Göttern, und sein Name wird im Qenya-Lexikon mit dem Wort für ›Adler‹, *earen(-d)* assoziiert; siehe auch den Eintrag *Ioringli* als »true Gn[omic] form of Earendel's name« unter *ior* ›Adler‹ (Tolkien, *I·Lam* 51). Erst später wird dies als *Earendil* ›Meerfreund‹ umgedeutet.

Turambar ist, wie oben erläutert, ursprünglich eine Lehnübersetzung. Die Figur hat mit dem germanischen Vorbild das Motiv des Drachentöters gemein, auch wenn sie selbst eher dem unglückseligen Kullervo aus der finnischen

---

1   Beispielsweise ist im Quenya der Aorist als Zeitform dem Griechischen entlehnt, wo er einmalige abgeschlossene Handlungen in der Vergangenheit bezeichnet. Im Quenya stellt er, im Wortsinne von ἀόριστος ›unbegrenzt, unbestimmt‹, ein Tempus ohne Zeitbezug zum Ausdruck allgemeiner Wahrheiten dar. Im Sindarin sind die Anlautmutationen dem Walisischen entlehnt, aber nicht mit ihnen identisch, und haben zum Teil zudem grammatische Funktion.

Kalevala nachempfunden ist. Später wird daraus ein Beiname, den Túrin sich selbst zulegt, welcher in einer dramatischen Ironie auf die Tatsache verweist, dass sein Träger eben nicht Herr seines Schicksals ist, sondern dem Fluch des gefallenen Vala Melkor unterliegt, der sich als »Master of the fates of Arda« (S 197) bezeichnet.

Wie haben wir aber, auch im Lichte von Le Guins Aussage, dass ein falscher Name auch eine falsche Figur impliziert, solche Wandel und Verschiebungen von Namen in der Entwicklung von Tolkiens Werk zu verstehen? Es ist ja keineswegs der einzige Fall. So hat Tolkien mitunter lange an Namen und Begriffen festgehalten, bevor er sie geändert hat, angefangen von den »Gnomes«, abgeleitet von dem griechischen γνώμη ›Weisheit, Wissen‹, mit denen er die Elben bezeichnete, die später »Noldor« genannt wurden, weil der Autor schließlich doch einsah, dass die Assoziation zu *gnome* (im Sinne von ›Zwerg, Wicht‹) zu stark war, um sie durch einen bloßen deklaratorischen Akt außer Kraft zu setzen. Ein ähnliches Festhalten an Namen findet sich auch in der Geschichte des Herrn der Ringe, etwa bei »Bingo« für *Frodo* oder »Trotter« für *Strider*.[2] »Aragorn« war ursprünglich der Name für Gandalfs Pferd, bevor die Figur so benannt wurde (RS 351). Auf der anderen Seite haben wir den Fall der Entstehung von *The Hobbit* aus einem spontanen Akt des Schreibens (»In a hole in the ground there lived a Hobbit«), und alles, was daraus folgt, kann als ein Versuch betrachtet werden, diesen Namen zu erklären. Dem entspricht auch Tolkiens eigene Aussage:

> Names always generate a story in my mind. Eventually I thought I'd better find out what hobbits were like. But that's only the beginning.   (Carpenter 230)

Viele Ideen und Figuren bei Tolkien sind als phantasievolle Auflösungen einer philologischen *crux* anzusehen. Darunter versteht man »a plain corruption in a text, or a contradiction between two versions of a text, from which at first sight it seems impossible to recover the author's original meaning« (Simon 12). Für Tolkien als Philologe war nichts provokativer als ein Name, der Rätsel aufgab, der sich nicht deuten ließ oder keinen offensichtlichen Referenten hatte (Shippey 275f.). Wenn es ein Wort gibt, dann gibt es auch ein Denotat, ein Verweisobjekt. Die Philologie ist da exakt und ausnahmslos – und Tolkien überträgt dieses Prinzip auch auf sein literarisches Werk. In *The Lord oft he Rings* kennt Théoden von Rohan den Namen »Entwood«; so ist es nur folgerichtig, dass Gandalf, der unter anderem, wie sein ursprünglicher Name »Olórin« – von Quenya *olos* ›vision, »phantasy«‹ (UT 396) – zeigt, die Funktion einer Verkörperung

---

2   *Bingo* wurde bei der dritten Überarbeitung des Ersten Buches, ca. 1939, geändert (RS 309), *Trotter* erst, nachdem der Roman weitgehend vollendet war (SD 78, Anm. 4).

der Fantasie hat, ihm auch die entsprechenden Referenzobjekte, die Ents, vorweist. Rainer Wimmer hat bereits in einem wenig beachteten Artikel von 1982 darauf hingewiesen, dass die Konstitution der fiktionalen Welt bei Tolkien im Wesentlichen im referenziellen System der Sprache geleistet wird. Tolkien weist daher auch Coleridges Formel der »willing suspension of disbelief«, mit der er als Spätromantiker automatisch assoziiert wird, für sich ausdrücklich zurück. So schreibt er in *On Fairy-stories*:

> Children are capable, of course, of *literary belief*, when the story-maker's art is good enough to produce it. That state of mind has been called 'willing suspension of disbelief'. But this does not seem to me a good description of what happens. What really happens is that the story-maker proves a successful 'sub-creator'. He makes a Secondary World which your mind can enter. Inside it, what he relates is 'true': it accords with the laws of that world. You therefore believe it, while you are, as it were, inside. The moment disbelief arises, the spell is broken; the magic, or rather art, has failed.   (60)

Sobald der Leser aufhört zu glauben, dass es für einen Namen ein Referenzobjekt gibt, bricht sein Glaube an die Sekundärwelt zusammen. Wie Wimmer schreibt: »Über Wahr und Falsch oder Glauben und Nicht-Glauben im Sinne der Coleridge-Formel kann ich nur entscheiden, wenn die Entscheidungen über die Gegenstandswelt, die mir für eine Bezugnahme überhaupt zur Verfügung steht, bereits gefallen ist« (555). Mit diesem Hintergrund gewinnt auch Tolkiens Aussage »To me a name comes first and the story follows« (L 219) eine neue Bedeutung. Sein immenser Aufwand an Nomenklatur dient letztlich auch der Bekräftigung der referenziellen Gültigkeit; dies ist seine spezifische Art von Realitätsfiktion. Objekte treten in die Geschichte ein, sobald sie einen Namen erhalten, wie in dem Lied von Durin, einem der Stammväter der Zwerge, der nach seinem Erwachen die namenlosen Hügel und Täler benennt.

> The world was young, the mountains green,
> No stain yet on the moon was seen,
> No words were laid on stream or stone
> When Durin woke and walked alone.
> He named the nameless hills and dells;
> *He drank from yet untasted wells;* ... (LotR 315 f.)

Die Benennung macht die Welt begreifbar und ergreift zugleich von ihr Besitz. Durin ist hier vergleichbar mit Adam, der den Tieren Namen gibt: »Gott, der Herr, formte aus dem Ackerboden alle Tiere des Feldes und alle Vögel des Himmels und führte sie dem Menschen zu, um zu sehen, wie er sie benennen

würde. Und wie der Mensch jedes lebendige Wesen benannte, so sollte es hei-
ßen« (Einheitsübers., 1 Mose 2.19).

Namen sind eine besondere Klasse von Bezeichnungen. Die Quellen von
Namen sind in der Regel sogenannte Appellative. Dies sind Begriffe, denen
eine lexikalische Bedeutung im engeren Sinne zukommt, wohingegen Namen
in erster Linie identifizieren, aber nicht charakterisieren. In der Auffassung der
modernen Linguistik besteht der Name »nur aus der Beziehung eines materiellen
(phonischen oder graphischen) Ausdrucks zu einem konkreten Objekt und hat
sich aus diachronischer Perspektive des bedeutungshaltigen Überbaus entledigt«
(Nübling 32). Namen haben in diesem Sinne keine lexikalische Bedeutung,
auch wenn eine solche assoziiert werden kann, »doch leistet diese keineswegs
(mehr) den Bezug zum Objekt« (33). »Hund« und »Katze« sind Appellative;
eine Katze wird nicht zum Hund, wenn man sie als solchen bezeichnet, aber
man kann Katzen alle möglichen Namen geben wie in dem Musical *Cats*, das
auf Eliots Gedichten beruht.

Eigennamen haben in der Regel einen monoreferenziellen Bezug, was bei
Appellativen für gewöhnlich nicht zutrifft. In einer Welt, in der Schöpfung und
Benennung eins sind, greift daher auch das magische Prinzip, dass zwischen
Benennung und Benanntem eine innere Beziehung besteht. Daher gibt es in
der Welt der Fantasy auch geheime Namen, die nie einem Außenstehenden
bekannt werden dürfen, weil er sonst Macht über deren Objekt gewinnt. Der
Ent Treebeard ist überrascht, dass ihm die Hobbits so einfach ihren Namen
verraten: »I am honoured by your confidence; but you should not be too free
all at once« (LotR 465). In Le Guins *Earthsea*-Romanen hat jedes Ding einen
wahren Namen in der Wahren Sprache, und ein Ding zu ändern, heißt, seinen
Namen zu ändern und damit die ganze Welt.

Zur Alleinstellung greift die Namengebung oft auf die Kombination mehrerer
Elemente zurück. Altgermanische Namen sind häufig aus zwei sinntragenden
Bestandteilen zusammengesetzt. Wir finden dieses Prinzip auch bei den Namen
von Rohan wie Theodred (›Volk-Rat‹), Theodwyn (›Volk-Wonne‹), Eomer (›Pferd-
Ruhm‹), Eowyn (›Pferd-Wonne‹) oder Eomund (›Pferd-Schutz‹), bei denen das
Altenglische als sprachliche Analogie zu ihren »wirklichen« Namen in einem
Dialekt des »Westron«, der Gemeinsamen Sprache, herangezogen wird, welche
im Text als erzählerische Fiktion durch das Englische ersetzt wurde. Auch die
Verbindung von verknüpfenden Alliterationen und Variationen sind typisch
für germanische Genealogien (vgl. Lee 51f.).

Eine vergleichbare Vorgehensweise findet sich auch bei den Namen der Elben.
Die Namen der ersten Generation wie *Elwë*, *Finwë* oder *Olwë* sind linguistisch
primitiv in dem Sinne, dass sie nur aus einem bedeutungtragenden Element
und einem Bildungsmorphem -*wë* bestehen, das die Grundbedeutung ›jemand‹,
›Person‹ hat. Bereits die Namen der nächsten Generation haben eine höhere
Komplexität, da sie zum Teil die Namen des Vaters als Bestandteil enthalten,

wobei *Fingolfin* und *Finarfin* (als Sindarin-Formen der ursprünglichen Quenya-Namen *Finwë Ñolofinwë* und *Finwë Arafinwë*) ihn zusätzlich ein zweites Mal voransetzen, um ihren Anspruch auf das Königtum zu dokumentieren. Bei den Halbelben *Elrond* und *Elros* dient das Element *el-* zur Bezeichnung ihrer elbischen Abkunft, während die Namen selbst etymologisch aus den Umständen ihrer Geburt in einer Höhle mit Wasserfall gedeutet werden (als ›Stern-Kuppel‹ und ›Stern-Gischt‹). Die Namen der Zwillinge *Elladan* und *Elrohir* sind im Grunde beide Varianten von ›Elb-Mensch‹. Mit der zunehmenden Dissoziation der Namen geht zugleich eine Herabstufung im Rang einher, wie sie sich an den Wahrzeichen der Eldar zeigt, die mit jeder neuen Generation eine geringere Komplexität aufweisen. Darin finden sich Reflexe der Sprachphilosophie Owen Barfields wieder, in der der Verlust der alten semantischen Einheit von Wörtern mit der Abschwächung von Bedeutungen einhergeht (vgl. Flieger 38f.). Verlyn Flieger sieht in der historischen Tendenz zur Differenzierung, die sie an der Brechung und Abschwächung des Lichts, aber auch sprachlichen und historischen Entwicklungen – »[m]odification and proliferation of language, fragmentation of perception of meaning, division and subdivision of peoples« (97) – festmacht, ein Leitmotiv des *Simarillion*. Tolkien selbst konstatiert, mit Rückgriff auf Barfield, in der poetischen Sprache eine Verbindung zwischen Form und Inhalt, die sich vor allem in einfachen, historisch verwurzelten Wörtern erschließt und den komplexen Begriffen der modernen Sprache fehlt (SV 67f.).

Tolkien schuf darüber hinaus ein eigenes System der Nomenklatur für die Eldar, welches an das römische System erinnert, das aus *Praenomen* (Vorname), *Nomen gentile* (Familienname) und *Cognomen* (Beiname) bestand, zu dem noch ein *Agnomen* (Ehrenname) hinzukommen konnte. Der »Vatername« wurde vom Vater in einer Zeremonie namens *Essecarmë* (›Namenschöpfung‹) kurz nach der Geburt verkündet, ähnlich wie der römische Vorname. In einer weiteren Zeremonie, *Essecilmë* (›Namenwahl‹), die zu einem späteren Zeitpunkt stattfand, wenn das Kind der *lámatyávë*, der »individuellen Freude an den Lauten und Formen von Wörtern« (MR 215), fähig war, wählte sich der Einzelne selbst einen zweiten Namen. Darüber hinaus gab es den »Mutternamen«, der als »Name der Voraussicht« prophetischen Charakter haben konnte. Weitere »verliehene Namen« konnten im Laufe des Lebens hinzukommen, galten aber nicht als »wahre« Namen. Als Beispiel nennt Tolkien Túrins Beinamen *Mormegil* (›Schwarzes Schwert‹) oder Aragorns Beinamen *Strider* (›Streicher‹) der in der Quenya-Form *Telcontar* zum Namen seines Geschlechts werden sollte.

In der Praxis finden wir allerdings etwa bei den Nachkommen Finwes den »Namen der Wahl« kaum vor. Bei den Vaternamen gibt es, ähnlich wie bei den adeligen Römern, die nur über eine kleine Zahl von Vornamen verfügten, die Tendenz, Kinder einfach durchzunummerieren, in diesem Fall generationenübergreifend. In der Regel ist es der Muttername, der den Vaternamen im Gebrauch ersetzt. Im Falle der Zwillinge *Pityafinwë* (›Kleiner Finwë‹) und

Telufinwë (›Letzter Finwë‹) gab ihre Mutter Nerdanel beiden den Namen *Amba-russa* (›Oben-Rotbraun‹) wegen ihres roten Haars und weil sie einander so ähnlich waren. Als darauf der Vater Feanor sie bat, wenigstens einem einen anderen Namen zu geben, sagte Nerdanel nach einigem Zögern: »Then let one be called… *Umbarto* [›the Fated‹, ›der vom Schicksal Bestimmte‹] but which, time will decide« (PM 353). Feanor änderte den Namen in *Ambarto*, aber Nerdanel blieb dabei: »*Umbarto* I spoke; yet do as you wish. It will make no difference«[3] (354).

Als die Noldor nach Mittelerde zurückkehrten, passten sie ihre Namen in der Form dem Sindarin an, mit der Folge, dass diese nicht mehr unmittelbar als sinnhaft erkennbar waren. Bei einem Namen wie *Galadriel* handelt es sich um einen Wahlnamen, der im Sindarin gebildet wurde und sich als Quenya-Form allenfalls rekonstruieren lässt.

Ein besonderer Fall sind auch die Königsnamen, weil sie programmatischer Natur sind. Elros, der Bruder Elronds, der sich für die Zugehörigkeit zu den Menschen entschied, legte sich als König den Namen *Tar-Minyatur* (›Hoher Erster Herrscher‹) zu, und seine Nachfolger folgten diesem Beispiel, indem sie sich gleichfalls Königsnamen gaben. Allein an diesen Namen lassen sich die Geschichte des Reiches und die Beziehung der Herrscher zu den Mächten des Westens ablesen. Herrschen in den ersten Generationen Namen wie *Tar-Amandil* (›Freund von Aman‹) oder *Tar-Meneldur* (›Diener des Himmels‹) vor, werden die Bedeutungen in den nächsten Generationen schon weniger offen-sichtlich – *Tar-Súrion* (›Sohn des Windes‹) kann eine Anspielung auf Manwë Súlimo sein, muss es aber nicht – und konzentrieren sich in der Folge ganz auf das eigene Reich wie in *Tar-Ciryatan* (›Schiffsbauer‹). Es folgt eine Reihe von Namen, in denen sich die Selbstverherrlichung spiegelt, wie in *Tar-Alcarin* (›Der Glorreiche‹) oder *Tar-Ardamin* (›Pfeiler der Welt‹). Die späteren Könige wählen ihren Namen nicht mehr in Quenya, sondern in ihrer eigenen Sprache, Adûnaïsch, um ihre Abkehr von den Valar zu dokumentieren, auch wenn sie aus abergläubischer Furcht noch immer auf Quenya in die offizielle Königs-rolle eingetragen wurden. Ein Name wie *Ar-Adûnakhor* (Qu. *Tar-Herunúmen*, ›Herr des Westens‹) kommt eigentlich nur Manwë, dem König der Valar, zu. Nach einer kurzen Restauration unter *Tar-Palantir* (›Der Weitsehende‹) endet das Reich mit *Ar-Pharazôn* (›Der Goldene‹), möglicherweise eine der wenigen beabsichtigten Assoziationen in Tolkiens Nomenklatur.[4]

---

3   *Umbar* ist dasselbe Wort wie *ambar* ›Schicksal‹, erweitert um die assimilierte negative Vorsilbe *u-*.

4   Das Wort erinnert an den ägyptischen Titel »Pharao«. Tolkien sagt dies nirgendwo expli-zit, wenngleich er die númenórische Kultur mit der ägyptischen vergleicht (L 281). Eine weitere bewusste Entsprechung ist *Atalante* ›die Gefallene‹ für das versunkene Númenor, als Anspielung auf Atlantis. Tolkien spricht selbst von einem wiederkehrenden Traum einer hohen Welle, die alles verschlingt, als seinem »Atlantis-Komplex« (L 213).

Auch bei den Namen der Könige des Dritten Zeitalters ist es signifikant, welcher Sprache sie sich bedienen und mit welchem Anspruch dies einhergeht. Die Namen der Könige von Gondor sind im hochelbischen Quenya gehalten, die Stewards tragen dagegen Sindarin-Namen, die zum Teil Namen von Helden aus dem Ersten Zeitalter aufgreifen. Nach dem Zerfall des Nordreiches Arnor geben sich die Könige von Arthedain ihre offiziellen Namen nicht mehr auf Quenya, sondern auf Sindarin und setzen zudem in der Folge das Präfix *aran*, *ar(a)* voran, um ihren Anspruch auf das Königtum von ganz Arnor zu dokumentieren (PM 193). Diese programmatischen Namen gehen zum Teil in prophetische über, etwa wenn der Seher Malbeth dem letzten König von Arnor bereits bei der Geburt den Namen *Arvedui* ›Letztkönig‹ gibt.

Je älter ein Name ist, desto größer ist die wahrscheinliche Dissoziation zwischen Benennung und Bedeutung. Im Dritten Zeitalter haben sich in Gondor die Namen schon so weit abgeschliffen, dass sie in ihren Bestandteilen nicht mehr unbedingt erkennbar sind. Als erstarrte Formen betonen sie den konservativen Charakter der Benennung: Denethor nennt seinen ersten Sohn *Boromir*, weil es im Ersten Zeitalter schon einmal einen Denethor gab, dessen Sohn Boromir ein großer Held war. Dies erschließt sich aber nur, wenn man die Historie kennt, was bei den meisten Lesern nicht der Fall sein dürfte. Auch der Name von Boromirs Bruder, *Faramir*, ist zunächst nicht interpretierbar, außer dass er eine Familienzugehörigkeit suggeriert. Dass der erste Bestandteil im Sinne von ›hinreichend, genügend‹ aufzufassen ist, und zwar im positiven Sinne, erschließt sich erst aus dem Studium der Elbensprachen selbst.

Selten wird innerhalb der Geschichte über den Charakter von Namen reflektiert, und dies meist am Rande des Geschehens. In *The Hobbit*, wo Namen häufig generischer Natur sind, reicht schon eine monoreferenzielle Bezeichnung aus, um aus einem Appellativ einen Namen zu machen. »He called it the Carrock, because carrock is his word for it. He calls things like that carrocks, and this one is he Carock because it ist he only one near his home and he knows it well« (H 102).

In *The Lord of the Rings* ist es Tom Bombadil, der über die Natur von Namen philosophiert. Als Frodo ihn fragt: »Who are you, Master?«, gibt er zur Antwort: »Don't you know my name yet? That's the only answer. Tell me, who are you, alone, yourself and nameless? But you are young and I am old. Eldest, that's what I am« (131).

Der Name *Tom Bombadil* ist innerhalb der literarischen Welt von Mittelerde weitgehend sinnfrei. Im Kapitel »The Council of Elrond« wird er als »Iarwain Ben-adar«, der Älteste (eigentlich der Alt-Junge) und Vaterlose, bezeichnet und mit anderen Namen, die »alt« oder »uralt« bedeuten (300).

Als Ältester von Mittelerde steht er am Anfang der Geschichte, und sein Name *ist* zugleich seine Geschichte; etwas, das ein junger, geschichtsloser Hobbit nicht nachvollziehen kann. »Real names«, sagt der Ent Treebeard, »tell you the story of the things they belong to in my language...« (516).

Dies ist etwas, dem Tolkien in seinen philologischen Arbeiten ein Leben lang nachgegangen ist und dem er auch in seinen fiktionalen Werken treu bleibt. Den Kern seiner Fiktion bildet die Vorstellung, dass jede Geschichte einen Namen enthält und jeder Name eine Geschichte.

Bibliographie

Carpenter, Humphrey. *J.R.R. Tolkien: A Biography*. 1977. London: HarperCollins, 2002

De Camp, L. Sprague. »Two Men in One: Lord Dunsany«. *Literary Swordsmen and Sorcerers: The Makers of Heroic Fantasy*. Sauk City, WI: Arkham House, 1976. 48-63

Dunsany, Lord. »The Sword of Welleran«. 1908. *The Sword of Welleran and Other Stories*. Mineola, NY: Dover, 2005. 1-15

Einheitsübersetzung der Heiligen Schrift. Katholische Bibelanstalt. Stuttgart 1980. Web. 1. Mai 2016

Eliot, T.S. »The Naming of Cats«. *Old Possum's Book of Practical Cats*. 1939. New York: Harcourt Brace Jovanovich, 1982, 11

Flieger, Verlyn. *Splintered Light: Logos and Language in Tolkien's World*. 1983. Rev. Ed. Kent, OH: Kent State Univ. Press, 2002

Lee, Stuart D., & Elizabeth Solopowa. *The Keys to Middle-earth: Discovering Medieval Literature Through the Fiction of J.R.R. Tolkien*. Houndmills, Basingstoke, Hants.: Palgrave Macmillan, 2005

Le Guin, Ursula K. »Dreams Must Explain Themselves«. 1973. *The Language of the Night: Essays on Fantasy and Science Fiction*. Hg. Susan Wood. New York: Putnam, 1979, 47-56

Le Guin, Ursula K., Todd Barton, Margaret Chodos-Irvine & George Hersh. *Always Coming Home*. New York: Harper & Row, 1985

Nübling, Damaris, Fabian Fahlbusch & Rita Heuser. *Namen: Eine Einführung in die Onomastik*. Tübingen: Narr, 2012

Scull, Christina, & Wayne Hammond. *The J.R.R. Tolkien Companion and Guide: Reader's Guide*. London: HarperCollins, 2006

Shippey, Tom. *The Road to Middle-earth*. 1982. Rev. Ed. London: HarperCollins, 2005

Simon, Tom. *Writing Down the Dragon and Other Essays*. Calgary: Bondwine Books, 2013

Tolkien, J.R.R. *The Hobbit*. 1937. London: HarperCollins, 1991

---. »I·Lam na·Ngoldathon: The Grammar and Lexicon of the Gnomish tongue«. Hg. Christopher Gilson, Patrick Wynne, Arden R. Smith, Carl F. Hostetter. *Parma Eldalamberon* 11 (1995)

---. »Laws and Customs Among the Eldar«. *Morgoth's Ring. HoME X*. Hg. Christopher Tolkien. London: HarperCollins, 1993, 207-253

---. *The Letters of J.R.R. Tolkien*. Hg. Humphrey Carpenter with the assistance of Christopher Tolkien. Boston: Houghton Mifflin, 1981

---. *The Lord of the Rings*. 1954/55. London: HarperCollins, 2004

---. *The Lost Road and other writings. HoME V*. Hg. Christopher Tolkien. London: Unwin Hyman, 1987

---. *On Fairy-stories* 1947. Grand Rapids, MI.: Eerdmans, 1966, 38-89

---. *The Peoples of Middle-earth. HoME XII.* Hg. Christopher Tolkien. London: HarperCollins, 1996

---. »Qenyaqetsa: The Phonology and Lexicon together with The Poetic and Mythologic Words of Eldarissa«. Hg. Christopher Gilson, Carl F. Hostetter, Patrick Wynne, Arden R. Smith. *Parma Eldalamberon* 12 (1998)

---. *The Return of the Shadow. HoME VI.* Hg. Christopher Tolkien. London: Unwin Hyman, 1988

---. *A Secret Vice: Tolkien on Invented Languages.* Hg. Dimitra Fini, Andrew Higgins. London: HarperCollins, 2016

---. *Sauron Defeated. HoME IX.* Hg. Christopher Tolkien. London: HarperCollins, 1990

---. »The Shibboleth of Feanor«. *The Peoples of Middle-earth.* 331-366

---. *The Silmarillion.* Hg. Christopher Tolkien. London: George Allen & Unwin, 1977

---. *Unfinished Tales of Númenor and Middle-earth.* Hg. Christopher Tolkien. London: Allen & Unwin, 1980

Wimmer, Rainer. »Aus Namen Mythen machen: Zu J.R.R. Tolkiens Konstruktion fiktionaler Welten«. *Erzählforschung: Ein Symposion.* Hg. Eberhard Lämmert. Stuttgart: Metzler, 1982, 552-567

Mediation of Names in *The Lord of the Rings*

Allan Turner (Gateshead)

It has often been pointed out that the names in *The Lord of the Rings* through their internal consistency play a significant part in the creation of a credible secondary world. In particular, the contrast between names which are in some way meaningful to an English-speaking reader and those which are clearly exotic are important in separating the familiar world of the Hobbits, through whose eyes we see the events of the narrative, from the strange environments to which their adventures lead them. But even within the exotic names, both personal and geographical, it is possible to distinguish between different cultures such as Rohan and Gondor, as well as between the various non-human beings, Elves, Dwarves, and Orcs. The principle is explained by Tolkien, or rather by his editor/translator persona, in *Appendix* F.

I have already examined in *Translating Tolkien* the question of verisimilitude and historical depth in the English-based names in order to analyse how far it has been thought possible or desirable to preserve this effect in a selection of published translations in such a way that it is accepted as familiar by the reader of the target text. An in-depth analysis of all the Shire names is also provided by Nagel. The exotic names present a different problem of acceptance, since as Schmitz and Graziano claim in this volume, in some cases they are very far removed from the putative reader's linguistic norms.

In the last 60 years or more we have certainly become more accustomed to a plethora of invented names in many different styles from the large amount of fantasy and science fiction that has been launched on to the popular market during that time, but Tolkien had to take into consideration a public with less exposure to the unusual, a public more used to historical novels or adventure stories in the style of Rider Haggard, in which the names most often reflected the period and place of the primary world in which they were set. In fact, Tolkien's choices may well have eased the path, but also set a standard for the fantasy writers who followed in his footsteps.

There are some names from *The Lord of the Rings* that have been taken to people's hearts more than others. As a purely anecdotal example, I have seen pleasure boats in British marinas called Éowyn and Faramir, the latter three or four times; this was in the days before Peter Jackson's films, when Faramir perhaps appeared as a more sympathetic character. In contrast, names from *The Silmarillion* have proved harder to assimilate, suggesting that the public shares the view of the publisher's reader Edward Crankshaw, who complained about the "eye-splitting Celtic names". ("Needless to say they are not Celtic!" was Tolkien's retort.) (L 25f.)

This may have something to do with the sheer number of unfamiliar names in *The Silmarillion*. In a highly informal check, I compared the number of non-English names in the Index of *The Silmarillion* with that in the old Index of *The Lord of the Rings* compiled by Nancy Smith for the second edition, not counting names which appear only in the *Appendices*. I counted about 430 in *The Lord of the Rings*, while there were 634 in *The Silmarillion*, although 132 of these had already appeared in the earlier book because *The Silmarillion* is a compilation which includes re-tellings of tales from the Second and Third Ages, which meant that only 502 names were completely new. However, in the editions that I used the 430 were spread over 1,056 pages, whereas the 502 were compressed into 289 pages, representing a much higher density. The two assumptions behind this count are a) that readers find it easier to assimilate names in their own language, or at least have forms similar to those of their own language, and b) that most readers come to *The Silmarillion* only after reading *The Lord of the Rings*, so that they have some acquaintance with Tolkien's nomenclature.

The figure for *The Lord of the Rings* is approximate because it is not always easy to decide whether a name counts as English or not. *Brockenbores* may mean nothing to some readers, but the morpheme *bore* and the plural *-s* give it a familiar shape. I counted *Hollin* as English, because even though it is a dialect form that may be unfamiliar to many, there is a Hollin Lane in several towns in the north of England. I did not count *Isengard* because the morphemes constituting it are not found at all in English of the modern period. Since Old English can normally be read only by those who have learnt it specially, even though some words may be the same as in the modern language, I have counted the Old English of Rohan as exotic. This problem does not exist for *The Silmarillion* because there are no characters like the Hobbits who act as intermediaries to give a sense of familiarity.

There is a significant difference of textual and narrative structure between the two books that affects their readability. *The Lord of the Rings* is essentially novelistic in style, whereas *The Silmarillion* is (deliberately) not: it is very densely written, in a compressed style rather like notes or a summary, with very little dialogue. This means that names cannot appear in the personal context of a conversation, but are delivered by a detached narrative voice. However, Tolkien never managed to prepare a finished version for publication, so we cannot be sure of his final intentions. Therefore from now on I will concentrate on *The Lord of the Rings*, the definitive version of which was deliberately crafted for the general reading public as a sequel to *The Hobbit*.

Strategies of Mediation

I will argue that the strategies by which the many names are presented add to the readability of the narrative and to their acceptance by the reader in the first place, while on repeated readings they enhance the reader's interest in the names as an integral part of a planned whole. They are mediated in a number of different ways which make them less opaque and easier to remember. The process works in parallel to the way in which the archaic world itself is mediated to the modern reader by the Hobbits, through whose eyes the reader discovers the wider world of the romance; Tom Shippey, who first pointed out this important function, uses the term "reflector" (6). The names also gain in resonance through being presented in a context which shows them to be significant markers in a complex pattern of interrelationships in the history of the secondary world.

Since *The Lord of the Rings* is novelistic in style, the names are often presented by means of dialogue, particularly by an authoritative character such as Gandalf or Aragorn, which underlines their significance and therefore encourages their acceptance by the reader. For example, in the second chapter Gandalf introduces three characters who will never appear in the events of the narrative but who are important for the history of the Ring:

> It was Gil-galad, Elven-king and Elendil of Westernesse who over-threw Sauron, though they themselves perished in the deed; and Isildur Elendil's son cut the Ring from Sauron's hand...   (52)

The names occur in an account of the history of the Ring, the discourse structure of which makes it clear both to Frodo within the narrative and to the reader outside it that important information is being conveyed. The three characters also also identified with an alliance. This is sufficient to recall and reinforce the names when two of them next occur, fully nine chapters later at Weathertop, where the original alliance was formed, in another historical explanation, this time by Aragorn (185). The poem about Gil-galad, which gains in authority through its association with Bilbo, consolidates this name even further by embedding it in a context. The mediation of place names is often similar, for example:

> We have now come to the River Hoarwell, that the Elves call Mith-eithel. It flows down out of the Ettenmoors, the troll-fells north of Rivendell, and joins the Loudwater away in the South. Some call it the Greyflood after that... That is Loudwater, the Bruinen of Rivendell.   (200)

Aragorn's geography lesson serves a multiple purpose: it not only introduces some relevant names to the reader but also enhances his status as someone with knowledge of the wild country. It also shows him to be familiar with the Elvish language and culture, as does his telling of the tale of Beren and Lúthien, while it foreshadows the revelation of his status as the descendant of the legendary characters he tells about, and as the claimant of the thrones of both Gondor and Arnor.

This form of presentation is not peculiar to Tolkien, since any romance in an unfamiliar setting has to do something similar: the reader has to be led into an understanding of the unfamiliar. This is true regardless of whether the world of the text is an invented one or a less well known aspect of the real world, or at least a literary representation of it. A similar technique can be found in historical novels such as Sir Walter Scott's *Waverley* and *Rob Roy*, in which a young Englishman, mediating for Scott's contemporary English readership, is introduced to the complexities of Scottish Highland history and culture, a culture which had all but disappeared as a result of the political events of the 60-100 years between the publication of the novels and the period in which they were set.

Doublets

In Tolkien's world the reception of the names is sometimes complicated by the doublet forms in which they appear: Loudwater/Bruinen, Hoarwell/Mitheithel, where one in each pair is more immediately recognisable than the other (even if *Hoarwell* is less transparent in meaning than *Loudwater*, nevertheless each of the constituent morphemes is clearly identifiable as an English word). This contributes to the realisation of the secondary world by making it clear that it is a polyglot civilisation, where different characters and cultural groups have different native and acquired languages.

More relevantly for the present discussion, for the reader the pairing with a familiar form serves the function of making the exotic linguistic shape easier to assimilate and providing a smoother transition into the exotic, archaic world, as proved by the preponderance of English-based equivalents in Books I and II. It can perhaps be explained by the analogy of the German word pair for the school subject geography. In primary school, children learn *Erdkunde*, where the transparent word in the mother tongue represents a more concrete approach to the phenomena of the natural world that children are likely to encounter at that stage of their development. At secondary school, however, the subject becomes *Geographie*, where the Greek-derived word symbolises a more distanced, academic approach.

The choice of doublet can have an additional function in characterising a person or situation. So Gandalf in "The Shadow of the Past" talks to Frodo of Westernesse, which can be recognised as an island far in the Western sea, whereas Númenor, the more frequent Sindarin equivalent, appears only later in Aragorn's tale of Beren and Lúthien, where it is immediately glossed: "And of Eärendil came the Kings of Númenor, that is Westernesse" (194). However, in Frodo's conversation with Faramir they use only Númenor, which characterises the tone of interaction with this learned young man from a more ancient culture, at a stage of the narrative where the reader has become much more used to Sindarin names and their phonological shape.

The volcanic mountain in Mordor is also rendered pictorially by the use of contrasted styles of naming. Gandalf, in the same conversation with Frodo, introduces the Sindarin *Orodruin*, but sandwiches it between two homely English-based names: "the Cracks of Doom in the depths of Orodruin, the Fire-mountain" (61).[1] The venerable Elrond twice refers to it as Orodruin, but subsequently it is most often known as Mount Doom. However, when Sam rescues Frodo in the Tower of Cirith Ungol, he says: "But you're in the land of Mordor now, sir; and when you get out, you'll see the Fiery Mountain and all" (911). This touch of rustic Hobbit informality ("and all") in the choice of name constitutes an astute flash of characterisation in passing for the character who has just sung "In western lands" to a simple Shire tune.

A different case altogether are the Dwarvish names spoken by Gimli in his trilingual evocation of the mountains of Moria, which, since they are almost the only words of Dwarvish ever spoken in the narrative, express in succinct linguistic form the longings of all the Dwarves for their ancient home:

> …under them lies Khazad-dûm, the Dwarrowdelf, that is now called the Black Pit, Moria in the Elvish tongue. Yonder stands Barazinbar, the Redhorn, cruel Caradhras; and beyond him are Silvertine and Cloudyhead: Celebdil the White, and Fanuidhol the Grey, that we call Zirakzigil and Bundushathûr.   (283)

This is not really a case of mediation, since the names are probably meant to remain completely alien to the reader, although they should be memorable because of their very different phonological shape.[2] This memorability is particularly

---

1   The Cracks of Doom are particularly familiar in that they echo a colloquial English expression: We shall be here until the crack of doom (= for a very long time). The reference is to the last trumpet on the Day of Judgement (OE dōm 'judgement').

2   The description in *Appendix* F of the Dwarves' pronunciation of the Common Speech as "harsh and guttural" is no doubt meant to suggest interference from the phonology of their own language. It seems probable that the Elvish names in *The Lord of the Rings* were deliberately selected to present as few phonological difficulties as possible to speakers of

important for Gimli's later words: Dark is the water of Kheled-zâram... and cold are the springs of Kibil-nâla" (283), as four chapters further on these very words are echoed by Galadriel, who continues: "and fair were the many-pillared halls of Khazad-dûm in Elder Days before the fall of mighty kings beneath the stone" (356). These Dwarvish names suffice to defuse a tense situation within the narrative, while for the reader they establish the empathetic nature of Galadriel and signal the deep rapport established here between the two characters.

Glossing

We have already seen several examples of direct glossing as a means of mediating non-English names to the reader. However, there are other cases where the gloss is so indirect as to become clear perhaps only on a third or fourth reading. This can be seen on several occasions where Old English is used to represent the language of Rohan; since it is exotic to the (English-speaking) reader but not perhaps wholly strange, it is meant to convey the impression of the Hobbits, particularly Merry, that there is something which reminds them distantly of their own language. The glosses serve to nudge the reader towards a semi-conscious recognition of the similarity. Some are very literal, whereas others rely on a small periphrasis; in each case the gloss is italicised:

> the Firienfeld men called it, a green *mountain-field* of grass and heath   (794)

> ... the peaks of Thrihyrne: now very near they stood on the northern-most arm of the White Mountains, *three* jagged *horns*   (527)

> ... she whom he had called Dernhelm. But *the helm of her secrecy* had fallen from her, and her bright hair, released from its bonds, gleamed with pale gold upon her shoulders
> (841) [dern-helm = secret helm]

> the *saw-toothed* mass of Irensaga   (794) [iren-saga = iron saw]

> [they] came to the Dimholt. There under *the gloom of black trees...*
> (786) [dim-holt = dark wood]

English, whereas those in *The Simarillion* are Quenya and Sindarin served pure with no concessions to the reader. Compare the comment at the beginning of *Appendix* E that Quenya has been spelt similarly to Latin "to produce words and names that do not look uncouth in modern letters".

These are some of the most overt examples. However, the same technique is occasionally used to gloss Elvish names too: "the loud-flowing Bruinen" (239); "the Rohirrim, the Horse-lords" (507); or less directly, "Ered Lithui, grey as ash" (636) [Ered Lithui = Ash Mountains]. There is even a gloss of a slightly obscure English-based name: "the cloven vale of Rivendell" (281).

Some of these glosses reveal themselves only to readers who have discovered information about Tolkien's invented languages from other sources, such as *Unfinished* Tales or the "Etymologies" in *The Lost Road*:

> Lebennin with its five swift streams
> (750) [*leben* = 5, *nîn*, plural of *nen* = waters, streams; cf. *UT* 449]

> the dark sad waters of Lake Núrnen
> (923) [*nen* as above; cf. *UT* 458]

> the bleak hills of the Emyn Muil
> (373) [*emyn*, pl. of *amon* = hills, *muil* = drear, bleak; cf. *UT* 434]

So the interest of Tolkien's techniques of mediation can be maintained even after many readings and continues to give insight into the complex craftsmanship of the text.

Although it has already been established that there are approximately 430 non-English names spread over more than 1,000 pages, the distribution is not even. In Book I, for example, they are concentrated towards the beginning and towards the end. Of the first three chapters, Chapter 1 contains a great deal of nomenclature, as might be expected in the exposition of a narrative, but the names refer almost exclusively to the Shire and are therefore English-based. Chapter 2 introduces a number of new, exotic names, mediated by Gandalf as demonstrated above. Chapter 3 returns largely to Shire names, except for the episode with Gildor and the Elves, and from then on there are no more exotic names until the last two chapters of the book.[3]

Aragorn introduces a dense cluster in his tale of Beren and Lúthien, which is followed a few pages later by the geography lesson examined above, and the meeting with Glorfindel, who with the help of a footnote reveals to us that the slightly eccentric Shire name *Brandywine* is in fact a folk-etymology of the Sindarin *Baranduin*. This distribution pattern is obviously determined by the shape of the narrative, but it also raises the question of how the clustering, which also occurs elsewhere in the text, can influence the reader's acceptance of unfamiliar names. At first sight, a high density of unfamiliar names might

---

3   This is ignoring the name Bombadil, for which there is no adequate explanation.

be thought to cause difficulties, but in fact the opposite may well be the case: the interest aroused by a new and enthralling topic such as the romance of two characters from the remote past could lead to a much smoother assimilation.

Names with Obscure Referents

The tale of Beren and Lúthien is significant for the plot as a whole because it underpins the legitimacy of Aragorn's claim both to the joint thrones of the West and to the hand of Arwen, so it is important that their names at least should be well imprinted on the reader's mind. However, not all the information in Aragorn's tale is equally essential; as a final point, I will point out how Tolkien occasionally uses the clustering technique for a different purpose:

> But the enemy was victorious and Barahir was slain, and Beren escaping through great peril came over the Mountains of Terror into the hidden kingdom of Thingol in the forest of Neldoreth. There he beheld Lúthien singing and dancing in a glade beside the enchanted river Esgalduin; and he named her Tinúviel, that is Nightingale in the language of old.   (193)

Apart from Lúthien, none of these names is mentioned again in the remaining 800 pages of the main narrative; their resonances can be picked up only in the *Appendices* or *The Silmarillion*. This passage can be compared with the earlier description of the constellations:

> Away high in the East swung Remmirath, the Netted Stars, and slowly above the mists red Borgil rose, glowing like a jewel of fire. Then by some shift of the airs all the mist was drawn away like a veil, and there leaned up, as he climbed over the rim of the world, the Swordsman of the Sky, Menelvagor with his shining belt. The Elves all burst into song.   (81)

Although it is perfectly possible to identify these names with known stars, as Kristine Larsen has done, within *The Lord of the Rings* itself the unfamiliar names are there to convey pure sound and atmosphere, to be compared for example with Coleridge's "Kubla Khan"

> In Xanadu did Kubla Khan
> A stately pleasure-dome decree:
> Where Alph, the sacred river, ran
> Through caverns measureless to man
> Down to a sunless sea.   (Wordsworth & Coleridge, 254)

Anyone who reads this does not immediately turn to an atlas to find out exactly where Xanadu is and where the Alph rises, or to a reference book on religions to discover who it is sacred to, since that is of no relevance to the poem itself. Similarly with Tolkien, the precise reference of the names is not of direct significance at this point in the text, although in contrast to Coleridge, Tolkien is always at pains to imply that it is nevertheless knowable.

There are other places where Tolkien appears to be using the techniques of mediation, but deliberately withholds the significance that they are normally intended to provide for the sake of cheating the reader's expectations and thereby heightening the tension. A simple instance of this is the narrator's presentation of the entrance to the tombs in Minas Tirith: "Fen Hollen it was called, for it was kept ever shut" (826). What looks like an explanation ("for") is not one at all, since the reader at this point has no way of knowing the meaning of the Sindarin words. It is only two pages later that it turns out to have been a cryptic gloss when Beregond refers to it as "the Closed Door" and the reader is left to make the identification.

A more complex case is the deliberate obscuring of the meaning of Cirith Ungol. When Gollum tells Frodo about a little-known route into Mordor but refuses to give it a name, the narrator provides one:

> Its name was Cirith Ungol, a name of dreadful rumour. Aragorn would perhaps have told them that name and its significance; Gandalf would have warned them.   (644)

Tolkien deliberately gives the name and the veiled warning, but not the significance, and in so doing he creates suspense. Later he heightens it through the mysterious comment of Faramir, who as a speaker of Sindarin should at least have known the literal meaning of the words:

> But there is some dark terror that dwells in the passes above Minas Morgul. If Cirith Ungol is named, old men and masters of lore will blanch and fall silent.   (692)

Finally one part of the name is glossed by the narrator when Frodo and Sam are led into the tunnel by Gollum: "He did not speak its name: Torech Ungol, Shelob's Lair". However, this is a gloss that gives absolutely no information, because the reader cannot know at this stage who or what Shelob is; almost no-one will surmise that it means "female spider" without having been told first. Only the word "lair" sounds ominous, in common with the previous references. It is a classic example of the use of language to avoid giving information.

Conclusion

In comparison with many other fantasy writers, Tolkien is generally acknowledged to have been particularly successful in the creation of names that have been readily received as credible by readers, who in many cases have taken them to their hearts. There are possible reasons for that which have not been examined here, such as the evident consistency of their formation and their pleasing phonological structure. However, a major contribution to their acceptance is the various techniques of mediation that Tolkien used, on the one hand embedding them into the texture of the narrative, often through the sub-narration of individual characters, and on the other subtly lifting them out through glosses, often in the form of equivalents in another language of the secondary world, to make them appear, almost below the level of consciousness, as artefacts in their own right.

Bibliography

Carpenter, Humphrey (Ed.). *The Letters of J.R.R. Tolkien*. London: Allen & Unwin, 1981

Larsen, Kristine. 'A Definitive Identification of Tolkien's "Borgil": An Astronomical and Literary Approach'. *Tolkien Studies 2* (2005): 161-170

Nagel, Rainer. *Hobbit Place-names. A Linguistic Excursion through the Shire*. Zurich/Jena: Walking Tree Publishers, 2012

Shippey, Tom. *J.R.R. Tolkien: Author of the Century*. London: HarperCollins, 2000

Tolkien, J.R.R. *The Lord of the Rings* (50th Anniversary Edition). London: HarperCollins, 2005

Turner, Allan. *Translating Tolkien: Philological Elements in* The Lord of the Rings. Frankfurt: Peter Lang, 2005

Wordsworth, William, & Samuel Taylor Coleridge. *Lyrical Ballads and Other Poems*. Ware: Wordsworth Editions, 2002

Ein heimliches Laster
oder der Untergrund der Sprache

Eine Untersuchung zu Tolkiens Semiotik

Wilhelm Kuehs (Klagenfurt)

Eine linguistische Häresie

In seinem 1955 gehaltenen Vortrag »English and Welsh« kommt Tolkien auf die Schönheit einzelner Wörter zu sprechen. Im Englischen, so meint er, empfinden die meisten Sprecher »cellar door« als schön, wohingegen »beautiful« sich nicht durch besondere Schönheit auszeichne (EW 190).

Was für einzelne Wörter gilt, gilt auch für ganze Sprachen. Walisisch, meint Tolkien, sei eine verführerische Sprache und dem Gotischen sei er schon bei der ersten Begegnung verfallen. Damit bezieht sich Tolkien zunächst auf die musikalische Qualität, den Sound, der jeweiligen Sprache (EW 191).

Die linguistische Häresie[1], wie Shippey das nennt, geht aber weit über die Frage hinaus, ob man den Sound einer Sprache als schön oder hässlich empfindet. Denn Shippey stellte fest, dass Tolkien die Frage nach der Schönheit des Sounds mit der Frage verknüpft, ob Phoneme an sich eine Bedeutung tragen können.

Wir wollen Tolkiens Argumentation hier kurz aufrollen und sehen, ob sich darin aus heutiger Sicht tatsächlich eine linguistische Häresie verbirgt, oder ob Tolkien vielmehr einen Punkt anspricht, der uns die Verbindung von Sprache und Mythologie auf neue und ungewöhnliche Weise erhellt.

Wenn Tolkien diese Häresie begeht, so sie überhaupt eine ist, dann in seinem Aufsatz »A Secret Vice«. Dort nämlich beschäftigt er sich unter anderem mit den speziellen Eigenschaften erfundener Sprachen. Hier stellt Tolkien die Frage nach dem Zusammenhang zwischen »sound symbol« und einer damit verknüpften Vorstellung (associated notion; SV 204). Bei einer erfundenen Sprache könne man solche sinnerfüllten Verbindungen zwischen Lautgruppen und den damit verbundenen Vorstellungen herstellen. Als Beispiel führt Tolkien das Wort »lint« an: »Lint« bedeutet in der Kunstsprache Nevbosh so viel wie »schnell, fix, gescheit«. Tolkien bereitete die Verknüpfung von Lautgestalt und Sinn außerordentliches Vergnügen und dieses Vergnügen

---

1   This was Tolkien's major linguistic heresy. He thought that people could feel history in words, could recognise language ›styles‹, could extract sense (of sorts) from sound alone, could moreover make aesthetic judgements based on phonology. He said the sound of ›cellar door‹ was more beautiful than the sound of ›beautiful‹. He clearly believed that *untranslated* elvish would do a job that English could not. (Shippey 104)

wurzelt in »the sense of fitness«, also in der passenden Entsprechung von Laut und Sinn (SV 205).

Freilich räumt Tolkien gleich ein, dass dieser Zusammenhang in einer natürlichen Sprache sehr bald verloren ginge und ein arbiträres Verhältnis zwischen Wort und Sinn entstünde. Aber grundsätzlich hält Tolkien es für möglich und wahrscheinlich, dass es Phoneme gibt, die besser oder schlechter zu einem bestimmten Sinn passen. Tolkien nennt das »phonetic fitness« (SV 211).

Schon hier können wir zwei voneinander geschiedene Argumente Tolkiens bezüglich der Ausdrucksebene der Sprache festmachen. Zum einen stellt Tolkien fest, dass der Sound einer Sprache uns Vergnügen bereiten kann. Zum anderen sagt er, es gebe so etwas wie eine nicht-arbiträre und damit privilegierte Verbindung zwischen Lautgestalt und Sinn.

Diese beiden Argumente verschmilzt Tolkien nun in einem dritten: Die geglückte Kombination von Phonemen und Sinn erzeuge etwas, das über den unmittelbaren Sinn hinausweise: Die Lautmelodie selbst trage eine Bedeutung (SV 218).

Shippey meint, Tolkien habe diese Idee mehrfach im *Herrn der Ringe* umgesetzt. Besonders deutlich wird dieser Effekt bei Théodens Begräbnis (HdR III 308). Die Beschreibung der Zeremonie scheint geradezu die Anwendung jener oben zitierten Stelle zu sein. Gléowines Lied, das hier von den Reitern von Rohan gesungen wird, erzählt nicht nur im Text die Geschichte des verstorbenen Königs, es erweckt auch in jenen Zuhörern, die die Sprache nicht verstehen, eine Ahnung von den Taten der Rohirrim und König Théodens.

Phonosemantik

Die Häresie, die Tolkien hier begeht, nennt man gemeinhin Phonosemantik. Häretisch nennen wir diese Position, weil wir seit Ferdinand de Saussures *Grundfragen der Allgemeinen Sprachwissenschaft* davon ausgehen, dass die Beziehung zwischen Vorstellung und Lautbild grundsätzlich arbiträr ist. Das sprachliche Zeichen setzt sich demnach aus der Vorstellung und einem Lautbild zusammen; diese sind aber nur per Konvention miteinander verbunden (de Saussure 76ff).

Man könnte nun meinen, Tolkiens Theorie von der »phonetic fitness« stelle diesen ersten und überaus wichtigen Grundsatz der Semiologie und Semiotik in Frage. Ich meine, das ist nicht der Fall. Als Philologe wusste Tolkien über die Veränderlichkeit von Sprache selbstverständlich Bescheid. Immer wieder beschreibt er die Veränderung von Wörtern, die komplexen Verflechtungen von Ablautreihen mit anderen linguistischen Gesetzmäßigkeiten, und als Kenner und Nutzer verschiedener Sprachen war ihm bewusst, dass verschiedene Lautmuster auf ein und denselben Inhalt hinweisen können.

Es scheint mir fast überflüssig, diese Dinge überhaupt anzusprechen. Denn auch wenn Tolkien an verschiedenen Stellen immer wieder seine Skepsis gegenüber strukturalistischen Methoden äußert, so war ihm so etwas Offensichtliches wie die Unmotiviertheit des sprachlichen Zeichens selbstredend bewusst.

So einfach ist Tolkiens Argument also nicht gestrickt, dass man es mit einem simplen Verweis aus der Welt schaffen kann. Selbstverständlich kann man für die Vorstellung /Baum/ verschiedene Lautmuster verwenden, um sie zu bezeichnen. Ob wir »Arbor«, »Tree« oder »Drvo« sagen, wir verweisen immer auf mehr oder weniger dasselbe Denotatum, so man das Denotatum nicht als Singularität, sondern als Kontinuum auffasst. Denn wie Hjelmslev zeigt, verweisen Begriffe wie das dänische »Trae« auf ein etwas größeres Segment der Enzyklopädie als der französische Begriff »Arbre«. Während »Arbre« in etwa das gleiche Segment der Enzyklopädie trifft wie der deutsche Begriff »Baum«, umfasst »Trae« einen weiteren Bedeutungsraum und schließt auch jenes Segment der Enzyklopädie mit ein, das im Deutschen mit »Holz« bezeichnet wird (Hjelmslev 57).

Auch diachron kann man einen solchen Bedeutungsunterschied leicht belegen. Der mhd. Begriff »hochzit« umfasste einen viel weiteren Abschnitt der Enzyklopädie als der nhd. Begriff »Hochzeit". Während nhd. »Hochzeit« sich lediglich auf die Vermählung und die damit einhergehenden Feierlichkeiten bezieht, meinte das mhd. »hochzit« jegliche Art von kirchlichem oder weltlichem Fest.

Soweit ich sehen kann, bestreitet Tolkien all das nirgends. Ganz im Gegenteil: Bei der Konstruktion verschiedener Sprachen und ihrer Abhängigkeiten setzt er die Wandlungsfähigkeit von Ausdrucksform und Ausdrucksubstanz in Bezug auf die Bedeutung ganz gezielt ein.

Sound und Bedeutung

Louis Hjelmslev fasst de Saussures Definition des Zeichens genauer und wirft einen Blick auf die innere Struktur von Signifikat und Signifikant. Er erstellt ein semiotisches Modell der natürlichen Sprache, das das Zeichen grundsätzlich als eine Kombination von Ausdruck und Inhalt definiert. Soweit decken sich die Auffassungen von Hjelmselv und de Saussure. Aber nun unterteilt Hjelmslev jede diese Komponenten in zwei weitere Ebenen: Der Inhalt eines Zeichens teilt sich demzufolge in Inhaltsform und Inhaltssubstanz. Unter Inhaltsform ist der Begriff, die mentale Einheit, die auf ein Faktum der Außenwelt verweist, gemeint; dieses Faktum der Außenwelt ist die Inhaltssubstanz (Hjelmslev 57).

Die Form des Inhalts eines Zeichens legt eine Ordnung über die an sich ungeordnete uns zugängliche Wirklichkeit. Sie ist ein Code, der die Welt segmentiert und sie zu einer Enzyklopädie macht. Beispiele solcher Inhaltsformen sind Nomenklaturen, Ordnungssysteme etwa der Tier- und Pflanzengattungen und dergleichen mehr.

Ebenso wie den Inhalt segmentiert Hjelmslev auch die Ausdrucksseite des Zeichens. Unter Ausdrucksform verstehen wir wiederum ein System von ordnenden Codes. Im Fall der natürlichen Sprachen handelt es sich um die Regeln der Grammatik, um phonologische Systeme etc. (Eco, *Sprache* 34). Die Ausdruckssubstanz ist die materielle Seite des Ausdrucks. Das gesprochene oder gedruckte Wort, die aktualisierte Lautfolge ist die Substanz, die durch die Ausdrucksform ermöglicht wird.

Ausdruck	Ausdrucksform
	Ausdruckssubstanz
Inhalt	Inhaltsform
	Inhaltssubstanz

Grafik 1: Zeichen nach Hjelmslev

Betrachten wir Hjelmslevs Modell hinsichtlich der Arbitrarität der Komponenten, so stellen wir fest, dass die Beliebigkeit der Verbindungen weit in das Zeichen selbst eingedrungen ist. Zwar regulieren die Codes auf der Ebene der Inhalts- und Ausdrucksform bis zu einem gewissen Grad die Möglichkeiten der Inhalts- und Ausdruckssubstanz, aber gleichzeitig eröffnen sie auch einen Spielraum der Performance.

Mit Hjelmslevs Modell können wir Tolkiens Vergnügen am Klang der Sprache besser verorten. Wir befinden uns auf der Ebene des Ausdrucks und wenn Tolkien sagt, im Walisischen gebe es Wörter, die dem Stil der Sprache so unmittelbar entsprechen, dass nicht nur die Rezeption dieser Wörter ein größeres Vergnügen mache, als das bei vergleichbaren englischen Wörtern der Fall sei, sondern dass diese Wörter über ihren unmittelbaren Sinn hinausweisen (EW 193), dann setzt sein Argument genau hier auf der Ausdrucks- und nicht auf der Inhaltsebene des Zeichens an.

Der Klang weist über die unmittelbare Bedeutung hinaus. Tolkien hat damit zweifellos recht. Aber wie kann man dieses Phänomen mit den Mitteln der Semiotik erklären? Zunächst ein paar Beispiele:

Wenn ich etwa eine fremdsprachige Unterhaltung mit halbem Ohr höre, dann kann ich dem Klang nach feststellen, um welche Sprache oder wenigstens um welche Sprachfamilie es sich handelt. Auch wenn ich selbst nicht Italienisch kann, reicht der Sound, also die Ausdruckssubstanz, um mich auf das mentale Muster /italienische Sprache/ zu verweisen.

Ich führe, um mit Eco und Peirce zu sprechen, eine Abduktion durch. Ich stelle eine Hypothese darüber auf, welche Sprache ich höre, und ziehe dabei die

Wahrscheinlichkeiten innerhalb des gegebenen Kontextes und die möglichen Codes in Betracht (Eco, *Interpretation* 312ff).

Vom Zeichen ist mir zunächst nur die Ausdruckssubstanz gegeben, und dennoch kann ich aufgrund meiner Kenntnis der Enzyklopädie eine Schlussfolgerung auf ein Gesetz bzw. einen Satz von Gesetzen ziehen. Ich weiß also nun mit einiger Sicherheit, welche Sprache da gesprochen wird, und habe ein Denotatum in der Enzyklopädie festgemacht.

Dieser Vorgang wird ganz unwillkürlich von weiteren Abduktionen begleitet. Diese binden weitere Codes und Codestrukturen ein und legen dabei ein Netz an Konnotationen frei. Das Denotatum ist wie der Ring eines Schlüsselbundes, an dem ein Strauß von Konnotaten hängt. Diese Konnotate umfassen Nebenbedeutungen, Assoziationen, Interpretanten, die zu Subtexten führen. Sie sind es, die mir u.a. Vergnügen oder Unlust beim Hören einer Sprache bereiten.

Lust und Unlust müssen aus einem Kontext heraus verstanden werden. So könnte mein Vergnügen beim Hören der italienischen Sprache aus einem ganz persönlichen Teil der Enzyklopädie entspringen. Der Klang könnte mich an Sonne und Meer erinnern, an Opernbesuche in Verona usw. Diese Elemente sind darüber hinaus etablierte Bestandteile der Enzyklopädie unserer Semiosphäre und daher für jeden leicht nachvollziehbar.

Die Konnotationen beziehen sich auf mentale Muster, die ihrerseits mit Interpretationen aufgeladen sind. So wie Italien für viele auf die Hauptkonotation Urlaub verweist, lässt sich in Westeuropa z.B. oft ein Missbehagen gegenüber slawischen Sprachen feststellen.

Jahrzehnte lang durchgehaltene Narrative von der Grausamkeit russischer Soldaten, der Rückständigkeit der ehemaligen Ostblockstaaten und sinistren Gastarbeitern haben dafür gesorgt, dass allein der Klang einer slawischen Sprache manchem immer noch Angst macht.

Der Klang, die Aktualisierung der Phoneme, die maßgeblich die Ausdruckssubstanz einer Sprache bestimmen, verweist also seinerseits auf einen Inhalt, der nicht unmittelbar mit der Inhaltsebene des sprachlichen Zeichens zusammenhängt, zu dem sie eigentlich gehören. Wenn ich also sage »ti si moje malo sonce, lubica«, so kann sich vor dem Inhalt dieser Aussage (Du bist meine kleine Sonne, Liebling) kaum jemand fürchten. (Wobei natürlich ein Kontext denkbar ist, in dem eine solche Aussage nicht als Liebeserklärung, sondern als Drohung gemeint sein könnte.) Der Sound allerdings könnte beim einen oder anderen Angst oder Wut erzeugen: In Kärnten ist es durchaus möglich, für ein freundliches »dober dan« von einem deutschnational gesinnten Mitbürger auf der Straße angespuckt zu werden. Hier wird die Ausdruckssubstanz selbst zu einem Zeichen.

Der Klang als Zeichen

M an könnte nun meinen, man habe hier ein sekundäres semiologisches System im Sinne Roland Barthes' vor sich (Barthes 92). Unser Fall ist ähnlich, aber doch etwas anders gelagert. Ein sekundäres semiologisches System im Sinne Barthes' nimmt ein Zeichen, also die Kombination von Signifikat und Signifikant, als Einheit und behandelt das Zeichen, als sei es nur Signifikant. Das Zeichen wird zum Bedeutenden innerhalb eines neuen Zeichens und verwischt somit die ursprüngliche Zeichenstruktur.

Bei Tolkiens Argument haben wir es aber nicht mit einer Überstülpung, sondern mit einer Ausfaltung zu tun. Das neue Zeichen wird als fraktale Wiederholung und Abwandlung in eine der Komponenten des ursprünglichen Zeichens eingepasst.

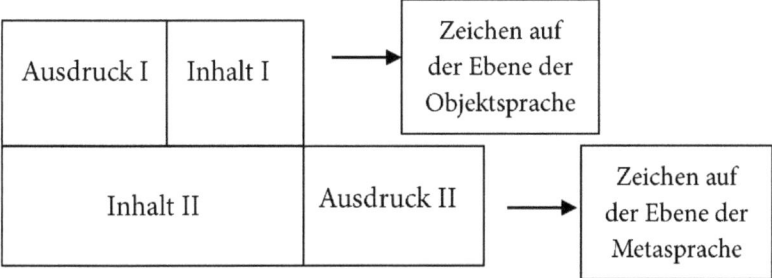

Grafik 2: Sekundäres semiologisches System nach Roland Barthes

Die Ausdruckssubstanz wird Ausgangspunkt eines neuen Zeichens. Der Klang selbst verweist auf ein kulturelles Muster, auf einen Teil der Enzyklopädie.

Tolkien nutzt diesen Mechanismus auf vielerlei Weise. Sein *Legendarium* ist auch und war zumindest für seinen Schöpfer zu einem Gutteil ein Essay über linguistische Ästhetik (L 202). Angesichts des bis jetzt Gesagten können wir diesen Hinweis neu deuten. Die linguistische Ästhetik, der Klang, der Tolkien solches Vergnügen bereitet, ist ein wichtiges Bindeglied zur Mythologie, die laut Tolkien immer mit einer Sprache verknüpft ist (SV 210).

Dies sei zunächst nur an einem Beispiel demonstriert: Bei der Konstruktion seiner Sprachen hat Tolkien sich von existierenden natürlichen Sprachen inspirieren lassen. So nahm er bei der Konstruktion der Deklination im Quenya Anleihen am Finnischen. Im Quenya wird deshalb der einfache Lokativ mit der Endung -sse gebildet. Für den Plural wird die Endung mit -n erweitert. Diese Konstruktion nimmt Anleihen am Inessiv des Finnischen, der mit den Endungen -ssa oder -ssä gebildet wird (Allan 17).

Hier liegt sowohl im Klang (Ausdruckssubstanz) wie auch in der grammatischen Form (Ausdruckform) eine Übereinstimmung zwischen Quenya und Finnisch vor.

Aber auch auf der Ebene der Lexeme nimmt Tolkien Anleihen am Finnischen. So verwendet er die Silbe tul- in der Bedeutung »kommen«. Das finnische Verb »tulla« bedeutet ebenfalls »kommen«.

Auf der Ebene der Grammatik scheint es einen starken Einfluss des Altgriechischen zu geben, wie Andrea Andreou ausführt. Es lassen sich hier u.a. Ähnlichkeiten bei Pluralbildung, Tempusformen und Fällen ermitteln.

In einem Brief an Naomi Mitchison vom 25.04.1954 geht Tolkien näher auf seine Beweggründe und seine Methoden bezüglich der beiden Elbensprachen Quenya und Sindarin ein: Quenya sollte als »Elven-latin« fungieren (L 175), also als eine Sprache, die zum Zeitpunkt der Handlung des HdR als antiquiert galt und nur noch von Gelehrten verstanden und gesprochen wurde. In ihr wurden Überlieferungen, Sagen und andere Berichte aus der Vergangenheit festgehalten. Damit tritt Quenya auch auf der Ebene der Pragmatik in Tolkiens *Legendarium* an jene Stelle, die in unserer westlichen Zivilisation Latein und Altgriechisch innehaben. Sindarin hingegen ist die lebende Sprache der Elben Mittelerdes und sie weist ausreichend Ähnlichkeiten mit dem Walisischen auf, um als Folie für einen »Celtic type of legends and stories« zu dienen (L 176).

Sprache und Mythologie

Eine Sprache muss notgedrungen eine Mythologie ausbrüten (SV 211). Und wenn sich Sprache und Mythologie nicht arbiträr zueinander verhalten, dann müssen wir auch in einer Kunstsprache, die von mehreren natürlichen Sprachen inspiriert ist, Spuren der Mythologie dieser natürlichen Sprachen finden.

Dass dies bei Tolkien so ist, lässt sich leicht zeigen. Tolkien hat sowohl die Sprachen als auch die dazugehörige Mythologie konstruiert. Ob das bei natürlichen Sprachen und natürlichen Mythologie ebenfalls so ist, scheint einen genaueren Blick wert.

Tatsächlich legt die vergleichende Erforschung von Mythologien nahe, dass hier ein Zusammenhang bestehen könnte. Alle Mythologien, die indoeuropäische Sprachen als Medium benutzen, ähneln sich nicht nur im Aufbau des Götterhimmels, der Verteilung von Zuständigkeiten unter den niederen Wesen der Mythologie, sondern bis weit hinein in die Geschichten einzelner Figuren. Georges Dumézil hat in seiner Arbeit immer wieder Vergleiche zwischen der nordischen und indischen Mythologie gezogen und bis in die Motive hinein Übereinstimmungen gefunden (Dumézil 53ff).

Die finnisch-ugrische Mythologie z.B. müsste sich dieser These nach allerdings in einigen wichtigen Punkten von der Grundstruktur der indoeuropäischen Mythologie unterscheiden. Wenn die finnisch-ugrische Mythologie aus der Matrix der finnisch-ugrischen Sprachen erwachsen ist, dann sollten wir ein Desiderat vorfinden, das sich grundlegend von der indoeuropäischen Mythologie abhebt.

Die Frage ist, auf welcher Ebene wir dieses Desiderat zu suchen haben. Verschiedene Versuche, eine Grammatik des Mythos herauszuarbeiten, haben wenigstens vier Grundkategorien entdeckt, die den meisten Mythologien gemeinsam sind. Es gibt so gut wie immer einen Schöpfungsmythos und verschiedene Geschichten, die in die Kategorie des Heldenmythos fallen. Außerdem finden wir den Göttinnenmythos und die Geschichte vom Weltende in jeder Mythologie (Kuehs 87f).

Wir können also davon ausgehen, dass wir auf dieser Analyseebene keine nennenswerten Unterschiede finden. Selbst eine so ferne und lange Zeit isolierte Mythologie wie jene der australischen Ureinwohner füllt alle diese Kategorien mit Erzählungen aus (Eliade, *Religions* passim). Wir müssen also das Material sichten, mit dem diese Kategorien gefüllt sind, und können uns hier von so globalen Kategorien wie dem System der Götter bis hinunter zu einzelnen Handlungssträngen und Motiven vorarbeiten.

Aus Platzgründen sei auch hier wieder nur ein Beispiel genannt. Die Geschichte Kullervos, so stellt Verlyn Flieger fest, war für Tolkien die Matrix für die zentrale Geschichte des *Silmarillions*, nämlich die Herstellung und den Kampf um die Silmarilli und für die Legende von Turin Turambar (Flieger 101).

Wenn wir Feanor mit Seppo Ilmarinen aus der *Kalevala* vergleichen (Himes 69ff), stellen wir eine Reihe von Gemeinsamkeiten fest. Als (Halb-)Götter des Handwerks verfügen sie auch über magische Fähigkeiten, sind daher in Schrift und Musik bewandert und nehmen eine besondere Stellung in der Gesellschaft ein. Damit unterscheiden sie sich allerdings noch nicht vom herkömmlichen Schmied und Schamanen, wie er weltweit in verschiedenen Mythologien vorkommt (Eliade, *Schmiede* passim). Sie sind aber durch ihr Produkt und die Geschichte, die sich um dieses Produkt rankt, aus der Masse der zaubermächtigen Schmiede herausgehoben.

Feanor bewahrt in den Silmarilli das Licht der Bäume von Valinor und rettet damit den Rest des kostbaren Schatzes über die Zeiten hinweg. Er verbindet damit die Zeitalter und hält die Konflikte zwischen Melkor und den anderen Göttern am Leben (S 72f).

Der Sampo ist ein ähnlich seltsames Gebilde wie ein Silmaril: Aus der Spitze einer Schwanenfeder, aus der Milch einer unfruchtbaren Kuh, einem einzigen Gerstenkorn und der Flocke aus dem Fell eines Schafes soll Ilmarinen den Sampo schmieden und dafür die Tochter der Beherrscherin des Nordlandes erhalten (Lönnrot 69).

Der Sampo gleicht den Silmarilli aber nicht nur in seiner überaus seltsamen Beschaffenheit. Wie die Silmarilli kann der Sampo nicht von den Göttern hergestellt werden. Es braucht ein Wesen der mittleren Mythologie. In der zehnten Rune der *Kalevala* sucht Väinämöinen Illmarinen in dessen Schmiede auf, um ihn bei der Herstellung des Sampo zu beobachten. Auf dem Weg dorthin erschafft Väinämöinen durch sein Singen eine Birke und auch den Mond singt er an den Himmel (Lönnrot 94). Es fällt dem Zaubergott also nicht besonders schwer, Dinge zu erschaffen, aber den Sampo kann er nicht herstellen. Darin gleicht Väinämöinen dem Vala Aule, der Feanor unter seine Fittiche nimmt, aber nicht selbst in der Lage ist, die Silmarilli herzustellen.

Dass sich nun sowohl um den Sampo als auch um die Silmarilli ein heftiger Kampf entspinnt, ist kein besonderes Spezifikum. Auch die Eigenschaft des Sampo, Wohlstand hervorzubringen, scheint ein Eintrag indoeuropäischer in die finnisch-ugrische Mythologie zu sein. Beispiele dazu finden sich vom *Mahabaratha* bis hin zum Gral des Wolfram von Eschenbach und dem Tischlein-deck-dich des Volksmärchens.

Was aber sehr wohl eine motivische Besonderheit darstellt, ist das schreck-liche und dunkle Schicksal, das die Silmarilli und der Sampo auslösen. Gemein-sam mit dem Andvaranaut der nordischen Sage gehören sie zu den Gegenständen der Mythologie, die dauerhaft Unglück und Niedergang stiften. Vom Ring der Nibelungen unterscheiden sie sich aber deutlich. Denn sowohl der Sampo als auch die Silmarilli wurden hergestellt, um Gutes zu bewirken. Der Andvaranaut war von Anfang an verflucht und sollte Lokis Verbrechen rächen.

Wir bewegen uns hier auf der Ebene der Motive und ihrer Transformationen. Wenn wir den Mythos als semiotisches System betrachten, dann können wir die Motive als Äquivalent zur Ausdrucksebene des Zeichens verstehen.

Auf der Ebene der Textsemiotik können wir ebenfalls sagen, ein Text besteht aus einer Inhalts- und einer Ausdrucksebene. Auf der Inhaltsebene des Textes finden wir wiederum Inhaltssubstanz und Inhaltsform.

Als Inhaltssubstanz können wir größere mentale Muster ausmachen. Nicht einzelne Begriffe, sondern kulturell und persönlich festgelegte Verknüpfungen bilden das Substrat, aus dem mittels der Inhaltsform Plots hergestellt werden. Die Mythen als para-digmatisches Kontinuum werden durch Regeln der Weltwahrnehmung erst in eine enzyklopädische Ordnung gebracht und diese organisieren sich mittels der Inhaltsform zunächst zu rudimentären Plots.

Campbell und Propp haben diesen Vorgang beschrieben und die Grund-legende Struktur des Erzählens, die Grammatik des Mythos aufgedeckt.

Ausdruck	Ausdrucksform	Szenen, Motive
	Ausdruckssubstanz	Erzählfunktionen
Inhalt	Inhaltsform	Plot
	Inhaltssubstanz	Fabel

Grafik 3: Struktur des Textes in Anlehnung an Hjelmslev

Was wir hier vor uns haben, ist aber noch keine Erzählung. Es ist die unanschauliche Struktur einer Erzählung, die erst durch eine Analyse sichtbar gemacht werden kann. Um dieser Struktur einen Ausdruck zu verleihen, muss auf der Ausdrucksebene zunächst mittels der Codes der Ausdrucksform ein Desiderat hergestellt werden, das letztlich mittels Ausdruckssubstanz zu einer Erzählung im herkömmlichen Sinn wird.

Auf der Ebene der Ausdrucksform werden aus den Erzählfunktionen die passenden ausgewählt und auf der Ebene der Ausdruckssubstanz mit Szenen und Motiven gefüllt. Der Einfachheit halber können wir sagen, dass Szenen und Motive sowie die Verknüpfungsregeln, denen sie unterliegen, die Hauptbestandteile der Ausdruckssubstanz bilden. Dass der Sampo aus der Spitze einer Schwanenfeder usw. geschmiedet wird, ist eindeutig ein Detail, das wir auf der Ebene der Ausdruckssubstanz verorten können.

Ausdruckssubstanz in Sprache und Mythos

Die »phonetic fitness«, also die Passung von Bedeutung und Klang, können wir nun neu definieren als Passung zwischen dem Klang und der Bedeutung, die dieser Klang in der Enzyklopädie aufruft. Der Klang als Ausdruckssubstanz wird in diesem Zusammenhang selbst zum Zeichen und verweist auf ein kulturelles Muster. In diesem Sinne kann man sagen, eine Lautfolge, etwa aus dem Sindarin, erinnert an das Keltische und ruft damit eine Reihe von Assoziationen auf.

Die Lautmelodie wird aus dem sprachlichen Zeichen herausgelöst und fortan als sekundäres hypoikonisches Zeichen behandelt. Unter einem Ikon verstehen wir ein Zeichen, das durch eine Ähnlichkeit hinsichtlich seines Referenten motiviert ist. Da ein Ikon aber nur in einer Firstness auftreten kann, also maximal als Idee einer möglichen Verwirklichung, ist uns ein Ikon als solches nicht in der Wahrnehmung zugänglich. Was wir vor uns haben, ist ein Ikon in der Verwirklichung der Thirdness. Das nennt Peirce ein Hypoikon (CP. 2.276). Die Klasse der hypoikonischen Zeichen kann laut Pierce in drei Unterklassen geteilt werden: So ist ein Hypoikon entweder ein Diagramm, ein Bild oder eine Metapher (C.P. 2.277).

Die Lautmelodie fungiert nun also nicht mehr als Teil eines sprachlichen Zeichens, sondern verweist mittels einer kulturell motivierten Ähnlichkeit auf ein kulturelles Muster und wird so in der Folge als Hypoikon verwendet. Dabei wird die primäre Bedeutung des sprachlichen Zeichens, zu dem die Lautmelodie gehört, verwischt oder sogar ausgelöscht. Der Inhalt der sprachlichen Botschaft spielt keine Rolle. In diesem Sinne haben wir es mit einem sekundären semiologischen System nach dem Modell Roland Barthes' zu tun. Das Hypoikon wird nur noch durch kulturelle Muster regiert, die ihm sekundär beigesellt wurden. Der Klang einer Sprache verweist z.B. auf die Mentalität der Sprecher, die Länder, in denen sie gesprochen wird, und auf ideologische Muster, die mit Sprache und Sprechen in Verbindung gebracht werden. So scheint auf dieser sekundären Ebene etwa die Verbindung zwischen arabisch klingenden Sprachen und dem Verdacht des Terrorismus nicht mehr als mögliche Konnotation, sondern wird in diesem von hypoikonischen Zeichen beherrschten Diskurs nun zu einem Denotatum. Ebenso ruft eine keltische Lautmelodie in so einem sekundären semiologischen System zum Beispiel nicht nur die keltische Sagenwelt, sondern auch jede Menge esoterische Assoziationen auf den Plan.

In gleicher Weise können Motive und Details einer Geschichte zu hypoikonischen Zeichen werden, die auf bestimmte kulturelle Muster verweisen. Die Motive werden aus dem Zusammenhang der Geschichte herausgelöst und fungieren in einem sekundären semiologischen System nun als Verweise auf andere Inhalte. Wir haben eben gerade die Simarilli und den Sampo aus Sicht der vergleichenden Mythologie als hypoikonische Zeichen betrachtet. Freilich haben wir die primäre Bedeutung nicht verwischt, aber außerhalb des wissenschaftlichen Diskurses geschieht so etwas sehr leicht. Ein prominentes Beispiel dafür ist der Umgang mit dem Vidovdan und der Schlacht am Kosovo Polje in der serbischen Mythologie. Die primäre Bedeutung, die historische Faktizität, nämlich die Niederlage der Serben im Kampf gegen die Osmanen, wird ausgeblendet und der heldenhafte Kampf der Serben zum Gründungsmythos erklärt.

Tolkien zeigt eine andere Verwendung der hypoikonischen Zeichens auf der Ebene der Motive. Er löst die Motive nie ganz aus ihrem ursprünglichen Kontext, so dass immer Teile der Erzählung, andere Motive und manchmal auch nur Details von der natürlichen Mythologie in die künstliche Mythologie mit übernommen werden. Er wendet hier also ganz genau dieselbe Technik an wie bei seiner Konstruktion künstlicher Sprachen. Er modifiziert und transformiert Elemente der Ausdruckssubstanz und macht sie zu Teilen seiner künstlichen Sprachen und Mythologie.

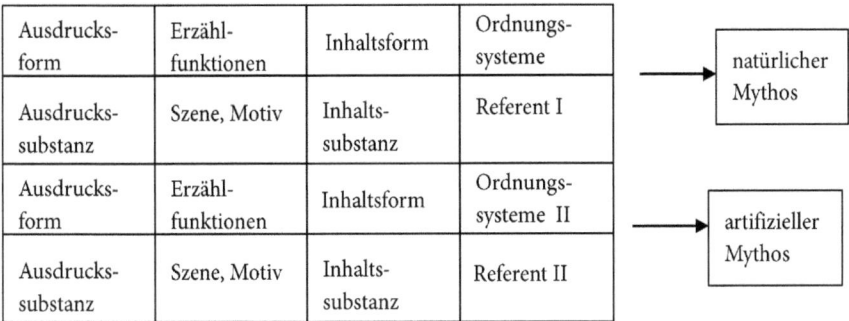

Grafik 4: Mythopoietische Strategie bei Tolkien

Durch dieses Verfahren stellt er einerseits ein in sich konsistentes System her. Er erschafft eine reiche Enzyklopädie von Sprachen und Erzählungen, die auf komplexe Weise miteinander verwoben sind. Andererseits gelingt es ihm mit dieser Methode, die Verbindung zu natürlichen Sprachen und Mythologien aufrecht zu erhalten, er borgt sich sozusagen einen Teil der Authentizität und macht seine kleine narrative Welt dadurch glaubwürdiger. Gleichzeitig weisen die Bezüge zu anderen Mythologien eben auch über Tolkiens *Legendarium* hinaus und stellen eine Verbindung zu natürlichen Mythologien her. Dadurch erscheint das *Legendarium* nicht nur größer, sondern wie natürlich gewachsen.

Damit haben wir eine durchgängige Methode der Konstruktion bei Tolkien aus semiotischer Sicht beschrieben. Die Entdeckung, dass Tolkien die Ausdruckssubstanz als hypoikonisches Zeichen verwendet, lässt die linguistische Häresie vielleicht in einem anderen Licht erscheinen. Jedenfalls haben wir hier eine Generierungsmethode von Sprache und Mythologie gefunden, die Tolkiens Behauptung untermauert, jede Sprache würde unweigerlich eine Mythologie ausbrüten.

Man müsste die hier aufgestellte These von der Ausdruckssubstanz und den hypoikonischen Zeichen noch an weiteren Beispielen überprüfen und sicherlich bedarf es noch etlicher Anpassungen und Erweiterungen. Aber ich denke, hier ein Werkzeug gefunden zu haben, das nicht nur bei Tolkien, sondern auch bei anderen Autoren, die sich der Mythopoiesis verschrieben haben, von Nutzen sein kann. Denn so wird es möglich, den Weg eines Motivs von einem mythologischen System in ein anderes semiotisch zu beschreiben und die Herstellungsweise von erzählerischen Systemen und von Idiolekten einzelner Autoren besser zu verstehen.

Bibliographie

Andreou, Andreas. *Quenya: The Influence of the Greek Language*,
    http://home.agh.edu.pl/~evermind/pdf/andreou.pdf (abgerufen am 12.04.2016)

Allan, Jim. *An Introduction to Elvish*. Helios, Glenfinnan, Inverness-shire: Bran's Head
    Books Ltd, 1978

Barthes, Roland. *Mythen des Alltags*. Frankfurt a. M.: Suhrkamp, 1964

Campbell, Joseph. *The Hero With a Thousand Faces*. London: HarperCollins, 1993

Dumézil, Georges. *Gods of the ancient Northmen*. Los Angeles: University of California
    Press, 1977

Eco, Umberto. *Die Suche nach der verlorenen Sprache*. München: C.H. Beck, 1994

---. *Die Grenzen der Interpretation*. München: dtv, 1995

Eliade, Mircea. *Australian Religions. An Introduction*. Ithaca/London: Cornell University
    Press, 1973

---. *Schmiede und Alchemisten*. Stuttgart: Ernst Klett Verlag, 1956

Himes, Jonathan. "What Tolkien really did with the Sampo". *Mythlore* 22.4 (Spring 2000):
    69-85

Hjelmslev, Louis. *Prolegomena zu einer Sprachtheorie*. München: Hueber, 1974

Kuehs, Wilhem. *Mythenweber*. Wiesbaden: Springer, 2015

Lönnrot, Elias. *Kalevala. The Land of the Heroes*. Vol. I. New York: J.M. Dent, 1907

Peirce, Charles Sanders. *Collected Papers of Charles Sanders Peirce*. 8 vol. Cambridge MA:
    Harvard University Press, 1931-1958

Propp, Vladimir. *Morphologie des Märchens*. München: Hanser, 1972

de Saussure, Ferdinand. *Grundfragen der Allgemeinen Sprachwissenschaft*. Berlin:
    Walter de Gruyter, 1972

Shippey, Tom A. *The Road to Middle-earth*. London: Grafton/Harper Collins, 1992

Tolkien, John Ronald Reuel. *The Monsters and the Critics,* London: HarperCollins, 1997

---. *The Return of the King – Being the third Part of The Lord of the Rings*. London:
    HarperCollins, 1993

---. *The Letters of J.R.R. Tolkien*. Ed. Humphrey Carpenter. London: HarperCollins, 1995

---. *The Silmarillion*. New York: Random House, 1981

---. *The Story of Kullervo*. Hg.: Verlyn Flieger. London: HarperCollins, 2015

Thresholds and Departures

Narrative Functions for Non-Westron Languages in Tolkien's *The Lord of the Rings*

Jonathan Nauman (Vaughan Association, USA)

On 20 October 1955, the publication of *The Lord of the Rings* came to completion with release of its final volume, *The Return of the King*. On the very next day, its author gave a talk entitled "English and Welsh,"[1] fulfilling a long-deferred duty to inaugurate an endowed lecture series in Celtic Studies. This engaging speech very much performed its intended function. It advocated rapprochement between philological studies in both languages; it fended off persistent cultural stereotypes of "the wild incalculable poetic Celt, full of vague and misty imaginations, and the Saxon, solid and practical when not under the influence of beer" (MC 172); and it fine-tuned its audience's understanding of the human complexities of the fifth-century incursion of invaders of Germanic tongue on territories for many centuries linguistically Celtic.

But framing and undergirding the address as a whole was, most clearly, Tolkien's own linguistic admiration for the Welsh language, his appreciation of its "words in which there is pleasure in the contemplation of the association of form and sense" (MC 191), his recount of escaping institutional constraints at Oxford in order to encounter Welsh in its medieval form, his extensive catalogues of Welsh words whose functional aesthetic he compared favorably against English usage—"*Nef* may be no better than *heaven*, but *wybren* is more pleasing than *sky*"; *atgyfodiad* is in linguistic style "far more Welsh" than *resurrection* is English (MC 193). In a final comment, and with a note that explicitly referenced *The Lord of the Rings*, Tolkien further surmised that his own linguistic attractions "to the western mountains and to the shores that look out to Iwerddon" (MC 192) were not an isolated phenomenon.

> My pleasure in the Welsh linguistic style, though it may have an individual colouring, [is largely a historical product,[2] and] would not, therefore, be expected to be peculiar to myself among the English. It is not. It is present in many of them. It lies dormant, I believe, in many more of those who today live in Lloegr and

---

1   See L 227 and Carpenter 223-224.

2   Earlier in his talk, Tolkien had pointed out that Celtic speech, due to its development through two millennia specifically on the island of Britain, was effectively the land's indigenous language. "It has, and had long ago, become, as it were, acclimatized to and naturalized in Britain; so that it belonged to the land in a way with which English could not compete, and still belongs to it with a seniority which we cannot overtake" (MC 177).

speak Saesneg. It may be shown only in uneasy jokes about Welsh spelling and place-names; it may be stirred by contacts no nearer than the names in Arthurian romance that echo faintly the Celtic patterns of their origin; or it may with more opportunity become vividly aware.   (MC 194)

Tolkien here acknowledged that *The Lord of the Rings* had been produced within a sensibility quite vividly aware of Cymric, "the senior language of the men of Britain" (MC 189); and he received the nascent and unanticipated success of his work as a confirmation that the strong attractions he had experienced toward Gothic and Finnish and most of all Welsh were not merely specific to himself. His art had stirred "deep harp-strings in our linguistic nature" (MC 194) and had thereby attained genuine popular appeal.

"English and Welsh" thus provides, along with Tolkien's 1965 Foreword to *The Lord of the Rings* (LotR I 8-12) and numerous passages in his *Letters*,[3] clear authorial testimony to love for the aesthetics of language as the basis for his art, an angle for examination of Tolkien's texts that is probably even wider than has yet been recognized. What Tolkien's readers usually—and quite accurately—mean when they say that the author's interest in philology influenced his fiction is that his invented cultures, nomenclatures, and geographies ultimately derived from his aesthetic responses to historical and modern languages, and that these responses energized his lifelong enthusiasm for inventing private languages, which in turn generated mythological narratives. "For perfect construction of an art language," Tolkien said in his early essay "A Secret Vice," "it is found necessary to construct at least in outline a mythology concomitant" (MC 210); and conversely, "language construction will *breed* a mythology" (MC 211). However, this specific cascade of creative endeavor—philological appreciation, linguistic invention, mythological composition—traces only one route of influence through which Tolkien's unusually intense experience of language affected *The Lord of the Rings*. This particular sequence is in fact most directly and properly associated in Tolkien's oeuvre with the foundational texts of *The Silmarillion*; and though these texts were for Tolkien of the highest importance and would easily and almost inevitably influence his other literary endeavors, they were not at any point in his career the only sort of creative composition he pursued. Tolkien also had considerable talent and interest in the fairy tale, personal spiritual allegory, farce with implicit social critique, and children's story. *The Hobbit*, Tolkien said, "was not intended to have anything to do with" the mythologies of *The Silmarillion*, though hints from those earlier texts were allowed to intrude (L 346). And *The Lord of the Rings*, Tolkien would recall a

---

3   See for example L 345, 374-375, 379-380.

decade after its publication, was a product of negotiations with its publishers, Allen and Unwin.

> When I offered them the legends of the Elder Days, ... their readers turned that down. They wanted a [*Hobbit*] sequel. But I wanted heroic legends and high romance. The result was *The Lord of the Rings*.   (L 346)

Though Tolkien was at the time disappointed with Allen and Unwin's rejection of his "primarily linguistic" (LotR I 8) "legends of the Elder Days,"[4] being forced to work within reader demand enabled him to attempt different avenues of philologically-driven invention, including one which I intend briefly to spotlight here: linguistic incursion as a means toward transformation of character and innovation of genre.

The Hobbit, as a children's *bildungsroman*, attended to questions of language only in regard to communicating with animals, a fairy-story motif[5] that Tolkien presented in that book humorously and with incidental variety. Gandalf's comprehension of wolf speech during the Warg meeting in the glade (H 105f) could either be construed as magical or as acquired knowledge of the sort implied in *The Lord of the Rings* when he shouted the word *open* at Moria Gate "in every language that had ever been spoken in the West of Middle-earth" (LotR I 401); Beorn's shape-changing provides magical basis for his interaction with his serving-beasts using "a queer language like animal noises turned into talk" (H 126); the warrior Bard is surprised to find himself understanding thrush speech, an ability inherited through descent from "the race of Dale" (H 237); while Balin's exchange with Bilbo at the thrush's return to the Lonely Mountain seems to portray converse with animals as an ability that dwarves could expect of anyone.

> "I believe he is trying to tell us something," said Balin, "but I cannot follow the speech of such birds, it is very quick and difficult. Can you make it out Baggins?"
> "Not very well," said Bilbo (as a matter of fact, he could make nothing of it at all); "but the old fellow seems very excited." (H 243)

---

4 See L 134-161 for Tolkien's passing attempt to get *The Silmarillion* printed simultaneously with *The Lord of the Rings* by changing publishers. He would later admit that Allen and Unwin had been right to refuse the legends of the Elder Days, as they were in an unfinished state and "needed re-writing and more thought" (L 374).

5 In *On Fairy-stories*, Tolkien maintained that "the magical understanding by men of the proper languages of birds and beasts and trees" served "one of the primal 'desires' that lie near the heart of Faërie" (MC 117).

In this practical linguistic difficulty, the Westron-speaking Raven Roäc steps forward—presumably, like the eagles and other communicative beasts, one of the *kelvar* specially animated (S 46)—and interspecies language issues are thereafter easily laid by. In no case in *The Hobbit* do these posited animal languages manifest any hint of the grammars or vocabularies of Tolkien's actual linguistic inventions.

As a *Hobbit* sequel, *The Lord of the Rings* begins in a manner generically reminiscent of the earlier work: the chapter "A Long-Expected Party" is set firmly in hobbit culture, so much so that one of Tolkien's friendliest reviewers termed it a risky way to begin a longer and much more serious work.[6] While the party scenes and their aftermath do effect a widening and foreboding commentary on Bilbo's past adventures, the narrative ethos moves only gradually away from the earlier work's domestic frame, the first truly notable check coming in Chapter Two with the identification of Frodo's ring, elevating it to the status of an active agent and character-in-story, a transition emphasized with words of power written in a foreign language.

> "I cannot read the fiery letters," said Frodo in a quavering voice.
> "No," said Gandalf, "but I can. The letters are Elvish, of an ancient mode, but the language is that of Mordor, which I will not utter here."   (LotR I 80f)

Gandalf's translation of the inscription on the One Ring, however, and also the prescient fear felt by Frodo as "a dark cloud rising in the East and looming up to engulf him" (LotR I 81), look backward as well as forward, having some antecedents in scenes and emotions in *The Hobbit*, where Bilbo "who liked runes and letters and clever handwriting" viewed along with Gandalf and Thorin the hidden inscription on the map of Erebor and heard it translated by Elrond (H 62); and where the dwarves reacted with instinctive dread to Gandalf's account of receiving the same Erebor map from Thrain "in the dungeons of the Necromancer" in Dol Guldur:

> "Whatever were you doing there?" asked Thorin with a shudder, and all of the dwarves shivered.   (H 37)

---

6   This review by Tolkien's friend C.S. Lewis, first published in *Time & Tide* on 14 August 1954 with title "The Gods Return to Earth," finally considered the light tone of Tolkien's first chapter a worthwhile risk, as it provided an effective and insightful contrast between "the frivolity, even (in its best sense) the vulgarity of the creatures called Hobbits" and "the appalling destiny to which some of them are called, the terrifying discovery that the humdrum happiness of the Shire, which they had taken for granted as something normal, is in reality a sort of local and temporary accident, that its existence depends on being protected by powers which Hobbits dare not imagine, that any Hobbit may find himself forced out of the Shire and caught up into that high conflict." (Lewis 112f)

Even in Chapter Three, where (as we shall see) the narrative finally and effect-ively moves beyond the ethos of *The Hobbit*, one last curious gesture recalls the limited linguistic preoccupations of the earlier book, while leading immediately toward the wider vision of the developing sequel. Frodo and Sam and Pippin sleep under a tree first night out on their cross-country hike to Buckland, and

> they set no watch; even Frodo feared no danger yet, for they were still in the heart of the Shire. A few creatures came and looked at them when the fire had died away. A fox passing through the wood on business of his own stopped several minutes and sniffed.
> "Hobbits!" he thought. "Well, what next? I have heard of strange doings in this land, but I have seldom heard of a hobbit sleeping out of doors under a tree. Three of them! There's something mighty queer behind this." He was quite right, but he never found out any more about it.   (LotR I 108)

This unique[7] and passing comedic incident acts as a threshold: on one hand, it is a formal valediction to the fairy-story emphases of *The Hobbit*; on the other, a dark foreshadowing of the approaches of the Ringwraiths immediately to follow, the curious and innocuous sniffing of the fox anticipating the preda-tory sniffings of disembodied sorcerors who "smell the blood of living things, desiring and hating it" (LotR I 256).[8]

Frodo's first encounters with the Nazgûl give Tolkien's readers an initial experiential taste of the higher and darker theme of *The Lord of the Rings*, with the hobbit's lack of ability to resist the wraiths's spiritual compulsions balanced fortuitously, as it were, with the tale's introduction to the Elves, their language sounding in the distance "like mingled song and laughter" (LotR I 117), its very presence sufficient to make the Black Rider retreat and vanish. Tolkien believed as a linguist that languages "have a virtue of their own, independent of their immediate inheritors" (MC 171); and it seems to be something of this

---

7   Although there are implications of communication with animals in other passages in *The Lord of the Rings*—Saruman with the *crebain*, Tom Bombadil with Fatty Lumpkin and other ponies, Gandalf with Shadowfax—animals are not, except in this passage, shown to communicate articulately themselves. The only notable exceptions are the Eagles, whose role throughout Tolkien's legendarium manifests the willed interventions of the Lords of the West (S 46, 110).

8   The manuscript histories offered by Christopher Tolkien in RS seem compatible with perceiving this narrative moment as importantly transitional. The vignette is a survival from the earliest stages of the book's composition (p. 51), with the innocent sniffing of the fox implicitly taking up an action first attributed to Gandalf in an even earlier draft, in which the pursuing wizard underwent a remarkable and "unpremeditated" mutation into a Black Rider (pp. 44-48).

experience of the powers of a language *per se* that the traveling hobbits feel in response to the elvish voices, each according to his own capacity.

> One clear voice now rose above the others. It was singing in the fair Elven-tongue, of which Frodo knew only a little, and the others knew nothing. Yet the sound blending with the melody seemed to shape itself in their thought into words which they only partly understood. This was the song as Frodo heard it:
>
> Snow-white! Snow-white! O Lady clear!
>   O Queen beyond the Western Seas!
> *O Light to us that wander here*
>   *Amid the world of woven trees!*
>
> *Gilthoniel! O Elbereth!*
>   *Clear are thy eyes and bright thy breath,*
> *Snow-white! Snow-white! We sing to thee*
>   *In a far land beyond the Sea*   (LotR I 117)

Although this passage quotes no actual words "in the fair Elven-tongue," it creates through subjective description a linguistic experience unprecedented either in *The Hobbit* or in earlier chapters of *The Lord of the Rings*.[9] The effect for the reader is a sudden expansion and deepening of the fictional experience, both through contemplating along with known characters the words of an elvish hymn "only partly understood," and through the song's subtle framing "as Frodo heard it," implying memory and translation after the fictional moment, perhaps with a hint even of Tolkien's bibliographical device of the "Red Book of Westmarch" (LotR I 37). The narrative then highlights in turn enduring memories kept by each of the three hobbits of this first encounter with High Elves—Pippin's recollection of "light upon the elf faces," Sam's inability to "describe in words" or to "picture clearly to himself" what "remained in his memory as one of the chief events of his life" (LotR I 121), Frodo's greeting

---

9   There is however a parallel in the later-published *Silmarillion*, when Bëor's tribe of men awaken to find Finrod Felagund singing to them of the Blessed Realm: "Now men awoke and listened to Felagund as he harped and sang, and each thought that he was in some fair dream, until he saw that his fellows were awake also beside him; but they did not speak or stir while Felagund still played, because of the beauty of the music and the wonder of the song. Wisdom was in the words of the Elven-king, and the hearts grew wiser that hearkened to him; for the things of which he sang, of the making of Arda, and the bliss of Aman beyond the shadows of the Sea, came as clear visions before their eyes, and his Elvish speech was interpreted in each mind according to its measure" (S 140f). One notes that Gildor Inglorion identifies himself to Frodo as "of the House of Finrod" (LotR I 118), and therefore as a relative of King Felagund.

Gildor Inglorion in the Quenya *"Elen síla lúmenn omentielmo"* (LotR I 119)[10] and his conversations with Gildor and requests for advice. One feels perhaps through the experiences of the characters and the motives reverberating through the story from this event something analogous to Tolkien's own philological experiences, pleasure and "satisfaction (as of a want fulfilled)" (MC 193) in encountering the aesthetics of a new language. The incident, in its unanticipated and lasting implications within the narrative, actually functions as the true moment of departure for the heroic romance at large.

Linguistic incursion, then, is distinctive and determinative to the ethos of *The Lord of the Rings*; but this does not of course mean that it is in every case constructive. As Gandalf implied when he chose at Bag End to render the Rune of the Rings of Power in Westron only, Sauron's device of the Black Speech has a power for evil aggression just as unanticipated to the narrative as the visionary power of Elvish. It is probably because they have been fortified by experience of High-elven linguistic vision, hospitality, and aid, that Frodo and his companions are able to weather the verbal assaults of the Nazgûl, a wailing "like the cry of some evil and lonely creature," rising and falling and ending "on a high piercing note," concealing words that Frodo can detect but not understand (LotR I 131). Gandalf's grim utterance of the Ring inscription in Black Speech at the Council of Elrond briefly imposes a similar evil spell even under clear autumn skies in Imladris.

> The change in the wizard's voice was astounding. Suddenly it became menacing, powerful, harsh as stone. A shadow seemed to pass over the high sun, and the porch for a moment grew dark. All trembled, and the elves stopped their ears.   (LotR I 333)

Inevitably, one notes the contrast with the wholesome song of the High-elves, much-repeated in Rivendell, which could take heartening verbal shape even for those without literal knowledge of the language.

That the tale's linguistic initiation should occur through a translated invocation of Elbereth Gilthoniel (i.e., Varda) is also very much worth noting, as the Star-Kindler (of whom there is no rumor in *The Hobbit*) will become a figure of momentous importance throughout the romance. The advent of Elvish language becomes in fact a bridge between the legendarium's benevolent Valar and Tolkien's characters of mortal race. Frodo (for example) invokes Elbereth in the words of the High-elven hymn even after having given way to the compulsion to put on the Ring and just prior to being wounded by the Lord of the Nazgûl at Weathertop, an action that apparently helps to protect him from

---

10 The Ballantine edition has *"omentilmo"* here, but I give Tolkien's spelling from the first edition which in a later note he endorsed as the form Frodo probably used; see L 447.

being seized by the Nazgûl (LotR I 293).[11] And the song of Gildor Inglorion and his company, as heard in the Shire, is specifically and effectively recalled and revoiced by Sam, first as he fights to protect Frodo in Shelob's lair,[12] and then when he and Frodo defeat the evil vigilance of the Silent Watchers in the Tower of Cirith Ungol (LotR III 234). The motif of linguistic incursion emerges in *The Lord of the Rings* just as consistently as aid arrives from the Eagles throughout the legendarium. Glorfindel's intervention on Frodo's behalf, prompted by and completing Gildor's, situates enheartening elvish linguistic incursions at arrival as well as at outset on the first leg of Frodo's quest, neatly framing Book One. Galadriel, renewing the quest's vision by her rejection of the Ring and her acceptance of an uncertain and diminished future, solemnizes her choice in a final song "in the ancient tongue of the Elves beyond the Sea" (LotR I 488). And the heroic romance ends with a meditative reprise of its departure, carefully placed at the exact location of the meeting with Gildor in the Shire's Woody End (LotR III 380-383).

In short, Tolkien used the languages he had constructed in the context of personal linguistic tastes much taken with Gothic, Finnish, and especially Welsh, to create fictional encounters that would change and ennoble the comfortable and rustic hobbits he had previously invented for a children's story. The benevolent linguistic incursions, and the visions of transcendent virtue and beauty that those incursions deliver, became the means whereby a sequel to an adventure story about a hobbit living up to his potential could modulate into the saga of a hobbit accomplishing through humility and acceptance of help a quest completely beyond his ability.

---

11   As Aragorn remarks after the attack, Frodo's sword stroke did not harm the Witch-king, but "the name of Elbereth" was deadly to the wraith (LotR I 265).

12   LotR II 430. This incident and the similar one preceding it, in which Frodo cries "*Aiya Eärendil Elenion Ancalima!*" but "knew not what he had spoken; for it seemed that another voice spoke through his, clear, untroubled by the foul air of the pit" (LotR II 418), show linguistic incursion in its strongest form in Tolkien's legendarium, a benevolent commandeering of the characters's voices for spiritual aid in response to invocations of Galadriel (which are, presumably, directed through her to Varda and Eru Ilúvatar).

Bibliography

Carpenter, Humphrey. *Tolkien: A Biography*. Boston: Houghton Mifflin, 1977

Lewis, Clive Staples. *Essay Collection: Literature, Philosophy and Short Stories*.
    Ed. Lesley Walmsley, London: HarperCollins, 2002

Tolkien, John Ronald Reuel. *The Fellowship of the Ring*. New York: Ballantine Books,
    1965

---. *The Hobbit*. New York: Ballantine Books, 1966

---. *The Letters of J.R.R. Tolkien*. Ed. Humphrey Carpenter. Boston: Houghton-Mifflin,
    1981

---. *The Monsters and the Critics and other Essays*. Ed. Christopher Tolkien. London:
    HarperCollins, 2006

---. *The Return of the King*. New York: Ballantine Books, 1965

---. *The Return of the Shadow: The History of The Lord of the Rings, Part One*.
    Ed. Christopher Tolkien. Boston: Houghton Mifflin, 1988

---. *The Two Towers*. New York: Ballantine Books, 1965

Hermeneutical Perspectives on Tolkien's Rhetorical Craftsmanship

Annie Birks (Angers)

Tolkien's love of words and languages is reflected in many facets of his work and constitutes a (self-admitted) major driving force behind the unfolding of his *Legendarium*. By putting his own linguistic ingredients into the Cauldron (invented words and languages, onomastics, rhetorical devices…), as most would agree, Tolkien simmered a most potent work of imagination whose spell has clearly not broken and whose enchantment has clearly not worn off. From this perspective we can wonder to what extent Tolkien's linguistic horizon and the reader's perception or sensitivity can merge and—more likely than not—engage with the text in a hermeneutically productive way.

The American philosopher Jens Zimmermann defines the goal of hermeneutics as "understanding", not just as "the mere passing or receiving of information", but as "knowledge in the deeper sense of grasping not just facts but their integration into a meaningful whole" (2). As grasping is mostly based on personal capacity, life experience and cultural references, hermeneutics can therefore refer to…, "the kind of practical operation that provides knowledge in the sense of deep familiarity with something" (2), when something "makes sense within our own life context and thus speaks to us meaningfully"(7).

Hermeneutics thus considers that the comprehension process goes primarily and naturally through a practical mode of perception depending on "our current desires and interests" (8) and will only adopt a more abstract, scientific or theoretical approach when we disconnect the object under scrutiny from our personal experience.

Fusion of Horizons

From a hermeneutical point of view, entering into a dialogical relationship with Tolkien's *Legendarium* does not only make us participate—on a wider scale—in "the production of a richer, more encompassing context of meaning" (started decades ago) but also helps us "gain a better and more profound understanding not only of the text but also of ourselves" (Ramberg). That is what the German hermeneutic thinker Gadamer (1900-2002) referred to as a "fusion of horizons" (Zimmermann 50).

Although the paths of Tolkien's Middle-earth are trodden by Elves, Dwarves, Ents, Wraiths and Orcs, among other characters, the "arresting strangeness" (TL

50) initially felt by the reader can soon give way to both a feeling of immersion and of constant "interplay between past and present" (Ramberg).

The question we could ask is: "what is it precisely that makes Tolkien's work merge with the modern reader's horizon of expectancy?" In other words, and to refer to a concept dear to the Master of Middle-earth himself, what can be said about applicability in our reception, comprehension and interpretation of his work which he himself qualified as being "fundamentally linguistic in inspiration" (L 219)?

The story-line is so carefully elaborated and so convincing that we could mistake it for real History, as he himself hoped for—"I wanted people simply to get inside this story and take it (in a sense) as actual history" (Carpenter 198-199); the grand universal themes running through the trajectories of both peoples and characters appear to be of abiding significance given the prevailing academic and popular respect for and interest in his *Legendarium*; Tolkien's self-professed functions of a good fairy-story, namely fantasy, recovery, escape and consolation, impart a vigor to his work and enrich the reader's personal experience of life through what could be referred to as "horizon-fusing".

The Aesthetic Experience of Art and Literature

And this is precisely what hermeneutics aims to point at. Gadamer—following his teacher Heidegger—"regarded understanding as the basic movement of human existence that encompasses the whole of life experience" including therefore "the aesthetic experience of art and literature" (Zimmerman 40).

"To unfold the nature of human understanding", Gadamer's hermeneutics raises the following questions: "How do we experience truth through artistic creations? In what way is it possible for a text, play, symphony, or painting to impart real knowledge about ourselves and our world?" (40)

The answer might lie in the concept of mediation. Each time we visit or revisit the lands of Middle-earth, for example, we encounter new things (unnoticed during previous incursions) or else we find that familiar things speak to us differently owing to our own "shifting horizon" (53), thus possibly producing an ontological change. As Zimmermann explains "when we understand, we unite our own perspective with another's viewpoint into a greater unifying context, and this experience transforms us by expanding our own perspective on things" (48)[1].

---

1   In his paper on Gadamer and hermeneutics ("Reading the Text"), James Risser also comments: "For Gadamer, to reach an understanding is not so much the successful assertion of one's point of view, but a transformation into a communion in which we do not remain what we were." (105)

The constant dialogical interplay between the alien in a text (Elves, Dwarves, Hobbits, Ents, Wraiths, Orcs … or when we read an ancient philosophical text) and the familiar (our down-to-earth everyday life), operates a sort of similar mediation in so far as there can emerge a "fusion of horizons" (50) that connects alien and familiar, past and present, author and reader. This could be where hermeneutical perspectives meet Tolkien's views on fairy-stories.

If modern readers' horizons of expectancy (whatever their age, social background, interests …) merge with Tolkien's presentation of Middle-earth, it is because there is something for them. As Zimmermann remarks: "Is it not true that we only really engage a text or another's viewpoint when we want to know what meaning another's perspective has *for us?*" (51)[2]. Tolkien referred to the notion of applicability, which he notably opposed to allegory, and Gadamer referred to "application" which "motivates engaged reading and set in motion the mediation of another perspective with one's own" (51).

The Linguisticality of Understanding

As hermeneutics gives primacy to the "linguisticality of understanding" (Malpas) (in other words: understanding is linguistically mediated), it is through language that we may encounter not only the essence of say, the peoples of Middle-earth, but also ourselves. Language, for Gadamer, is "the medium through which reality comes into focus" (Nielsen). And the use of language is an art, and, as Zimmermann explains "in what is perhaps its greatest gift to us, art makes possible *recognition*, the power allowing us to say, 'Yes, that's how it is, now I understand'" (56).

Could we say that, when readers journey in Tolkien's Middle-earth, recognition and understanding pass through what the sub-creator calls "enchantment" in his essay *On Fairy-stories?* The enchantment of fantasy that "produces a Secondary World into which *both designer and spectator can enter, to the satisfaction of their senses* while they are inside", seeking "*shared enrichment, partners in making and delight*"[3] (TL 54-55).

Is it precisely Tolkien's linguistic artistry that makes enchantment so potent and a meeting of horizons even more tangible? When we come across a phrase such as "Keen are the eyes of the Elves" (LotR II 33), the image comes out with a profundity, musicality and impact that ordinary prose wordings might have difficulty producing. Had Aragorn, or should we say Tolkien, opted for "The

---

2   This seems to echo what Tolkien said about the critics of *Beowulf*: "Correct and sober taste may refuse to admit that there can be an interest for *us*". (Shippey 3)

3   *My* italics. Tolkien opposes enchantment to magic and regards it as "uncorrupted", not seeking "delusion, nor bewitchment and domination".

Elves have keen eyes" or "The Elves are well-known for their good eyesight", the result would have been a mundane character description based on mere physical attributes without any particular effect. Instead, the old-fashioned inversion of syntax (Shippey 108)[4], conjuring up the style of ancient legends, tends to inspire both respect and awe for the First Children of Ilúvatar.

The same comment could be made about Celeborn and Galadriel, when Frodo meets them for the first time in Lothlórien; their eyes appear "keen as lances in the starlight" (LotR I 460). In both examples, the Elves' power of observation thus described encapsulates their faculty of intuitive vision, their knowledge, vigilance, and watchfulness (Cooper 62)... all these capacities which go far beyond mere eyesight and the limitation of the purely visible.

In fact, although "the very wise cannot see all ends" (LotR I 89), on the paths of Middle-earth, readers are encouraged to beware the purely visible and perhaps to be more like Farmer Maggot with "earth under his old feet", "clay on his fingers", "wisdom in his bones", and "both his eyes... open", (LotR I 182)— again a much more potent description than if he had been literally presented as a down-to-earth, practical, sensible and vigilant farmer. Or like Barliman Butterbur (in spite of his blunder at the beginning of the story) who, according to Gandalf, "can see through a brick wall in time" (LotR I 289). By contrast, from Treebeard's point of view, Saruman has become "like windows in a stone wall: windows with shutters inside" (LotR II 90), revealing somebody who has decided to limit his field of vision to his own personal lucubrations. And Faramir addresses Gollum with a similar judgment: "There are locked doors and closed windows in your mind, and dark rooms behind them" (LotR II 373).

Enlarging Perspectives: Metaphors and Imagination

Most Tolkien readers would no doubt agree that the paths of Middle-earth have been carefully and subtly signposted with an abundance of similes, metaphors, aphorisms and other figures of speech—which do not only make things come alive but also encourage us to structure our thoughts according to our own individual applicability. Perspectives are enlarged through juxtapositions which invite us to "see similarity in difference" and thus to "see things otherwise" (Zimmermann 69). Doors get unlocked and windows open onto new ways of looking at things, so that, to quote another well-known of Tolkien's

---

4　In Chapter IV of *The Road to Middle-earth*, Shippey describes Elrond's speech at the Council as being "full of old-fashioned inversions of syntax...".

ideas: "the things seen clearly may be freed from the drab blur of triteness or familiarity—from possessiveness" (TL 59).

For example, among the archetypes found in *The Lord of the Rings*, the river or more generally water is often associated with the passing of time and the flowing of life. Among the metaphors linked to water, the tide is a recurring one. Lady Galadriel resorts to this literary trope when she tells Frodo and Sam what will happen to her Kingdom after the destruction of the One Ring: "The tides of Time will sweep it away"; a few moments later, she even encourages the two Hobbits to carry on with their mission without delay for "the tides of fate are flowing" (LotR I 474-475).

With its alternating pattern the tide conjures up a ceaseless in-coming and out-going movement against which nothing can be done. Even more so as tidal forces can prove to be immensely powerful.[5] Only King Cnut (1016-1035) thought that he might have had the power to hold back the tides. Contrary to the Viking monarch, Galadriel knows that in Middle-earth there are forces at work that nobody can control. This lucid observation from the Lady of the Galadhrim finds an echo in some of Gandalf's best-known aphorisms, namely when he tries to reassure Frodo about the return of Sauron in *The Fellowship of the Ring* (78):

> "I wish it need not have happened in my time," said Frodo.
> "So do I," said Gandalf, "and so do all who live to see such times. But that is not for them to decide. All we have to decide is what to do with the time that is given us."

Galadriel came in from Valinor with the flow—for legitimate reasons as Tolkien says in his correspondence (L 430), although not under the best circumstances— and she knows that she will have to go back with the ebb. If we look up various definitions and synonyms of the word *ebb* we notice how fitting the tidal metaphor turns out to be here: when something *ebbs*, it *declines, diminishes* or *flows away*. After passing the test of the Ring, Galadriel herself says to Frodo: "I will

---

5   Tolkien's recurring dream of the "Great Wave" inevitably comes to mind here. As he explained in his letter to W.H. Auden, on 7 June 1955: "I have what some might call an Atlantis complex. Possibly inherited, though my parents died too young for me to know such things about them, and too young to transfer such things by words. Inherited from me (I suppose) by one only of my children, though I did not know that about my son [Michael] until recently, and he did not know it about me. I mean the terrible recurrent dream (beginning with memory) of the Great Wave, towering up, and coming in ineluctably over the trees and green fields. (I bequeathed it to Faramir.) I don't think I have had it since I wrote the 'Downfall of Númenor' as the last of the legends of the First and Second Age" (L 213). Further references to the Great Wave can be found in other letters: p. 232, p. 347 and p. 361. See Charles Ridoux's comments on Tolkien's dream in Ridoux, *Vague*.

diminish, and go into the West, and remain Galadriel" (LotR I 475). There and back again, Galadriel's Tale.

When Ëomer asks Aragon for help, he uses the same figure of speech: "The Heir of Elendil would be a strength to the sons of Eorl in this evil tide" (LotR II 42). A few chapters later hope arises when Gandalf comes back victorious after his sacrifice in Moria and revives the flame of his companions: "Be merry! We meet again. At the turn of the tide. The great storm is coming, but the tide has turned" (LotR II 119). Whereas Frodo and Sam laboring on the stairs of Cirith Ungol feel 'as if… they had been swimming long against a heavy tide of water'.

To hermeneutic thinkers, literary texts can "demonstrate more intensely the power of language to turn our environment into a meaningful human world through symbolic representations" (68). To them "language is not primarily conceptual but metaphorical" (68). And throughout the story, the tidal metaphor serves as mediation which, as previously mentioned, invites us to structure our thoughts. Especially when Gandalf expands on what he hinted at earlier on:

> "It is not our part to master all the tides of the world, but to do what is in us for the succour of those years wherein we are set, uprooting the evil in the fields that we know, so that those who live after may have clean earth to till."   (LotR III 185)

Gandalf's resort to this metaphor is all the more potent as one might equate *tide* with *time*, given the two terms' euphonic similarity[6]. As Tolkien was a philologist, one might be tempted to trace back the origin of the word tide, which, surprisingly or most likely unsurprisingly, brings us precisely to the Old English noun 'tid' meaning "point or portion time, due time, period, season; feast-day, canonical hour" (etymonline.com). Therefore not only can we feel the characters' helplessness in referring to the powerful and ineluctable movement of the sea but we can also sense what could be described as nature's symbolical canonical rites. Hence Hirgon's use of both words in his injunction-like address to Théoden:

> Make haste! For it is before the walls of Minas Tirith that the doom of our time will be decided, and if the tide be not stemmed there, then it will flow over all the fair fields of Rohan, and even in this Hold among the hills there shall be no refuge.
>
> (LotR III 82)

---

6   Interestingly, Tolkien published his poem *Imram* (The Death of Saint Bredan) in the December 1955 issue of the British weekly political and literary magazine *Time and Tide* (cf. *Tolkien Gateway*; *The J.R.R. Tolkien Companion and Guide: I. Chronology*, p. 480). Reviews of *The Fellowship of the Ring*, *The Two Towers* and *The Return of the King* were also published by C.S. Lewis in 1954 and 1955 in this journal.

The emissary of Gondor thus efficiently expresses the gravitas of the choice about to be made (which will lead to good or bad *tidings*) for as the saying goes: "Time and tide wait for no man."

Therefore by integrating "something unfamiliar into our familiar way of seeing things", to quote Zimmermann again, "our own former perspective is altered by being enlarged and deepened" (68). And "hermeneutic philosophers consistently emphasize the power of the human imagination to envision and inhabit a meaningful world through language" (68-69). And: "At the heart of imagination lies metaphor."

Enlarging Perspectives: Onomastics, Etymology and Symbolism

For those among us who have a passion for etymology and symbolism, from a hermeneutical point of view, digging into Tolkien's onomastics may also enlarge our perspectives (cf. Birks, *Hobbit*). For example, if we closely examine the following anthroponyms and toponym found in the first chapter of *The Hobbit*—'The Hobbit' 'Bilbo' 'Baggins' from 'Bag-end'—, we might be inclined to consider that we are dealing with an apprenticeship novel with plenty of food for thought (cf. Green).

At the very beginning of the story, we are told that the eponymous protagonist lives in a hole and, thanks to the author's later etymological feedback (LotR III 518-519), we learn that he actually comes from a background of "hole-builders". If, on the one hand, the notion of 'hole' traditionally evokes emptiness, on the other hand, the hole in the earth can represent the feminine fertility principle and the hole in the roof of a temple, for example, the opening upwards to the celestial world (Cooper 83). Such considerations open up levels of understanding and potentialities we might not be aware of if we purely and simply stick to the storyline.

If we now consider the patronym Baggins, we obviously identify the word 'bag', and, as some readers have remarked, we can even reverse this word and go as far as to say "in the bag". Given Tolkien's obsession with words as a constant source of inspiration, we can nearly jump to the conclusion that, consciously or unconsciously, Tolkien created or, should we say, sub-created a hero whose story symbolically starts in a hole, or in a bag. From a symbolical point of view, bags are often associated with secrecy, hiding, and hidden treasures (Cooper 17). Interestingly, in the first chapter of *The Hobbit* Gandalf says to Gloin: "Let's have no more argument. I have chosen Mr. Baggins and that ought to be enough for all of you… There is a lot more in him than you guess, and a deal more than he has any idea of himself" (29). Later in *The Fellowship of the*

Ring, he says to Frodo: "'You take after Bilbo,' ...'There is more about you than meets the eye, as I said of him long ago.' Frodo wondered if the remark meant more than it said" (426).

Another clue which reinforces the first impressions gathered so far is the name of the hobbit's dwelling, "Bag End", which seems to infer that his home is itself a dead end. By staying there we can suppose that he will surely continue to lead a comfortable life but it is likely to lead nowhere.

Finally, as already pointed out by other Tolkien scholars and readers, *The Oxford English Dictionary* indicates that the noun 'bilbo' comes from the city of "Bilbao in Spain, long called in Engl. Bilboa" where they made "blades accounted of the best temper" (187). A 'bilbo' is therefore defined as "a sword noted for the temper and elasticity of its blade" (187). A connection can legitimately be established between Bilbo's name and his sword, Sting, which he finds in the Troll-cave. Correlating the traditional symbolism of the sword and Sting's new owner again goes without saying. The sword is often linked to power, leadership, courage, strength and vigilance, the penetrating power of the intellect, keen or piercing discernment, penetrating insight; victory over ignorance (Cooper 167). A very fitting image.

Consequently, for those who want to dig deeper by going inside Tolkien's language, etymology and symbolism seem to open up new hermeneutical perspectives. As illustrated above, the key words 'The Hobbit' 'Bilbo' 'Baggins' from 'Bag-end' can be perceived as reflecting the two sides of the hero's personality: on the one hand, we are introduced to a well-to-do Hobbit, content with his comfortable life (as testified in the first paragraph), however going nowhere, because he is stuck in a rut, a hole or a bag; and on the other hand, we might presume, at the very beginning of the story, that although he appears to be a bit of a coward at first glance, he might be concealing treasures in himself which are only waiting to be discovered. Hence the author's good reason for sending him ... "on a *journey* far from settled home into strange lands and dangers... On a journey of a length sufficient to provide the untoward in any degree from discomfort to fear the change in companions well-known in 'ordinary life' (and in oneself) is often startling" (L 240).

It would thus appear that Bilbo's development stands more chance to materialise during a journey to unknown lands than by staying at Bag End. The unfolding of the story proves this hypothesis right. Not only will he escape stagnation by leaving his "hole in the ground" at Bag-end (although he is in a way "bagged" by Gandalf and the Dwarves to start with), but, "once out", owing to the quality of his decisions, he will gradually become "hard to bag" (Greene 53). In fact he will become the one who "bags". As William Green explains in *The Hobbit: A Journey into Maturity*, "bagging and escaping bagging are strongly connected to the theme of Bilbo's maturation" (53). Furthermore as an echo to the (above-mentioned) symbolic elements associated to the hole (feminine fertility principle, opening upwards to the celestial world...) at the end of the story we observe that:

> "To mature, Bilbo must leave his ancestral home, the womblike hobbit-hole, and pass uncorrupted through the tomblike dragon lair, the mountain tomb that becomes the womb of heroic re-birth."   (43)

The tidal metaphor underlies Bilbo's cyclical trajectory: "*The Hobbit* or *There and back again.*"

Conclusion

It goes without saying that hermeneutical perspectives on Tolkien's rhetorical craftsmanship cannot be reduced to the above limited number of parameters. The selected illustrations are just a few drops of water in Tolkien's immense ocean of words or, could we say, they are just a few notes in a large symphony (BMC 192).

For instance, this would be without taking into account the "style and lexis" of characters like Saruman who, as Tom Shippey points out, talks like a politician encapsulating "many of the things the modern world has learnt to dread most: the ditching of allies, the subordination of means to ends, the 'conscious acceptance of guilt in the necessary murder...'" (108)[7]: a type of rhetoric which has become all too familiar in our society, a seminal observation of both political and modern economic discourse...

This would also be without taking into account the enchantment produced by Tolkien's phonosemantics, as explained by Ross Smith in his theoretical treaty *Inside Language* (57). How could we be insensitive to names like *Withywindle, Brandywine, Brandybuck, Barliman Butterbur, Rivendell* and the entire Elvish onomasticon (cf. Birks, *Transmission*)? How could we be insensitive to the aesthetics of Tolkien's prose as a whole, with its perfume of ancient legends and its hints of mystery and wonder?

Admittedly, the grand themes running through the history of Middle-earth are not new; they have been enacted and reenacted countless times in countless tales. What makes the difference here is precisely Tolkien's use of language, Tolkien's arresting language which, as Gadamer said about art, "draws us into its orbit" (Zimmermann 53), holds our attention and contributes to a meet-

---

7   In his turn, from a hermeneutical point of view, Shippey helps readers to further expand their horizons by highlighting rhetorical aspects they might not be aware of or sensitive to. The same thing could be said about other contributors to the study of Tolkien.

ing of horizons. From a hermeneutical point of view literature can work as an eye-opener, educate our imagination and challenge received ideas. There is no doubt that, in this respect, Tolkien is extremely rich. His use of language is such that we are constantly encouraged to clean our windows, to go beyond appearances, to dig deeper.

Hermeneutics is already at work when we consciously or unconsciously register Aragon's declaration to Legolas and Gimly: "Not idly do the leaves of Lórien fall" (LotR II 25) for we all know that "Not idly did Tolkien choose his words". The old-fashioned inversion again, the mystery attached to it, the hint of underlying wisdom which makes it sound like a well-known ancestral proverb, all this opens up a world of potentialities linguistically mediated. Should we decide to adopt a first degree approach and content ourselves with the bare storyline, it would still be a splendid experience. In this particular scene, Legolas and Gimli have found Pippin's brooch and Aragon explicitly adds: "This did not drop by chance: it was cast away as a token to any that might follow". Hermeneutically Aragon's second statement appears to also have the potential to open up new perspectives and find resonance in our own fields of applicability. Tolkien's literary legacy may be seen as a linguistic *token* cast away to anyone that might feel inclined to explore it in a hermeneutically productive way. As Peter Schakel pointed out in his study of C.S. Lewis's last novel *Till We Have Faces* (46):

> "Learning to see... is what... the novel—and all of life—is actually about".

Bibliography

Birks, Annie. "Figures de Rhétorique dans *Le Seigneur des Anneaux* de J.R.R. Tolkien: Approche exploratoire d'une œuvre d'inspiration fondamentalement linguistique". *Esprit des mots et mots d'esprit*. Ed. Daniel Lévêque. Paris: L'Harmattan, 2012, 189-207

---. "*The Hobbit* de J.R.R. Tolkien: Exégèse d'un roman d'apprentissage au fil des toponymes et anthroponymes". *Étymologie et Exégèse Littéraire*. Ed. Yannick Le Boulicaut. Paris: L'Harmattan, 2011, 37-57

---. "Transmission des écrits de la Terre du Milieu de J.R.R. Tolkien: Étymologie et questions de traduction". *Étymologie et Traduction*. Ed. Annie Birks. Paris: L'Harmattan, 2011, 137-151

Carpenter, Humphrey (Ed.). *J.R.R. Tolkien: A Biography* [1977]. London: Allen & Unwin, 1978

---. (Ed.). *The Letters of J.R.R. Tolkien*. London: George Allen & Unwin, 1981

Cooper, J.C. *An Illustrated Encyclopaedia of Traditional Symbols*. London: Thames & Hudson, 1978

Green, William H. *The Hobbit: A Journey into Maturity*. New York: Twayne Publishers, 1994

Hammond, Wayne G., & Christina Scull. *The J.R.R. Tolkien Companion and Guide. Chronology*. New York: Houghton Mifflin Company, 2006

Malpas, Jeff. "Hans-Georg Gadamer". *The Stanford Encyclopedia of Philosophy* (Summer 2015 Edition). Ed. Edward N. Zalta. http://plato.stanford.edu/archives/sum2015/entries/gadamer/ (28.07.2016)

Nielsen, Cynthia. http://percaritatem.com/2009/08/28/gadamer-on-language-and-being/ (28.07.2016)

Ramberg, Bjørn, & Kristin Gjesdal. "Hermeneutics". *The Stanford Encyclopedia of Philosophy* (Spring 2006 Edition). Ed. Edward N. Zalta <http://plato.stanford.edu/archives/spr2006/entries/hermeneutics/> (28.07.2016)

Ridoux, Charles. "Grande Vague/le complexe de l'Atlantide". *Dictionnaire Tolkien*. Ed. Vincent Ferré. Paris: CNRS Editions, 2012, 257-258

Risser, James. "Reading the Text". *Gadamer and Hermeneutics*. Ed. Hugh J. Silverman. New York/London: Routledge, 1991

Schakel, Peter. *Reason and Imagination in C.S. Lewis*. Grand Rapids: William B. Eerdmans, 1984

Shippey, Tom. *The Road to Middle-earth* [1982]. London: HarperCollins, 1992

Smith, Ross. *Inside Language*. Zürich/Bern: Walking Tree Publishers, 2007

The Oxford English Dictionary. Oxford: Clarendon Press, 1989

Tolkien, Christopher (Ed.). *The Monsters and the Critics and Other Essays*. London: HarperCollins, 1997

Tolkien, J.R.R. *The Hobbit or There and Back Again* [1937]. London: Allen & Unwin, 1981

---. *The Fellowship of the Ring* [1954]. London: HarperCollins, 1993

---. *The Two Towers* [1954]. London: HarperCollins, 1993

---. *The Return of the King* [1955]. London: HarperCollins, 1993

—. *Tree and Leaf* [1964]. London: Allen & Unwin, 1964

Zimmermann, Jens. *Hermeneutics. A very Short Introduction*. Oxford: OUP, 2015

Angeborene, natürliche und Heimatsprache – Native Language – und was die Wissenschaft heute davon hält

Friedhelm Schneidewind (Hemsbach)

I m Seminar 2016 beschäftigten sich mehrere Vorträge mit der von T.A. Shippey als Tolkiens »linguistische Häresie« bezeichneten Auffassung des Mittelerdeschöpfers, dass in einer Sprache zwischen Form und Inhalt ein innerer Zusammenhang bestehe. Dies steht im Gegensatz zur derzeit vorherrschenden Sprachtheorie, die seit Ferdinand de Saussure von der Arbitrarität der sprachlichen Zeichen ausgeht, also davon, dass sich Signifikat und Signifikant einer natürlichen Sprache grundsätzlich arbiträr zueinander verhalten. Nicht ausdrücklich eingegangen wurde im Seminar auf Tolkiens Vorstellung einer »Native Language« – im Deutschen unterschiedlich übersetzt (s.u.): »Heimatsprache« (B 418), »angeborene Sprache« (B 490) oder »natürliche Sprache« (HL 19f) –, die heute auch nicht mehr haltbar ist.

Zu Tolkiens Zeit war die Vorstellung einer gemeinsamen Ursprache, eben einer angeborenen und evtl. sogar von Volk, Ethnie oder Herkunft abhängigen Sprache in Linguistik, Anthropologie und anderen wissenschaftlichen Disziplinen durchaus verbreitet und wurde gerne im Zusammenhang mit einem postulierten Erbgedächtnis diskutiert; beides kann heute als widerlegt betrachten werden.[1]

Tolkiens Ideen zu einer „natürlichen Sprache« finden sich vor allem in dem Vortrag »English and Welsh« über den Zusammenhang der walisischen und der englischen Sprache, den er am 21.10.1955 hielt als Auftakt zu einer Vorlesungsreihe verschiedener Professoren über verbliebene Elemente der altenglischen und keltischen Sprache im modernen Englisch.[2] Hier heißt es u.a.:

> If I were to say ›Language is related to our total psycho-physical make-up‹, I might seem to announce a truism in a priggish modern jargon. I will at any rate say that language—and more so as expression than as communication—is a natural product of our humanity. But it is therefore also a product of our individuality. We each have our own personal linguistic potential: we each have

---

1   2007 veröffentlichte ich den Artikel »Erbgedächtnis und angeborene Sprache«. Anlass war, dass in den Seminaren davor immer wieder auf Tolkiens Vorstellungen von Erbgedächtnis und angeborener Sprache hingewiesen worden war. In Kurzform stellte ich dar, warum beides nicht mit modernen wissenschaftlichen Erkenntnissen vereinbar sei.

2   Der Vortrag wurde erstmals 1963 veröffentlicht in dem Sammelband *Angles and Britons: O'Donnell Lectures* (University of Wales Press, Cardiff) und dann 1983 in *The Monsters and the Critics and Other Essays.*

a native language. But that is not the language that we speak, our cradle-tongue, the first-learned. Linguistically we all wear ready-made clothes, and our native language comes seldom to expression, save perhaps by pulling at the ready-made till it sits a little easier. But though it may be buried, it is never wholly extinguished, and contact with other languages may stir it deeply.

My chief point here is to emphasize the difference between the first-learned language, the language of custom, and an individual's native language, his inherent linguistic predilections: not to deny that he will share many of these with others of his community. He will share them, no doubt, in proportion as he shares other elements in his make-up.[30]

Anmerkung 30: A difficult proportion to discover without knowing his ancestral history through indefinite generations. Children of the same two parents may differ markedly in this respect.

(EW 190, Anm. 197, Hervorhebung im Original)

Tolkien endet: »… for satisfaction and therefore for delight—and not for imperial policy—we are still ›British‹ at heart. It is the native language to which in unexplored desire we would still go home« (EW194).

Schon in seinem berühmten Essay »A Secret Vice«, der wohl 1931 entstand, aber erst 1983 veröffentlicht wurde, geht Tolkien, wenn auch nur kurz und oberflächlich, auf die angeborene Sprache ein, wenn er über Nevbosh redet, die erste seiner erfundenen Fantasie-Sprachen, die er in seiner Kindheit gemeinsam mit seiner Cousine Mary entwickelt hatte:

Clearly »phonetic predilection«—artistic phonetic expression—played as yet a very small part owing to the domination of the native language, which still kept Nevbosh almost in the stage of a »code«. The native language constantly appears with what at first sight appears casual unsystematic and arbitrary alteration. Yet even here there is a certain interest…   (SV 204)

Offenbar spielten »Lautsympathien« – die künstlerische Lautgestaltung – erst eine sehr unbedeutende Rolle, wegen der Oberhoheit der natürlichen Sprache, die das Nevbosh fast noch auf der Stufe eines »Kodes« festhielt. Die natürliche Sprache kommt in den auf den ersten Blick beliebigen und unsystematischen Abwandlungen immer wieder zum Vorschein. Doch selbst dies ist nicht ganz uninteressant…   (HL 19 f.)[3]

---

3   Ich führe jeweils die deutschen Übersetzungen an, da die verschiedenen Wörter, die Krege dafür gewählt hat (teilweise sogar innerhalb eines Werkes, bei den Briefen), die Problematik des Begriffs ebenso verdeutlichen wie seine mangelnde Genauigkeit.

Tolkien verwendet den Begriff immer wieder und auch sehr viel später noch, bspw. 1962 in einem Brief an seine Tante Jane: »… the theory that one's ›native language‹ is not the Same as one's ›cradle-tongue‹« (L 318, 1962) – »…die Theorie, daß jemandes ›Heimatsprache‹ nicht dasselbe ist wie seine ›Wiegensprache‹« (B 418, 1962).

Noch 1967 schreibt er: »It is these preferences, reflecting an individual's innate linguistic taste, that I called his ›native language'; though ›native linguistic potential‹ would have been more accurate, since it seldom comes to effect, even in modifying his ›first-learnt‹ language, that of his parents and country« (L 375). – »Diese Vorlieben, in denen sich der angeborene Sprachgeschmack eines einzelnen ausdrückt, habe ich seine ›angeborene Sprache‹ genannt; ›angeborenes Sprachpotential‹ wäre allerdings genauer gewesen, denn es wird selten auch nur insofern wirksam, daß es seine ›zuerst erlernte‹ Sprache modifizierte, die seiner Eltern und seines Heimatlandes.«

Tolkiens Vorstellungen von einer »native language« lassen sich auch in seinem belletristischen Werk, seiner Erfindung von und seinem Umgang mit Sprachen nachweisen, doch ist dies nicht Inhalt dieses Artikels. Hier geht es darum zu zeigen, dass diese Auffassung überholt ist.

Vom Nativismus bis zum Konnektionismus

Ob die »Sprache« mancher Tiere (Schimpansen, Bienen …) als solche zu bezeichnen und eine Sprache wie die der Menschen sei, ist ebenso umstritten[4] wie der Zeitpunkt, seit dem Menschen bzw. ihre Vorfahren die Fähigkeit zum Sprechen besitzen; die Hypothesen reichen von 30.000 Jahren bis zu »mindestens fünf bis sieben Millionen Jahre« (Niemitz 322).

Jahrhundertelang suchte man vergeblich nach einer »Ursprache«. Um 1900 stellte Berthold Delbrück fest: »Ob es eine Ursprache des Menschengeschlechts gegeben hat, wissen wir nicht; das aber wissen wir sicher, daß wir sie durch Vergleichung nicht wiederherstellen können« (Pinker, *Sprachinstinkt* 25).

In grundlegenden Punkten ist sich die Fachwelt heute einig: »Die zutreffendste Behauptung ist wohl, dass die Möglichkeit, Sprache zu erlernen, vererbt wird, während die Fähigkeit, tatsächlich Sprache zu verwenden, erlernt werden muss« (Herrmann 60).[5] »Sprache ist also die im geschichtlichen kulturellen

---

4   Es hängt stark von der Definition von Sprache ab (Überblick Herrmann 47f.).

5   Bestätigt wird die genetische Determiniertheit von Sprachfähigkeit u.a. durch Untersuchungen, wonach »Frauen bei Aufgaben zur Sprachflüssigkeit, zum verbalen Gedächtnis, zur Artikulationsgeschwindigkeit und zur Verwendung der Grammatik den Männern überlegen sind« (Hermann 64f.), und die Entdeckung von Genen für Sprachstörungen (inkl. Dyslexie/Legasthenie). Auch ein sprachrelevantes Gen wurde bereits entdeckt. Seit etwa 200.000 Jahren unterscheidet sich das FOXP2-Gen von der Variante der Schimpansen,

Lernprozeß erstellte Ausformung der anlagemäßigen Sprachfähigkeit« (Oeser 81). Einig ist man sich auch: »Ein Kind erlernt jede beliebige Sprache gleich gut« (Herrmann 60) und »als *wissenschaftlich irrig* gelten die Behauptungen«, Ethnien, sog. Rassen, klimatische oder gesellschaftliche Zustände »könnten den Sprachtypus gesetzmäßig bestimmen« (Vollmer, *Erkenntnistheorie* 151, meine Hervorh.).

Zwei Positionen zum Erwerb von Sprache stehen sich heute gegenüber: Die nativistische Auffassung geht davon aus, dass wesentliche strukturelle Aspekte der Sprache angeboren sind und dass Sprache anatomisch autonom repräsentiert ist (Stichwort Universalgrammatik). Wesentliche Vertreter sind Noam Chomsky und der Psychologe Steven Pinker. Die Auffassung der Epigenese, basierend auf Arbeiten von Jean Piaget und Conrad Hal Waddington, sieht Sprache »als Resultat dynamischer Interaktionen zwischen genetisch enkodierten Informationen, neuronalen Veränderungen und äußerer Umwelt« (Szagun, *Sprache* 5). So wichtig und spannend diese Kontroverse ist: Es geht nicht um wirklich gegensätzliche Auffassungen, sondern um Nuancen in der evolutionären Einschätzung (Dennett 340ff.).

Lassen sich diese beiden eben kurz dargelegten Positionen oder wenigstens eine davon mit Tolkiens Vorstellung von einer *native language*, einer angeborenen »Heimatsprache« in Einklang bringen? Wenn, dann wohl am ehesten der Nativismus.

Abgeleitet vom lateinischen *nativus* (angeboren, natürlich) bezeichnet Nativismus in Psychologie und Anthropologie die Auffassung, bestimmte (mehr oder weniger viele) Begabungen oder Fähigkeiten seien angeboren oder von Geburt an im Gehirn fest verankert – im Gegensatz zur Vorstellung der »tabula rasa«, nach der das Gehirn nur wenige angeborene Fähigkeiten besitzt und fast alles durch Interaktion mit der Umwelt lernt.

Für unsere Betrachtungen besonders wichtig ist das Werk des 1928 geborenen Avram Noam Chomsky, emeritierter Professor für Linguistik. Unter vielen anderen wesentlichen Beiträgen zur Sprachwissenschaft sticht die Universalgrammatik hervor. Nachdem Chomsky die Darstellung natürlicher Sprachen formalisiert, ihre einzelsprachlichen Ausdrücke mit Hilfe einer Metasprache rekursiv definiert und aus der Metasprache Klassen von Grammatiken abgeleitet hatte, ordnete er diese ein in die (heute so genannte) Chomsky-Hierarchie. Laut Chomsky ist die menschliche Fähigkeit, mit einem begrenzten Vorrat an grammatikalischen Regeln und einer endlichen Anzahl von Wörtern eine unbegrenzte Menge von Sätzen zu bilden, unsere Äußerungen zu strukturieren, angeboren und Teil der genetischen Ausstattung des Menschen. Dabei nimmt er an, dass

---

wahrscheinlich wird dadurch eine bessere Kontrolle von Mund- und Gesichtsmuskeln erreicht.

alle menschlichen Sprachen gemeinsamen grammatischen Prinzipien folgen und eben diese allen Menschen angeboren seien: als Universalgrammatik. Der Mensch wird nach dieser Theorie mit einer abstrakten Sprachfähigkeit geboren, die es ihm ermöglicht, eine konkrete Sprache zu erlernen; unterschieden wird zwischen dem angeborenen Sprachwissen, der Kompetenz, und dem Gebrauch dieses »Wissens«, der Sprachverwendung, der Performanz.

Es gibt viele gute Gründe für und auch manche, die gegen diese Theorie sprechen.

Sehr stark ist die Analogie zur Musikwahrnehmung, die von manchen als eine universale Sprache angesehen wird. Ausgehend von der Überlegung, dass Prozesse, die schon bei der Geburt funktionieren, sehr wahrscheinlich angeboren und damit unabhängig von Erfahrungen sind, zeigt sich, dass Musik zwar keine universale Sprache ist, es aber grundlegende Universalien der Musikwahrnehmung und -verarbeitung gibt. So gibt es den Einklang und die Oktave in praktisch allen und die Quinte und Quarte in den meisten Kulturen. Die Neigung zu Intervallen mit kleinen Frequenzverhältnissen (Oktave 1 : 2, Quinte 2 : 3, Quarte 3 : 4) ist wohl angeboren. Das gilt wahrscheinlich auch für das Bedürfnis, tonale Bezüge herstellen zu können, und dasjenige nach dem Wechsel von Spannung und Auflösung, weshalb es fast überall Skalen, also Tonleitern, mit ungleichen Tonabständen gibt. Schon Kleinkinder kommen besser mit Skalen mit ungleichen Abständen zurecht als mit einer gleichschrittigen Tonleiter. Universal scheint auch die prinzipielle Melodiewahrnehmung zu sein; die meisten Menschen merken sich die Kontur einer Melodie, also Richtungsänderungen der Tonhöhe, nicht die absolute Tonhöhe oder Geschwindigkeit, dies zeigt sich auch schon bei Kleinkindern. Schließlich ist der Einsatz auditiver Gruppierungsstrategien universal, also die Gruppierung und Strukturierung nach bestimmten Gestaltprinzipien; diese selbst aber sind wohl nicht universal. Diese Gruppierung von Ereignissen zu Wahrnehmungseinheiten, um Information zu reduzieren, spielt auch eine wichtige Rolle bei der Sprache, ebenso wie die Universalien der Rhythmuswahrnehmung – Menschen fassen eine Folge von Schlägen in der Regel zu Gruppen von unterschiedlichem Gewicht zusammen und versuchen immer, einen regelmäßigen Puls zu finden. Über 90 Prozent der Menschen schaffen es bei Versuchen, zu unbekannter Musik den Takt zu klopfen – und Säuglinge können ihre Saugrate an die Rate einer auditiven Sequenz anpassen.

Dies passt zu Erkenntnissen der Spracherwerbsforschung. Schon vom siebten Schwangerschaftsmonat an nehmen Babys die Sprachmelodie der Mutter auf und können bei Versuchen verschiedene Sprachen an Rhythmus und Sprachmelodie erkennen. Später unterscheiden Babys bekannte und neue Sprachrhythmen: Bei neuem Input nuckeln sie schneller. Dies sind eindeutig angeborene Komponenten der Sprachlernfähigkeit. Und zunächst sind Babys für jedes der etwa 100 Phoneme der Welt offen, können also jede Sprache akzentfrei lernen. In der

Regel fällt zwischen dem zehnten und zwölften Lebensmonat die Entscheidung für das Lautsystem einer oder bei zweisprachiger Umgebung zweier Sprachen. Durch den Abbau neuronaler Verbindungen, die nicht benötigt werden, reduziert sich die Vernetzungsdichte des neuronalen Netzes im frontalen Broca-Areal des Gehirns auf das Wesentliche; in dieses passen zwei Sprachen. Ab etwa dem fünften Lebensjahr muss für jede neue Sprache ein separates neuronales Netz geknüpft werden, ab ungefähr dem zwölften Lebensjahr wird das Sprachenlernen wegen verringerter Plastizität des Gehirns schwieriger; zweisprachig aufgewachsene Menschen haben es auch dann noch leichter.

Ganz sicher also gibt es angeborene Regeln. Inwieweit diese so strikt sind, wie es bei der Universalgrammatik angenommen wird, ist nicht gesichert.

Beispielsweise ist das Zählen wohl nicht angeboren; es gibt Ethnien, die nur bis zwei zählen und alle größeren Zahlen als »mehr« bezeichnen. Vergleichbares gilt für die nonverbale Kommunikation, es gibt sowohl universale, angeborene Gebärden und Körpersprache-Elemente wie sehr viel mehr erlernte.

Es gibt Forschungsansätze, die den Spracherwerb ohne die Annahme angeborener sprachspezifischer Gehirnstrukturen erklären. Epigene (vom Griechischen *epigenesis*: nachträgliche Entstehung) bezeichnet in Biologie, Psychologie und Anthropologie die schon von Aristoteles vertretene Ansicht, dass sich bei der Entwicklung eines Organismus neue Strukturen herausbilden können, die nicht vorher vorgebildet waren. Wenn die hohe Plastizität des Gehirns in den frühen Jahren auf anregende Lernumgebungen trifft, entsteht, so die Grundannahme, eine gemeinsame Sprache – wenn die Menschen in der Umgebung über vergleichbare geistige Strukturen, Absichten und Zwecke verfügen. Dies ist ein Beispiel für eine Emergenz-Theorie (vom Lateinischen *emergere*: auftauchen, emporsteigen), die die Herausbildung von neuen Eigenschaften oder Strukturen eines Systems durch das Zusammenspiel seiner Elemente erklärt, ohne dass diese direkt oder offensichtlich auf Eigenschaften der Elemente zurückzuführen sind. Hierzu gehört auch der Konnektionismus; er erklärt Sprache wie vieles andere mit dem Verhalten vernetzter Systeme bei Zusammenschlüssen von künstlichen Informationsverarbeitungseinheiten: Lernen und Verhalten wird als Produkt einer Vielzahl interagierender Komponenten verstanden, die sich wechselseitig beeinflussen, Menschen analog gesehen zu künstlichen neuronalen Netzen (oder umgekehrt).

Andere Alternativen zu Chomskys Theorien kommen vor allem aus der konstruktivistischen Kognitionswissenschaft, der Wahrnehmungspsychologie und phänomenologischen, existentialistischen und hermeneutischen Traditionen.

In letzter Zeit wird zunehmend auch in umgekehrter Richtung geforscht: dass und wie Sprache die Weltsicht bestimmt. Zweisprachig aufgewachsene Menschen bspw. wechseln mit der Sprache oft auch ihre Sicht auf die Welt, je nach grammatikalischem Aufbau der Sprache. Im Englischen gibt es z.B. die sogenannte progressive Zeitform, die eine andauernde Handlung beschreibt, im Deutschen nichts dergleichen. Deutsche haben daher eher eine holistische Sicht der Welt, betrachten eine Aktion als Ganzes und konzentrieren sich auf die Anfangs- und Endpunkte, englisch Muttersprachliche mehr auf die Bewegung an sich. Bilinguale Menschen, die natürlich in ihrer Muttersprache aufgewachsen sind, aber heute zwei Sprachen fließend sprechen, wechselten bei Experimenten je nach Sprache auch den Blickwinkel. Das Idiom, in dem Menschen sich ausdrücken, bestimmt also mit, zumindest unbewusst, was sie wie wahrnehmen, wie sie es darstellen und beschreiben. Und da Wahrnehmung die Grundlage jeder weitergehenden Analyse und Beurteilung ist, werden dadurch auch diese bis hin zu einer Bewertung und vielleicht sogar Werten beeinflusst.

Zwar gilt auch weiterhin und gerade im politischen Raum die alte Regel: Wer die Sprache beherrscht, beherrscht das Denken. Teilweise aber funktioniert es eben auch umgekehrt: Die Sprache kann sogar das Bewusstsein bestimmen.

Das kann vielleicht teilweise erklären, wieso Ideen wie die einer »natürlichen« oder »Heimatsprache« so weite Verbreitung finden konnten.

Außerdem muss bis heute der Streit darüber als unentschieden gelten, ob überhaupt denkbar ist, worüber nicht gesprochen oder zumindest in Sprachelementen gedacht werden kann. Kann, wer nur Zahlwörter bis zwei kennt, physikalische Formeln entwickeln? Andererseits haben Menschen das Rad und den Bogen erfunden, ohne dafür einen Namen gehabt zu haben. Und sie haben sich sicher schon geliebt und gehasst, bevor ihre Sprache Begriffe dafür kannte. Vieles spricht also für grundlegende und allen Menschen gleiche Prinzipien.

Fazit

Trotz aller Kritik an Chomskys Gedankengebäude sind die grundlegenden Prinzipien seiner Theorie heute allgemein anerkannt: dass der Geist kognitiv ist, also mentale Zustände, Überzeugungen, Zweifel usw. enthält und nicht nur als Rechenwerk funktioniert; dass ein Großteil dessen, was der erwachsene Geist kann, angeboren ist, zumindest als Fähigkeit und/oder Disposition; dass der Geist eine Ansammlung zusammenwirkender spezialisierter Subsysteme ist, die nur eingeschränkt miteinander kommunizieren.

Chomskys Theorie der Universalgrammatik wurde deshalb so ausführlich vorgestellt, weil sie noch am ehesten in der Lage wäre, die Idee einer *native language*, einer »Heimatsprache« im Sinne Tolkiens, zu erklären. Doch selbst diese Theorie, die von angeborenen Voraussetzungen ausgeht, lässt sich nicht vereinbaren mit den Vorstellungen von einer angeborenen Sprache, bei der Herkunft, »Rasse«, Ethnie, Abstammung oder was auch immer eine Rolle spielen sollen. Moderne Forschungsergebnisse liefern im Gegenteil Ansätze für Erklärungen, wieso man sich in »seiner« Sprache, der eigenen, wohl fühlt.

Tolkiens Vorstellungen von einer *native language* sind mit dem aktuellen wissenschaftlichen Kenntnisstand nicht vereinbar und somit widerlegt.

Bibliographie

Adams, Michael. *From Elvish to Klingon. Exploring Invented Languages.* New York: Oxford University Press, 2011

Athanasopoulos, Panos et al.: »Two Languages, Two Minds: Flexible Cognitive Processing Driven by Language of Operation«. *Psychological Science* 26 (April 2015): 518-526. DOI: 10.1177/0956797614567509

Beeh, Volker. »Was ich dir sagen will. Der Mensch und die Sprache«. *Funkkolleg Der Mensch. Anthropologie heute.* Studienbrief 7, Studieneinheit 21. Tübingen: Deutsches Institut für Fernstudien an der Universität Tübingen, 1993

Dennett, Daniel C. *Darwins gefährliches Erbe. Die Evolution und der Sinn des Lebens.* Hamburg: Hoffmann & Campe, 1997

von Ditfurth, Hoimar. *Der Geist fiel nicht vom Himmel. Die Evolution unseres Bewusstseins.* München: dtv, ^{12}1991

Eco, Umberto. *Die Suche nach der vollkommenen Sprache.* München: Beck, ^{3}1995

Eibl-Eibesfeldt, Irenäus. *Die Biologie des menschlichen Verhaltens. Grundriss der Humanethologie.* München/Zürich: Piper, ^{3}1997

Egenolf, Heinrich. *Die menschliche Stimme.* Stuttgart: Paracelsus, ^{3}1974

Falk, Dean. *Braindance – oder warum Schimpansen nicht steppen können. Die Entwicklung des menschlichen Gehirns.* Basel/Boston/Berlin: Birkhäuser, 1994

Glück, Helmut, & Michael Rödel (Hg.). *Metzler Lexikon Sprache.* Stuttgart: Metzler ^{5}2016

Hermann, Christoph & Christian Fiebach. *Gehirn und Sprache.* Frankfurt a. M.: Fischer, 2004

Jourdain, Robert. *Das wohltemperierte Gehirn. Wie Musik im Kopf entsteht und wirkt.* Heidelberg: Spektrum Akademischer Verlag, 2001

Karpf, Anne. *Frauen reden anders, Männer auch. Was die Stimme über unsere wahren Gefühle verrät.* Bergisch Gladbach: Ehrenwirth (Lübbe), 2006

Kuckenburg, Martin. *... und sprachen das erste Wort? Eine Kulturgeschichte der menschlichen Verständigung. Die Entstehung von Sprache und Schrift.* Düsseldorf: Econ, 1996

---. *Wer sprach das erste Wort? Die Entstehung von Sprache und Schrift.* Darmstadt: Theiss, ^{3}2016

Masson, Peter. »Anthropologische Dimensionen interkultureller Verstehensbemühungen«. *Philosophische Anthropologie der Moderne.* Hg. Helmut Gipper & René Weiland. Weinheim: Beltz Athenäum, 1995

Mayr, Ernst. *Das ist Evolution.* München: Bertelsmann, 2003

Miller, George A. *Wörter. Streifzüge durch die Psycholinguistik.* Heidelberg/Berlin/New York: Spektrum Akademischer Verlag, 1993

de la Motte-Haber, Helga. *Handbuch der Musikpsychologie.* Laaber: Laaber-Verlag, ^{2}1996

---. *Musikpsychologie.* Laaber: Laaber-Verlag, 2005

Niemitz, Carsten. »Evolution und Sprache«. *Sprache denken. Positionen aktueller Sprachphilosophie.* Hg. Jürgen Trabant. Frankfurt a. M.: Fischer, 1995: 298-327

Oeser, Erhard, & Franz Seitelberger. *Gehirn, Bewusstsein und Erkenntnis.* Darmstadt: WBG, ^{2}1995

Phelpstead, Carl. *Tolkien and Wales. Language, Literature and Identity.* Cardiff: University of Cardiff Press, 2011

Pinker, Steven. *Der Sprachinstinkt. Wie der Geist die Sprache bildet.* München: Kindler, 1996

---. *Das unbeschriebene Blatt. Die moderne Leugnung der menschlichen Natur.* Berlin: Berlin-Verlag, 2003

Riedl, Rupert. *Biologie der Erkenntnis. Die stammesgeschichtlichen Grundlagen der Vernunft.* Berlin/Hamburg: Paul Parey, 1980

---. *Wahrheit und Wahrscheinlichkeit. Biologische Grundlagen des Für-Wahr-Nehmens.* Berlin/Hamburg: Paul Parey, 1992

Schneidewind, Friedhelm. »Biologie, Genetik und Evolution in Mittelerde«. *Hither Shore* 2 (2006): 41-66

---. »Erbgedächtnis und angeborene Sprache«. *Hither Shore* 3 (2007): 235-238

---. »Stimmen die Stimmen? Dokumentation eines Scheiterns«. *Musik in Mittelerde.* Hg. Friedhelm Schneidewind & Heidi Steimel. Edition Stein und Baum. Saarbrücken: Verlag der Villa Fledermaus, 2014: 219-222

Smith, Ross. *Inside Language. Linguistic and Aesthetic Theorie in Tolkien.* Zürich/Bern: Walking Tree Publishers ²2007

Szagun, Gisela. *Wie Sprache entsteht. Spracherwerb bei Kindern mit beeinträchtigtem und normalem Hören.* Weinheim: Beltz, 2001

---. *Sprachentwicklung beim Kind. Ein Lehrbuch.* Weinheim/Basel: Beltz ⁶2016.

Tolkien, John Ronald Reuel. *The Letters of J.R.R. Tolkien.* Ed. Humphrey Carpenter. London: Allen & Unwin, 1981

---. *Briefe.* Hg. Humphrey Carpenter. Stuttgart: Klett-Cotta ²2002

---. *A Secret Vice. Tolkien on Invented Languages.* Eds. Dimitri Fimi & Andrew Higgins. London: HarperCollins Publishers, 2016

---. »A Secret Vice«. *The Monsters and the Critics and Other Essays.* Ed. Christopher Tolkien. London: Allen & Unwin, 1983: 198-223

---. »English and Welsh«. *The Monsters and the Critics and Other Essays.* Ed. Christopher Tolkien. London: Allen & Unwin, 1983: 162-197

---. »Ein heimliches Laster«. *Gute Drachen sind rar. Drei Aufsätze.* Stuttgart: Klett-Cotta, 1983: 7-49

---. »Über Märchen«. *Gute Drachen sind rar. Drei Aufsätze.* Stuttgart: Klett-Cotta, 1984: 51-140

Trabant, Jürgen (Hg.). *Sprache denken. Positionen aktueller Sprachphilosophie.* Frankfurt a. M.: Fischer, 1995

Vollmer, Gerhard. *Evolutionäre Erkenntnistheorie.* Stuttgart: Hirzel, ⁸2002

---. *Was können wir wissen? Bd. 1: Die Natur der Erkenntnis. Bd. 2: Die Erkenntnis der Natur. Beiträge zur modernen Naturphilosophie.* Stuttgart: Hirzel, ³2003

Wuketits, Franz M. *Der freie Wille. Die Evolution einer Illusion.* Stuttgart: Hirzel, 2007

---. *Evolution. Die Entwicklung des Lebens.* München: C.H. Beck, ³2009

The *Lord of the Rings* Stage Musical as a Fairy-story

Tobias Escher (Bingen)

The theatre stage has been a place for thrilling suspense, detailed character studies, and grand emotions to strive for centuries. Yet the realm of fantastic stories has been largely absent from theatre, which is noteworthy given the genre's penchant for especially grand emotion and character studies. J.R.R. Tolkien's works arguably bring a good deal of suspense into the fantasy mix, mostly by virtue of their exhaustive back story that makes every plot action an important part of a much larger narrative context. When a battle is lost (or won), it has major consequences and is not just one of the many battles good vs. evil. In his essay *On Fairy-stories*, Tolkien briefly talks about fantasy on stage and concludes that it simply does not work. While the specific examples mentioned certainly have merit, one might beg to differ on the general assumption.

The *Lord of the Rings* stage musical by Matthew Warchus and Shaun McKenna, with music by A.R. Rahman and the Finnish group Värttinä is perhaps the one stage play best fitted to serve for an analysis of both Tolkien's specific comments about theatre adaptations of fantasy elements as well as the treatment of the genre in general in regards to its creative potential. The concept of sub-creation, introduced by Tolkien in the same essay, as well, is of special interest here. After all, the stage show constitutes a world within a world within a world, one might say: Tolkien's literary work is rooted in the Primary World and the stage show is rooted in the literary work.

This essay aims to analyse several elements from the stage show—musical numbers, props, stylistic decisions—and compare them to both Tolkien's specific comments about theatre adaptations as well as the larger area of (successful) sub-creation. In this it becomes apparent that the stage show also serves as an example of a fairy-story following Tolkien's description of its properties.

The Stage Show

There have been a number of stage productions setting out to bring Tolkien's most well-known work to life, one of those being Bernd Stromberger's *The Lord of the Rings* in 1998, which however actually was a stage version of *The Hobbit* and was a commercial and artistic failure. Originally a part of the creative team of this production, writer Shaun McKenna then found his way to the big theatrical production of *The Lord of the Rings* (this time indeed based on the actual book). The *Lord of the Rings* stage musical opened in 2006 in Toronto CA and after a short and very unsuccessful run re-opened in London's West

End in 2007 with significant re-writes, only to close in July 2008. With a very large budget and a gigantic cast of fifty actors plus a sizable pit orchestra, along with a stage with three revolves and a sumptuous stage decoration, the show could be likened to a spectacle rather than a regular stage musical.

The music for the production was written by Indian composer A.R. Rahman in collaboration with Finnish world music group Värttinä. According to the producers, orchestrator Christopher Nightingale had a significant part in shaping the score (Russell 77), as well. He was tasked with the different styles of Rahman and Värttinä together, which suggests that his work went far beyond the realm of regular orchestration.

Even though only very few direct quotes from Tolkien's poems were used for the lyrics of the musical, the producers nevertheless maintain their desire to be true to Tolkien: "Was I ever tempted to use Tolkien's lyrics?" asks Shaun McKenna [Co-Writer]. "No, it wouldn't have been appropriate here..." (Russell 75).

According to Christopher Nightingale [Orchestrator], it was the very essence of Tolkien's world-scape that he wanted to capture in the music and themes (Russell 70). The composers of the musical approached the task of setting Tolkien's world to music from the angle of capturing the feeling and the underlying drama and culture, not by following the letters to the word. The songs were intended not as regular musical songs, progressing the story, but as the songs of the cultures itself: "...with this notion that the songs wouldn't do what songs do in musical theatre; instead they would be the old songs of Middle-earth; that people were singing them because they were singing the old songs" (Russell 49).

What Music is there in Middle-earth?

To look at what might make a musical in Middle-earth successful or not, first it is in order to look at the role or prevalence of music in Middle-earth in general. Music clearly is an important part of the narrative, especially in *The Hobbit* and *The Lord of the Rings*. There is a number of songs sung by protagonists in *The Hobbit* along with relatively detailed descriptions of instruments and the very large number of songs and poems in LotR clearly show the importance of the art form in Middle-earth. These songs span the full spectrum: Hobbit folk songs, what can be called Elvish art song, riddles, and many more. Music literally shaped the world through the Ainulindalë and arguably still shapes it. Some stylistic descriptions of music as well as instruments described by name or sound allow conclusions to the prevalence of instrumental as well as vocal music—the latter often performed a-cappella by force of circumstances, rather than as a sign of instrumental music being less prevalent. One might even add non-conscious sounds to the musical world of Middle-earth: Sound created by Orcs or by forces of nature cross the boundaries between sound and music, as for example shown by the Ents.

Sub-creation and Secondary Belief

When looking at an adaptation of any literary work, the most important pre-requisite to answering the question "Does it work?" is determining the level of inner consistency within the adaptation. In the case of a theatre play, this becomes even more important because of the direct connection between actors and spectators. Stage plays need to connect directly to the viewer because on the one hand they provide a largely pre-defined experience (as opposed to literature, which leaves much detailing to the reader), yet on the other hand work by their close proximity between stage and spectator. If that experience is unsatisfying, there is little chance of the spectators fleshing out things on their own as it would happen when reading a book.

In an adaption of a well-known work with a deep mythology like LotR, the end result can be described as a "world within a world". Tolkien describes the act of creating a consistent world within another world as "sub-creation". Every sub-creation is rooted in the Primary World. In the case of a stage play based on such a successful sub-creation (which we can safely assume LotR to be) a double sub-creation is encountered. In fact, on top of the first sub-creative layer (the Legendarium) and the second layer (the creative team by adapting the story through music, acting, props...) there arguably is a third layer, namely by the listener/spectator through connotations, own experiences, shared public knowledge, etc...

It is this "world" with its inner consistency that brings forth the much-discussed "suspension of disbelief". This concept basically assumes that a recipient needs to willingly make him/herself not realise that what is going on right now on stage is not in fact happening, but rather is fictional. It also accepts that believing something in the sense of having a fulfilling experience entails assuming it to be actual reality, suggesting a form of deliberate delusion. As soon as the fictional element loses the ability to be believable (or rather its inner consistency), the recipient supposedly suddenly becomes aware of the illusion and only then realises that everything was just fictional.

This view can be doubted, and in fact Tolkien himself does so when he says that "children are capable, of course, of literary belief, when the story-maker's art is good enough to produce it" (FS 37). This Secondary Belief is the key to understanding to which degree an adaptation such as the LotR stage show is successful. No spectator above a certain age would ever truly believe that such a show was actually real in the sense that it was factually happening. Instead the inner consistency of this Secondary World creates a Secondary Belief that—in this particular moment—is real, actual belief.

The Fairy-story as a Journey

Tolkien states that "Most good fairy stories are about the adventures of men [protagonists] in the perilous realm" (FS 9). In an at least partially interactive medium like a stage play, these adventures form the backbone of a journey the spectators take part in on a very emotional level. For this purpose, Tolkien's description can be amended: a good fairy story deals with the lived and shared adventures of protagonists and recipients in the perilous realm.

The journey and the recipient's wish to take part in it form the core of the appeal of a good story: "Fairy-stories are plainly not primarily concerned with possibility, but with desirability. If they awaken desire… they succeed" (FS 40).

In its ability to provide a flexible 360° view (the viewer is free to look at specific points contrary to for example a movie) and a direct eye to ear connection, there is no better place imaginable to share in an adventure than the stage.

Is an Adaptation a (Sub)-creation?

In *On Fairy-stories*, Tolkien addresses the wide-spread argument of originality. One criticism often levelled at the LotR stage show by critics is the show's frequent use of existing material—or the fact alone that it is based on a literary work, suggesting that this would prevent it to stand on its own artistically. Tolkien writes about this that "…it is precisely the colouring, the atmosphere, the unclassifiable individual details of a story… that informs with life the undissected bones of the plot, that really count" (FS 19). One may argue that it is exactly this usage of existing material, or, as Tolkien puts it the different ingredients of the soup, that together with the skills of the creative team manages to make the whole more than the sum of its parts. The following analysis of a number of elements from the show aims to prove this point.

Fantasy on Stage

While not specifically being concerned with Fairy-stories in the performing arts, *On Fairy-stories* nevertheless contains a number of pointers to Tolkien's views about the medium: "but drama is naturally hostile to fantasy… The nearer it is to 'dramatised fairy-story' the worse it is. It is only tolerable when the plot and its fantasy are reduced to a mere vestigial framework for farce, and no 'belief' of any kind in any part of the performance is required or expected of anybody" (FS 50).

Tolkien recalls a stage play of *Puss in Boots* and mentions the transformation of an ogre into a mouse as one example of a story element that simply did not work on stage. This example serves as a good reference point towards an explanation why Tolkien's view might have been justified in in his days, but today is not able to hold up in the lights of a changing medium.

1) The Inadequacy of Stage Effects

The above-mentioned transformation of an ogre into a mouse stands for the underlying cause of the failure of that particular scene: the inadequacy of (practical) stage effects. The kind of stage play, or "dramatised story" Tolkien seems to have in mind here uses rather small production values. Indeed with only simply trapdoors and lifts and a conventional theatre stage it would be quite hard if not impossible to convey a believable fantastic setting. The stage musical as a quite recent development of theatrical storytelling is very different from the traditional theatre. As far as the LotR stage show is concerned, the most important subtype of the stage musical is what might be called historical spectacle. Stage shows like *Les Misérables* and *The Phantom of the Opera* have brought a middle ground between stage drama and entertainment shows by combining an epic, coherent narrative with lavish production and entertainment. These productions not only usually employ a very large cast often comparable to a movie production as well as elaborate sets and props, but have also taken inspiration from the moving images in the realm of practical effects. While a transformation of an ogre into a mouse is still a major feat, with movie-inspired stage effects Tolkien today might actually be able to see a quite convincing *Puss in Boots*.

Compared to the kind of productions Tolkien refers to, modern stage musicals have a vastly bigger budget. At over 25 Million GBP, the LotR show was the most expensive such production of its time. A stage play today thanks to computer technology, projections, and full electronic control systems largely eliminating the need for hosts of stage hands or at least changing their area of work, is simply able to mount far higher production values. These high production values arguably are a prerequisite to a convincing fantasy world.

2) Characters vs. Things

Tolkien writes that "very little about trees as trees can be gotten into a play" (FS 52), addressing the fundamental difference in focus areas between for example a literary work and a stage play. While both are very capable of conveying a story, a literary work excels at describing things, be it landscapes, devices or any other more or less inanimate object. Stage plays, on the other hand, effortlessly transport characters, emotions, and every other living thing. Emotions do not need to be described because they are immediately, wordlessly, apparent by means of facial expression, posture etc... People, or more precise humans or humanlike characters are easy to introduce, also aided by costuming, props and of course acting cues. An Orc may require generous makeup and movement training, but is still essentially humanoid and therefore rather easy to portray—actually easier to grasp as a character by looking at him rather than reading, at least on a superficial level. Being essentially trees, the Ents are a different case: they clearly look like trees and in their outward appearance they are in fact trees. A play is not able to easily have talking trees, at least not without major practical effects. The stage show works around this issue by portraying the Ents with a tree's most apparent physical characteristic: its immense height. Ents in the musical are played by regular actors on very high stilts wearing long dark green coats and hats. So while for example the feature films focus on the tree component of the Ents, the stage show emphasises that they are tree *people,* again drawing on the more immediate interaction between actors and audience.

One thing that must not be forgotten, though, is that the difficulties of the theatre in portraying objects in essence refer to everything that is not a character. That is an acting and reacting element with its own goals and things that cause it to act. These characters may very well be usually inanimate objects (like trees) and certainly do not need to be people or human-like figures. The point is that they need to be an acting element rather than for example a static landscape (which works beautifully for example in a motion picture).

3) The Fourth Wall

Most traditional forms of western theatre rely heavily on the so-called fourth wall for their staging, meaning an imagined wall between the stage and the audience. Actors generally completely ignore the audience and pretend it is not even there, aided by the fact that from the brightly lit stage it is near impossible for actors to see anything in the dark audience. The use of the stage as the single area where any performance takes place is a limitation in itself, because—especially in a literally vast genre like Fantasy—it forces a story taking place in a very large space, for example Middle-earth, into a relatively tight space that is the polar opposite of any epic grandeur. The *Lord of the Rings* stage show breaks the fourth wall on many levels. The stage decoration itself extends into the auditorium, thus making the stage look larger than it actually is. Also by employing decoration to the side and even behind the audience, an all-encompassing effect is produced that makes the auditorium feel part of a much larger world. Middle-earth literally is all around and can still be seen when the audience turns around. This effect is amplified by the lighting, which not only extends into the audience but also comes from the audience itself. The Balrog, for example, enters with red light and mist from behind the rows. As most West End stages, the LotR stage is actually not completely straight, but features a rake, which creates the illusion of it being even larger.

The actors on occasion break the fourth wall themselves. Before the actual show begins, a number of Hobbits provide entertainment in the rows to engage the audience. Later during intermission, Orcs roam the theatre. The orchestra pit is covered and hidden from view, which, together with the very directional use of sound effects provides a 360° experience, rather than all sounds clearly emanating from the stage.

The Soup

Tolkien in *On Fairy-stories* frequently refers to "The Soup" to denote the story with its different ingredients that still bring a single (hopefully coherent) result—just like a soup should do. In fact, he clearly states, that looking at the soup as simply that—a soup—is perfectly fine. It is in fact (for the reader) the intended way to encounter it. Tolkien refers to the individual elements the story is made of as the "bones". All these bones are placed in one big pot, out of which the soup is cooked. This also connects to the above mentioned argument of originality. The same bones do not necessarily result in the same soup. The "bones" Tolkien specifically mentions are pseudo-historical elements like the archbishop and his unfortunate incident involving a banana skin. One might argue, though, that "bones" do not need to be story fragments or events (short narratives) in general. The very foundation of Tolkien's soup argument is that the individual elements within the pot get their own life, so to speak, apart from the original (possibly even historical) truth. Like Bertha was "attached" to the *Goosegirl* tale, elements develop a particular significance sometimes unrelated to the actual historical truth after having been thrown in the pot. One more recent example of such a "bone" that is not a story or tale is the use of the Irish Penny Whistle in Howard Shore's *Lord of the Rings* scores in the Shire theme. While there have been countless uses of this instrument both in other film scores as well as in numerous other musical genres, a large percentage of listeners immediately connect it with Hobbits. The very same can be said of the Celesta and Harry Potter, falsely in this case because "Hedwig's Theme", as it is called, employs a Celesta layered with a sine wave. A solo celesta sounds notably different, yet still in most listeners evokes "Hedwig's Theme". This shows that individual "bones" indeed have a life of their own that sometimes is far removed from actual reality. It can be argued that most listeners hearing a Tin Whistle are very much aware that this is not truly a Hobbit instrument, if just for the reason that Hobbits are fictional. But within the belief system constructed by the recipient, in this particular case it is indeed a Hobbit instrument—in-universe, so to speak.

For the purpose of this paper, as a selection from the multitude of elements the sage show is comprised of, four such "bones" come to mind:

- Characterisation through comparison, where the creative team characterises a culture by comparing it through musical stylistic elements to existing conceptions in the Primary World.
- Literal use of original elements, where direct quotes from the source material are used for dramatic effect and to underscore a plot development.
- Belief through credible realism, where actions of characters and elements from the world they live in are portrayed deliberately realistically to enhance believability.

- Emotional Involvement, where the personal feelings of the audience are used to enhance the plot, drawing on the strengths of the medium.

As shall be seen, these bones are all rooted in the Primary World and have an inner consistency within themselves. That means that taken on their own they make sense as a coherent element. Within the Secondary World of the stage play they use this consistency and realism to either point to a similarity to their state in the Primary World, or even to the complete opposite. This arguably makes a "good bone": that it works on its own just as well as within the larger soup, the story as well as possessing an internal realism.

Characterisation through Comparison

The *Lord of the Rings* stage show extensively uses comparisons to elements from the Primary World to characterise protagonists or even whole cultures. The most all-encompassing example is the representation of the Dwarves' culture as a people of craftsmen and fine artists rather than the nowadays more frequently employed portrayal as axe-wielding warriors. Obviously, Dwarves also perform quite a bit of axe-wielding, but the stage show as well as a large number of other adaptations clearly stress the focus of their culture on craftsmanship and art.

The stage show is notable for using a whole musical number embedded in a roughly seven-minute scene just to portray these cultural traits. The spot chosen is the place of the Song of Durin, which Gimli sings to Sam after the latter speaks of darksome holes. Just like in the book, Gimli in the stage musical corrects Sam and in the song tells him about how the Mines of Moria once looked. The very existence of this song says a lot about the desire of the show's creative team to keep the spirit of the books; after all seven minutes running time are a lot in a rather short show and this whole sequence does not actually add anything to the understanding or progression of the story. The song and the scene give the viewer deeper insight into the background, but are not needed for understanding the plot, especially considering two minutes after the song the fellowship is chased by a Balrog and will lose Gandalf.

The "Lament for Moria", as the song is called in the stage show, uses a different text from the book and is also sung as a duet between Gimli and Gandalf—Gimli curiously being a tenor. That Gandalf is able to join in suggests that the song is widely known in Middle-earth, or at least to a learned man like Gandalf. With the Dwarves' usual emphasis on secrecy about their culture—even their language is spoken by very few outsiders—it stands to reason that this song might be one of many representative songs used to describe their culture when dealing with outsiders. The intention to have the songs in the show represent actual songs sung by the people is made clear by the producer:

> …with this notion that the songs wouldn't do what songs do in
> musical theatre; instead they would be the old songs of Middle-
> earth; that people were singing them because they were singing
> the old songs.   (Russell 49)

It is also notable that the song describes the Balrog's destruction as an accident
("none could prevent"), focussing on the lost times of old rather than the
current state (like for example the motion picture does). This also adds to the
realism, because the Dwarves do not know for certain, if at all, that the evil in
the mines is actually a Balrog. By describing the architecture of the mines in
its glory days ("the vaulted roof, from pure basalt grown"), the lament deals
with the accomplishments of the Dwarves as well as their history (in this case
the Moria incident) instead of with the actually narrative.

On a related note, it is also interesting to see that quite a few musical rendi-
tions of the Song of Durin including this Lament use very hymn-like melodies
and elements commonly found in sacred music, as well as almost always mentioning the cathedral-like quality of Dwarvish architecture.

Literal Use of Original Elements

When adapting any work into a different medium or genre, the most obvious and probably easiest way to connect the two works is the literal use
of original elements. In the case of a book this may be word-by-word dialogs,
the extremely detailed reproduction of descriptions (for example by modelling
a building exactly like it is described rather than taking artistic license) or the
deliberate inclusion of expanded or even completely new arcs in the plot for
characters that would otherwise be little more than minor characters.

The LotR stage show has a large number of these, mainly made necessary
by the extensive cuts that had to be made to fit a very large book into a theatre
performance. This resulted in a lot of originally important characters to lose
significance because their back-story was largely cut. The creative team evidently
wanted to still keep these figures and found a way to show the audience that
these characters are actually important; they just happen to have more minor
roles in this particular story. The prime examples of this are Gimli, who gets a
lot of exposure through his Lament for Moria, as well as Legolas. Introduced as
the son of an elf-king, at first glance he does little more than shout "You have
my bow!" and use said bow to cut down Orcs en masse. The stage show uses
the fellowship's arrival in Lothlórien to provide more stage time for Legolas
by having him not only lead the first encounter with Galadriel, but also with
his song "Lothlorien" [sic!], in which he introduces the realm of Lothlórien
and how Galadriel came from the West and made it her home. The song both
gives Legolas more substance and introduces some mythology behind the play,

solidifying the presentation of the world, but not making the plot unintelligible to people not familiar with the subject matter. This adds to the depth of the adaption by providing crucial information about what happens outside the play, but still keeps it accessible to the audience not familiar with the Legendarium who might not know or even care where "the West" is or why Galadriel longs to go back. The stage show deliberately uses very few direct quotes from the book, according to writer Shaun McKenna: "Was I ever tempted to use Tolkien's lyrics?" asks Shaun McKenna. "No, it wouldn't have been appropriate here… (Russell 75). In fact, the only song to use any direct quote from Tolkien is "Wonder", which is sung by Galadriel in Lothlórien after Sam calls for her aid at Shelob's lair.

> I sang of leaves, of leaves of gold, and leaves of gold there grew:
> Of wind I sang, a wind there came and in them blew.

Apart from replacing "in the branches" with "in them" these lines are taken from Galadriel's Song of Eldamar, sung when the fellowship leaves her realm. In the show, they refer to Lothlórien, not to the Undying Lands, probably for reasons of exposition; hardly anyone would know what Galadriel is singing about, just like the Fellowship in the book, and in any case the text can be interpreted both ways. One might argue that choosing this quote as the only direct quote in the whole stage show clearly shows the importance the mythology behind the plot had for the creative team. The fact that this is the only quote viewers familiar with the book will recognise makes it stand out even more and therefore makes one of the shortest scenes in the play one of the most memorable.

Belief through Credible Realism

The importance of creating a believable world cannot be stressed enough, especially when also dealing with mass entertainment like a stage show that not only has to satisfy critics, but also a mass audience usually not familiar with the subject matter. Tolkien writes:

> …But at any rate it is found in practice that 'the inner consistency of reality' is more difficult to produce, the more unlike are the images and the rearrangements of primary material to the actual arrangements of the Primary World.   (FS 48)

That points to one of the strengths of theatre: portraying actions that are undertaken live in front of the audience. The actors may be supported by visual trickery, lighting FX and other tools, but everything still actually happens right before the eyes of everyone watching.

The LotR stage show provides this realism in a large part by carefully characterising the various cultures. The most prominent examples of this are Hobbits and Orcs. Conforming to the general image of Hobbits as essentially English country-folk, the show portrays them as rather easy-going, not very deep on the surface and with the well-known tendency to have quite some more meals a day than strictly necessary not to die of hunger. Tolkien himself confirms this view of the Hobbits when he writes that "the Shire ... is in fact more or less a Warwickshire village of about the period of the Diamond Jubilee" (L 230), referring to Queen Victoria's jubilee in 1897, of course. By its virtue as a musical and the fact that exuberant music is at home on a musical stage, the show extends this Hobbit image by also extensively using typical folk music instruments and tunes, beginning already before the performance with Hobbits dancing across the auditorium. Just like in the book, these songs also deal with subject matters such as drinking, a nice warm bed and other amenities.

The instrumentation in Hobbit-inspired musical pieces adds typical folk instruments like penny whistle, bouzouki and mandolin to the regular musical band. Employing these instruments is a crucial part of the realism because Hobbits would actually be able to play them very well, contrary to for example full-size guitars which would be a bit too large for them, despite also being used in folk music.

The musical's adaptation of Bilbo's Walking Song "The Road Goes On" is an upbeat traveling song in which all the Hobbits join in. It is notable in its use of close harmony, which similar to bluegrass or old time music allows the singers to join in polyphonically without actually needing to know the piece, aided by clear and concise cues to tell every participant what to do. Easy to remember (and predictable) chord progressions as well as a catchy melody mean that everyone familiar with close harmony rules can immediately join in.

The Orcs, on the other hand, are portrayed very differently. Their most striking feature is the use of sharp crutches which they use both to aid their walking as well as for defending themselves. This double use blurring the border between walking aid and weapon lets the human actors convincingly portray a non-human race. Especially on rough terrain or to propel oneself forward on the battlefield it is easy to imagine how a culture could choose to use this combination of tools. The sounds made by the crutches also serve as a kind of music, or at least sound of the Orcs. In the stage show, the Orcs do not actually sing, but instead have their own kind of music based on rhythmic sounds generated by their various warfare paraphernalia. Instead of solely relaying on makeup and the belief of the audience for the Orcs to make an impression, the creative team instead used their disparity to the humans, Hobbits and Elves to portray them as realistically as possible.

Emotional Involvement

Coming back again to the strengths of the medium, one final example of how the stage show manages to create a convincing Secondary World is by drawing on the emotional involvement on the part of the audience. As noted before, personal interaction is a virtue of theatre and nowhere can this virtue be used better than in one on one situations. In LotR the relationship between Frodo and Sam offers the best opportunities for such emotional involvement. The recurring theme here is friendship, one of the most basic and most universal concepts. Tolkien writes: "and actually fairy stories deal largely, or (the better ones) mainly, with simple or fundamental things untouched by Fantasy, but these simplicities are made all the more luminous by their setting" (FS 59). Concepts like friendship or loyalty work to engage sympathy in the audience and by this create actual belief. Nothing makes one believe more than personal involvement, either real or just wished for (as in this case because obviously the audience does not have any influence over what happens).

The stage show puts great emphasis on the friendship between Frodo and Sam to the point of giving them their own duet "Now and for always". These tend to happen with love interests usually, but in the show the relationship between Frodo and Sam is the closest of any characters in the musical. While on their way to Mount Doom, Sam just like in the book wonders if there will be songs about their adventure and then improvises this song together with Frodo at the campfire. In a way the musical validates its own existence this way—a musical or even theatrical retelling of stories is actually foreseen in the book with the Elves' concerts in Rivendell which also deal with musical stories. Accordingly, the lyrics of the song deal with this story of Frodo and Sam and how it is told. Frodo and Sam's friendship is confirmed again when Frodo makes up a verse of his own after Sam has fallen asleep:

> Sing me a tale of the bravest of them all
> Comrade and guide, at my side
> Stouthearted Sam who wouldn't let me fall
> Holding my life in his hand
> True to the end, no finer friend
> Now and for always

The song again employs a very catchy melody and uses a Bouzouki for accompaniment, drawing on musical elements attributed to the Hobbits. Gollum, once a Hobbit himself, uses the same melody shortly after the duet in an attempt doomed to fail to vanquish his dark side. The use of the same melody and distorted instrumentation along with Gollum's two personalities verbally fighting each other connects Sam's simple Hobbit song with Gollum's pitiful existence. Contrary to the book and movies, the stage show portrays Gollum as almost equal to Sam in terms of importance. He is far more than just the guy leading Frodo and Sam through Mordor and finally succumbing to the ring at Mount Doom. Many interactions with the audience as well as his inner monologue detailed in his song to the melody of "Now and for always" make him one of the most emotionally effective characters in the show. He hints to the eucatastrophe at the end with his line "precious and me alone will be", where he indeed will be reunited with the ring forever. In Sam's song, the same line is "stories we tell will cast their spell", which indeed they do.

Inner Consistency

Tolkien describes inner consistency as the primary mark of a good (fairy-) story: "the achievement which gives the inner consistency of reality is indeed another thing: art, the operative link between imagination and the final result, Sub-creation" (FS 47).

By virtue of its unavoidable reliance on practically performable actions—after all performers actually need to perform everything live without the aid of cuts or trick shots—as well as the direct contact with the audience, the LotR stage show fares very well when it comes to portraying reality. The use of crutches as both a means of showing the different movement style of the Orcs as well as serving as their weapon of choice adds a layer of believability to their portrayal that makes them actually work as a race. These are not just people walking in a crooked manner, a criticism which could be levelled at the motion pictures, but have their own identity. Similarly, the use of folk instruments as well as their general portrayal as basically English country folk makes the Hobbits convincing and appealing figures without the need for extensive explanations. In essence the "Cat and the Moon" song at the beginning of the show serves as the musical's counterpart for Tolkien's "Concerning Hobbits" prologue. This is but one example where the show uses its own medium's strengths instead of blindly copying the book with a spoken prologue.

The extensive use of the large auditorium and stage of the *Theatre Royal Drury Lane*, where the show was staged in London's West End makes Middle-earth literally surround the audience, adding to the immersion into the world.

Looking back at the elements of the production mentioned in this essay, it becomes apparent that the creative team clearly endeavoured (and arguably succeeded) to not just bring the book to the stage, but rather to translate and adapt it to the new medium. By adding the musical language of the various culture, the show features a dimension only hinted at in the book and mostly passed over in the feature films. Coupled with the extensive choreography of the various cultures, the auditory and physical characteristics take centre stage in the production. In this way one can truly call this a successful sub-creation as per Tolkien's description.

Bibliography

Bratman, David. "Liquid Tolkien: Music, Tolkien, Middle-earth, and More Music".
    Middle-earth Minstrel. Ed. Bradford Lee Eden. Jefferson: McFarland & Company,
    2010, 140-170

Russell, Gary. *The Lord of the Rings: The Official Stage Companion*. London, HarperCollins,
    2007

Tolkien, John R.R. *Tree and Leaf*. London: HarperCollins, 2001

---. *The Letters of J.R.R. Tolkien: A Selection*. Ed. Humphrey Carpenter with the assistance
    of Christopher Tolkien. Boston: Houghton Mifflin, 1981

Zusammenfassungen der englischen Essays

Hermeneutische Perspektiven auf Tolkiens rhetorische Kunstfertigkeit

Annie Birks

Tolkiens Liebe zu Wörtern und Sprachen schlägt sich in vielen Facetten seines Werkes nieder und konstituiert eine (von ihm selbst zugegebene) der wichtigsten Motivationskräfte hinter der Entfaltung seines Legendariums. Indem er seine eigenen linguistischen Zutaten in den Kessel gab (erfundene Sprachen, Onomastie, rhetorische Mittel...), schmorte Tolkien, wie viele übereinstimmen, ein höchst kräftiges Werk der Imagination, dessen Wirkung offenkundig nicht gebrochen ist und dessen Verzauberung nicht nachgelassen hat.

Dieser Beitrag hebt hervor, zu welchem Ausmaß der linguistische Horizont des Autors und die Wahrnehmung oder Empfindsamkeit des Lesers sich verbinden und mit dem Text auf hermeneutische produktive Weise in Kontakt treten können.

Das *Lord-of-the-Rings*-Musical als ein Märchen

Tobias Escher

Die Musical-Adaption des *Herrn der Ringe* durch Matthew Warchus und Shaun McKenna mit Musik von Värttinä, A.R. Rahman und Orchestrationen von Christopher Nighingale ist weitgehend unbeachtet als werkgetreu gedachte Adaption. Als eine High-Fantasy-Adaption auf der Bühne ist sie durch den Medienwechsel von Buch zu Bühne auch ein Beispiel für eine „sub-creation" im Sinne Tolkiens.

Das Selbstverständnis des Musicals als dem Geiste des Originals verpflichtet zeigt sich in der Aussage, dass „die Nummern die alten Lieder Mittelerdes seien; dass Handelnde sie singen, weil sie die alten Lieder singen". Die Musik wird hier also – thematisch zurückleitend zur „First Music" nicht als Notwendigkeit des Mediums Bühnenmusical, sondern als Folge des Inhalts gesehen. Dies findet sich ja ebenfalls in der Handlung im Buch, sogar erweitert zu nicht-musikalischen Klängen durch Orks, die Natur oder die musikalische Sprachmelodie der Ents.

Die „sub-creation" erhält im Musical eine spezielle Wichtigkeit, da die Bühnenhandlung direkt mit dem Zuschauer emotional interagieren muss und

seitens des Zuschauers eine stark imaginative Eigenleistung gefragt ist. Im Kontext der „sub-creation" ergeben sich so drei Schichten:
1. Die Buchhandlung bzw das gesamte Legendarium
2. Die Musicaladaption an sich
3. Die „Ausarbeitung" dieser Schichten durch den Zuschauer.

Hier muss sich dann die „suspension of disbelief" ergeben, um eine funktionierende Adaption darzustellen.

Tolkien selbst steht der Fantasy-Adaption auf der Bühne kritisch entgegen, doch können veränderte Produktionsweisen heute dies entkräften. Neben technischen Verbesserungen bei Bühneneffekten, Sound und Kostümen lassen sich mehrere funktionelle Arten aufzeigen, wie eine „Fairy-story" im Sinne Tolkiens auf der Bühne wirken kann:
1. Charakterisierung durch Vergleich, in welcher Elemente der Primären Welt der Handlung als Basis gestellt werden.
2. Wörtliche Nutzung von Original-Elementen.
3. Glaube durch realistische Darstellung, in der auf innerweltliche Konsistenz geachtet wird.
4. Emotionale Bindung, durch die der Zuschauer persönlich involviert wird.

Schwellen und Aufbrüche: Narrative Funktionen für Nicht-Westron-Sprachen in Tolkiens *The Lord of the Rings*

Jonathan Nauman

In seinem Essay "English and Welsh" bekräftigt J.R.R. Tolkien, dass sein Legendarium und die damit verbundene Fiktion von seiner Ästhetik der Sprache inspiriert wurde. Tolkien's Leser_innen charakterisieren diese Inspiration in der Regel in einer Weise, die vor allem auf das *Silmarillion* zutrifft: intensive ästhetische Antworten auf bestimmte historische und moderne Sprachen ermöglichten Tolkiens lebenslangen Enthusiasmus, Privatsprachen zu erfinden, die ihrerseits mythologische Narrative generierten.

Aber Tolkiens linguistische Prioritäten erweisen sich aus einem anderen Blickwinkel heraus auch als wirksam in der Entwicklung des *Lord of the Rings* als Fortsetzung des *Hobbit*. Linguistische Einfügungen innerhalb der Geschichte, beginnend mit der Begegnung der Hobbits mit den Hochelben im Auenland, verbinden das neue Narrativ stärker mit dem weiteren Legendarium und transformieren somit sowohl die Charaktere als auch das Genre der Fortsetzung.

Hinter den Namen von Torhthelm und Tídwald: Tolkiens Onomastische Vorstellungskraft in »The Homecoming of Beorhtnoth Beorhthelm's Son«

Łukasz Neubauer

Ob es Anthropo- oder Toponyme sind, Namen scheinen immer eine signifikante, zuweilen sogar formative Rolle in Tolkiens Werken zu spielen. In der Tat scheint es so, als böten sie dem Autor des *Lord of the Rings* regelmäßig einen Ausgangspunkt, um Fantasy zu verfassen. Manchmal jedoch war es das spezifische Thema – moralisch, ethisch oder ähnlich –, das Tolkien zu einem Namen veranlasste, der die onomastische Lücke füllt. In diesen Fällen nutzte der Oxforder Professor entweder einen Namen, der schon in mittelalterlichen oder anderen literarischen Quellen existierte (z.B. Gandalf) oder erfand einen eigenen, oft, indem er das Vokabular von meist (aber nicht ausschließlich) Alt- oder Mittelenglisch ausnutzte.

Es ist überflüssig zu betonen, dass sich in beiden Fällen die Namen gewöhnlich als hoch informativ über den Hintergrund und die Persönlichkeit der Charaktere erweisen.

Einige der besten Beispiele dieser Benennungsstrategien können in dem Werk gefunden werden, das vielleicht am wenigsten charakteristisch für Tolkien ist, nämlich der dramatische Dialog in alliterativen Versen, der seine zwei kurzen Essays begleitete, die kollektiv mit dem Titel »The Homecoming of Beorhtnoth Beorhthelm's Son« versehen wurden. Die beiden fiktionalen Charaktere, die kommen, um den Körper ihres gefallenen Anführers nach der Schlacht von Maldon zu holen, tragen die Namen Torhthelm (Totta) und Tídwald (Tída), beide offenkundig angelsächsischer Herkunft (wie es zu Engländern aus dem späten zehnten Jahrhundert passt).

Bislang haben die meisten Forscher lediglich versucht, kurze Überblicke über den tatsächlichen Sinn und/oder die Bedeutung der Namen zu geben. Dieser Beitrag versucht jedoch, den höchstwahrscheinlichen Sinn dieser Anthroponyme im Kontext von Tolkien's Untersuchung des »nördlichen heroischen Geistes« zu analysieren.

Eine Untersuchung über Tolkiens linguistisches *World-building*

Patrick Schmitz & David A. Graziano

Der vorliegende Aufsatz behandelt zwei Schwerpunkte. Zunächst wird die Theorie des *World-Building* vorgestellt und in den literaturwissenschaftlichen Kontext der Fantasyliteratur gerückt, denn es handelt sich bei der *World-Building Theory* in erster Linie um ein intermediales Feld, anwendbar auf Literatur, Film und weitere Medienformen. Durch eine Eingrenzung auf fiktionale Literatur des Genres Fantasy wird dabei insbesondere die Möglichkeit hervorgehoben, dass durch Analyse des *World-Building* einzelne Werke hinsichtlich des zugrundeliegenden Diskurses [zwischen der realen Welt und der vom Autor »erbauten« fiktionalen Welt] untersucht werden. Einerseits werden nach Meinung der bein Autoren dadurch viele Argumente von Kritikern obsolet, die die Fantasyliteratur als diskurslos darstellen wollen; andererseits legt die *World-Building Theory* den Grundstein zur Entwicklung einer Methodologie, die unabhängig vom jeweiligen Werk Anwendung finden kann und als »Messinstrument« zum Gegenüberstellen der fiktionalen und der realen Welt dienen kann.

Diese Ergebnisse können in Form von Korpora mit den jeweiligen Lesern der Werke in Relation gesetzt werden und lassen letztendlich Schlussfolgerungen und Interpretationen über Realweltliches zu. Sie ermöglichen dadurch einen literarischen Diskurs. Mit Blick auf die Leser-Werk-Relation, welche im Sinne Tolkiens Hypothesen über *sub-creation* eine wesentliche Rolle spielt, schlägt der Aufsatz eine begründete Weiterentwicklung des Ansatzes vor.

In einem weiteren Schwerpunkt wird ein beispielhafter Korpus, welcher linguistische Elemente ausgewählter Werke im Fokus hat, erarbeitet und analysiert. Hierbei findet die von Mark J.P. Wolf vorgestellte Kategorisierung von Elementen einer »erbauten Welt« Anwendung. Gleichzeitig werden begründete Vorschläge zur Präzisierung und Ökonomisierung der literaturwissenschaftlichen Methodologie angewandt. Die dabei präsentierten Ergebnisse aus Phonologie, Graphemik und Morphologie stützen beispielhaft die theoretischen Ansätze des vorliegenden Aufsatzes. Ferner stellen sie eine unmittelbare und empirische Anwendung der *World-Building Theory* dar und dienen der Exemplifizierung der Praktikabilität dieser Theorie.

Tolkiens Philosophie der Sprache

Ross Smith

Dieser Beitrag analysiert bestimmte Theorien, die zusammen als Tolkiens umfassende Sprachphilosophie betrachtet werden können, insbesondere die Überlegungen, wonach Wörter zentral für unseren Gemeinschaftssinn sind und der Laut des Wortes zentral für die Bedeutung ist. Das erste dieser Konzepte ist mit Tolkiens Konzept der »nativen Sprache« verbunden. Tolkiens Idee einer nativen Sprache stimmt nicht mit dem überein, was gewöhnlich darunter verstanden wird: Er bezieht sich nicht auf die Sprache, die Menschen als Kinder lernen, sondern eher auf eine individuelle, ererbte linguistische Identität. Die Idee einer nativen Sprache reflektiert Tolkiens Überzeugung, dass ein Volk, seine Sprache, sein Land und seine Mythologie ein Gesamt bilden, das auf eine weit zurückliegende Vergangenheit zurückgeht und in der Lage ist, unsere Gefühle zu wecken, ohne dass wir genau wissen, warum. Er hoffte, diese entfernten Resonanzen würden von den Lesern seiner Fiktion verspürt, und er nahm Passagen in Sprachen auf, die mutmaßlich keiner seiner Leser verstehen konnte, aber von denen er hoffte, sie seien ihnen auf einer tieferen Ebene als derjenigen gewöhnlicher linguistischer Bedeutung verständlich. In diesem Beitrag wird dargelegt, dass Tolkiens Theorie zu einem gewissen Maß aus seiner eigenen außergewöhnlichen Empfindsamkeit für die Klänge der Sprache folgt sowie aus seiner tiefen emotionalen Verbundenheit zu einer bestimmten geographischen Gegend Englands, die durch die Umstände seiner Kindheit betont wurde.

Das andere hier diskutierte wesentliche Konzept von Tolkiens Sprachphilosophie ist der phonetische Symbolismus. Für Tolkien war phonetischer Symbolismus nicht nur eine Theorie, sondern eine absolute Realität. Die Beziehung zwischen Bedeutung und Laut war die Grundlage seiner erfundenen Sprachen und ein wesentlicher Teil seiner linguistischen Überzeugungen.

Tolkiens Ideen über phonetischen Symbolismus waren zu seiner Zeit unorthodox und seine Ungewissheit hinsichtlich dieses Themas aus einem streng analytischen Blickwinkel kann seinen Schriften der 1930er und 1940er deutlich entnommen werden. Es wird dennoch argumentiert, dass im Verlauf des 20. Jahrhunderts der Schwerpunkt der Argumentation sich von einer völligen Zurückweisung jeglicher Beziehung zwischen Laut und Bedeutung zu einer Akzeptanz verschoben hat, wonach zumindest in bestimmten Fällen Wortform und Bedeutung wechselwirken. Die aktuelle Forschung auf diesem Gebiet wird zitiert und an Beispielen wird gezeigt, wie Tolkien seine phonosemantischen Theorien in seine Fiktion inkorporiert hat.

Vermittlung von Namen in *Der Herr der Ringe*

Allan Turner

Namen spielen eine wichtige Rolle bei der Ausarbeitung einer glaubhaften Sekundärwelt. Darum ist es notwendig, dass sie eine Form annehmen, die von einem breiten Publikum akzeptiert wird. In *Der Herr der Ringe* besteht ein klarer Unterschied zwischen den scheinbar bekannten Orts- und Personennamen aus dem Auenland und den exotischen, die die verschiedenen Kulturen der Elben und Orks sowie der Menschen von Rohan und Gondor auszeichnen.

Es besteht jedoch die Gefahr, dass zu viele Namen in einer fremden phonologischen Form den Leser überfordern und den Bann der Sekundärwelt zerfließen lassen. Deshalb verwendet Tolkien zwei Strategien, um neue Namen wirkungsvoll zu vermitteln.

Zum einen lässt er sie im Dialog durch eine Respektsperson wie Gandalf oder Aragorn vorstellen, z.B. in Aragorns Erzählung von Beren und Lúthien unter der Wetterspitze. Zum anderen lässt er sie als Zeichen einer polyglotten Welt erscheinen, so dass z.B. elbische Namen auch auf Englisch (= Gemeinsame Sprache) glossiert werden, was zu einer besseren Verständlichkeit und deshalb größeren Akzeptanz führt. In einem solchen Fall kann die Wahl der Sprache auch zur Charakterisierung beitragen. Die Glossen sind jedoch nicht immer offen zu erkennen; in manchen Beispielen wird die Bedeutung nur indirekt durch den unmittelbaren sprachlichen Kontext ausgedrückt. Schließlich gibt es einige Situationen, in denen die Bedeutung eines Namens absichtlich undurchsichtig bleibt, entweder um eine besondere Stimmung oder Wirkung mittels ungewohnter Klangmuster zu erwecken, oder um die Spannung zu erhöhen, wie im Fall vom nur scheinbar erklärten Cirith Ungol.

Summaries of the German Essays

Language and Worldview
Thomas Fornet-Ponse

This article gives an overview of the relationship between language and worldview in Tolkien's world. It begins with an introduction of the main characteristics of the linguistic relativism that proposes a connection or correspondence of language and thought, worldview or living environment and the Sapir-Whorf-hypothesis of linguistic relativity with its principles of languages relating differently to extralinguistic reality and linguistic determinism. Then it goes on to discuss some examples for the philosophical relevance of linguistic idiosyncrasies, like the challenge on Cartesian thought by African thought and its stress on collective and relational aspects or the interpretation of the *status constructus* by Xavier Zubiri.

Against this backdrop, the connection between language and worldview in Tolkien's invented languages is analysed by first mentioning the basis in Tolkien's linguistic philosophy and then discussing the different languages and their peculiarities. Although the extent to which the languages are fleshed out is very divergent, and the methodological limitations have to be regarded, it is possible to point out the many indications for a close connection between language and worldview in Tolkien's work, e.g. a structural and phonetic Indo-European character of the Elvish languages or a more Semitic note in Dwarvish or 'Mannish', the enormous phonological differences between Quenya and Black Speech etc. In particular, the phonological differences resound with central characteristics of the different peoples.

An Analysis of Tolkien's Semiotics
Wilhelm Kuehs

In Tolkiens so called "linguistic heresy" we find a very important instrument for the creation of mythology out of language. While searching for a semiotic foundation of Tolkiens idea of linguistic fitness we came across a pattern that could be used as matrix of artificial language as well as artificial mythology. So we can describe a secondary semiological system quite similar to the system of myths discovered by Roland Barthes that underlies Tolkien's lengendarium.

The semiotic inquiry starts with a comparison between Tolkien's theory of sign and Hjelmselv's structuralistic approach. Structuralism banished the idea of phonosematics, and so there seems to be no chance of agreement between these positions. But when we search deeper we see that Tolkien used the connection of phonological structure and meaning in a new and creative way. So he could not only create new languages but also new mythologies.

The semiotic analysis of Tolkien's technique provides us with an instrument to explore the deep structure of a text, so that we can explore the mechanism of creative mythology in a new and systematic way.

Function and Meaning of Names in Tolkien's Work

Helmut W. Pesch

Before *The Lord of the Rings*, names in fantasy fiction were mostly based on real-world names by connotation and association, a strategy still valid today. J.R.R. Tolkien bestowed not just one name upon characters and things he loved, but several, creating a systematic nomenclature by drawing on elements from his invented languages. Linguistic references to existing words are conspicuously absent, even in his early Elvish wordlists.

Two major exceptions are the names of Earendil and Turambar. The former is based on a line from an Anglo-Saxon poem but reinterpreted by Tolkien in several stages to comply with his own linguistic system, the latter a loan translation from a now obsolete interpretation of the name of Sigurðr, as 'master of fate', implying a certain dramatic irony since the actual, self-styled "Master of the fates of Arda" is Morgoth, Túrin's adversary.

For the High Elves, Tolkien devised a tripartite scheme of names reminiscent of the naming system of ancient Roman nobility, some given at birth, some self-imparted, some attributed at a later date. The increasing complexity and opacity of names in history reflects a fragmentation of an "ancient semantic unity" (in Owen Barfield's words) of form and content.

Still, all the names are to some extent true, displaying characteristic features of their owners. This even applies to the programmatic names of rulers, such as the Kings of Númenor, whose names show their shifting attitudes towards the Lords of the West. There is a thin line between telling and prophetic names since every name, in a way, tells the story of the person or the thing it belongs to.

Naming, in this sense, is but an extension of Tolkien's own scholarly work, where according to the strict rules of philology there is no name without a referent and a history behind it.

„Native Language"
and what Science thinks about it

Friedhelm Schneidewind

During Tolkien's lifetime, the idea of a shared "native language", i.e. an inherited language based on race and ethnic group, was common in linguistics, anthropology and other disciplines. Tolkien shared this idea at least temporarily.

After explaining the concept of "native language" this paper discusses two contemporary theories of language acquisition: first of all the nativist idea represented by Noam Chomsky, Steven Pinker and others based on the assumption that general structural aspects of language are native to human beings. A second theory called Genetic Epistemology is based on concepts of Jean Piaget and Conrad Hal Waddington and claims that language is the result of dynamic interaction between genetically encoded information, neuronal variations and social environment.

Both theories concur that the search for a "native language" has failed. Even Chomsky's theory of a universal grammar—which at first appearance seems to explain the concept of "native language"—does in fact not support this older idea. Tolkien's concept of a "native language" is therefore not compatible with contemporary linguistic state of knowledge.

Reviews/Rezensionen

Tolkien Studies: An Annual Scholarly Review, Vol. XII

Morgantown: West Virginia Univ. Press, 2015, 268 pp.

The delivery of the most recent issue of *Tolkien Studies* was delayed—in my case so much that my review did not make the deadline for the 12th issue of *Hither Shore*. Let's hope that this was a one-time occurrence and that they will be back on track again for volume XIII. Before turning to the content, a word or two about the 'new appearance'. *Tolkien Studies* is no longer a hardcover publication and West Virginia University Press has switched to a softcover and print-on-demand option. The latter poses no problem since the quality of print-on-demand products has increased significantly over the years and, to the untrained eye, there is little difference to a traditionally printed book. The change to softcover, however, is more noticeable. The layouters did their best, but volume XII looks rather undernourished next to the eleven hardcover volumes of the preceding issues. And the price has not gone down, which makes it a rather expensive publication to buy! I am not going to speculate about who is profiting from these changes—certainly not the editors and contributors, since they don't get any remuneration for their work.

But let us proceed to explore the contents. Three out of the six research papers that constitute the bulk of the volume belong to the category 'sources and analogues'. Kris Swank provides a thorough, systematic, and knowledgeable discussion of the *immrama* (Irish Otherworld voyage) elements in *Roverandom*. We know from other publications (most obviously the poem 'Imram') that Tolkien was familiar with the *immrama* tradition, but the extent to which it constitutes the structural basis for *Roverandom* has not been recognised until Swank's analysis. In addition, Swank's study provides further evidence for Tolkien's 'Celtic connection'.

The second paper in this group is by the historian and King Alfred specialist Alban Gautier, who investigates the possible parallels between the figure of King Alfred the Great and Aragorn. His discussion is characterised by great circumspection and he is aware of the potential pitfalls of such a comparison. Gautier thus distinguishes clearly between the 'historical' Alfred as we know him today, the Alfred as presented in popular historical fiction at the beginning of the 20th century, and also the Alfred in the biographies written by scholars up to the 1950s. He thus re-creates the matrix that could have influenced Tolkien's creation of Aragorn. The final result of Gautier's investigation would be disappointing if the reader had expected many clear and obvious parallels between Alfred and Aragorn: there are none with the exception of Alfred's campaign against and victory over the Vikings in 878. The value of the paper lies therefore more in the informative and knowledgeable discussion of the possible sources and analogues, and the scrupulous scholarly weighing and ultimate rejection of much of the evidence, which thus provide a model of how to conduct similar scholarly investigations. The fact that Gautier overlooked the obvious parallel in the deaths of the two monarchs—both died peacefully and were succeeded by their sons (which is, as Janet Brennan Croft correctly observed, "a notable accomplishment in his [i.e. Alfred's] warlike time" (*Mythlore* 128/34.2, Spring/Summer 2016, p. 203)—could be read positively as an indication of his deep-seated reluctance to see parallels that are not structurally grounded.

The third contribution in this category is by Simon J. Cook, though his line of argument differs from the traditional 'sources and analogues' pattern. Cook thinks that Tolkien, in his treatment of the pairings between mortals and immortals, drew (indirect) inspiration from H.M. Chadwick's account of the motif of the goddess Nerthus's mortal consort as found in his *The Origin of the English Nation* (1907). Chadwick established a dichotomy between immortal = divine (i.e. the goddess Nerthus) vs. mortal = human (her consort). Tolkien, by contrast, changed this by introducing the immortal but non-divine Elves. He thus altered and adapted Chadwick's view on the nature of the goddess's consort, yet retained the older scholar's concept of an original cultural-religious heritage shared by Swedes, Danes, and English, which allowed Tolkien to connect the Norse mythology with his own legendarium. Cook's paper is an interesting contribution to the exploration of the early stages of Tolkien's legendarium, most prominently investigated in the work of John Garth, to which it is a welcome supplement.

The second group of papers comprises a close reading of the events leading up to the breaking of the Fellowship, an investigation of the Gnostic and Manichaean elements in *The Silmarillion*, and an in-depth look at the connection between Tolkien's concept of the Faerian Drama and the Middle English lay *Sir Orfeo*. The last one mentioned takes its cue from my paper in *Tolkien Studies* VII (2010) where I pointed out for the first time the striking parallels between *Sir Orfeo* and Tolkien's concept of the prototypical fairy-story. Kelley Wickham-Crowley focuses on the idea of the Faerian Drama as a phenomenon that originates "from contact between two minds and modes of perception, mortal and immortal, where humans encounter a radical change of perception that remakes the world and its reality for them" (20). Thus literature at its best can impart a belief in a world of the mind, which in turn can have an impact on the lives of the readers. It is of interest to note that the question of Faerian Drama has also been dealt with in connection with *Sir Gawain and the Green*

Knight and *Pearl* by Janet Brennan Croft in her paper 'Tolkien's Faërian Drama: Origins and Valedictions". *Mythlore* 32.2 (2014):31-45, and I'm looking forward to further explorations in this field.[1]

The thorny yet at the same time fascinating question of the relationship between good and evil in Tolkien's universe provides the starting point for Carrol Fry's contribution. The topic has been discussed frequently, not least in connection with the question of Free Will (see Shippey, Flieger, Fornet-Ponse, Dickerson, to mention only the most important scholars), so Fry's paper is not really treading on new ground. He unfortunately fails to engage with this larger discourse and limits his analysis to a detailed discussion of parallels between the Gnostic and Manichaean traditions and ideas and concepts found in the first chapters of *The Silmarillion* and claims that the 'Ainulindalë' provides the framework for "monist and dualist interpretations of evil" (80). Fry's readings and examples can indeed be interpreted as possible evidence for a Gnostic or Manichaean view of good and evil, yet he overlooks the fact that most of these positions overlap with the orthodox view, so that my conclusion from the evidence presented in this paper would be (similar to Tom Shippey's argument in *Author of the Century*) that Tolkien was aware of and alluded to the dualistic view, but would and could do so from an undoubtedly orthodox standpoint.

The last paper by Sherrylyn Branchaw is based on a close reading of the events leading up to the breaking of the Fellowship on Amon Hen. Branchaw argues that it is not Boromir's fault that the eight companions split up and continue on two separate trajectories. I found her argument persuasive, yet was wondering why Tolkien would present events in such a way that so far all readers and critics "are agreed... that Boromir is responsible for the breaking of the Fellowship" (123). Branchaw is aware that her "conclusion may be counterintuitive" (138) and I for one would now like to find out why Tolkien left it thus.

The 'Notes and Documents' section contains a reprint of Tolkien's obituary of Henry Bradley, editor of the OED, with valuable commentaries by Tom Shippey and Peter Gilliver. This is followed by the extensive review section and the 'Year's Work in *Tolkien Studies* 2012'. Among the reviews I would like to draw special attention to Michael Drout's piece on Tolkien's *Beowulf* translation. With more than twenty pages it is more of a scholarly essay than a review and an illuminating discussion of Tolkien's engagement with the Old English epic.

All in all the twelfth issue of *Tolkien Studies* in its new outfit did not disappoint: it provides a selection of informative and well-researched papers on a variety of themes.

Thomas Honegger

---

1   Allan Turner suggests that future research may also include the tradition of Thomas the Rhymer and works such as 'La belle dame sans merci'.

Janet Brennan Croft (Ed.)
Baptism of Fire: The Birth of the Modern British Fantastic in World War I.

Altadena, CA: Mythopoeic Press, 2015, 326 pp.

This is a major collection of 17 articles edited by Janet Brennan Croft, herself the author of a monograph on war and the works of Tolkien. All the contributions build on the thesis first proposed by Tom Shippey in his *Author of the Century* that fantasy, far from being a mere escape from the crises of the 20th century, and in particular the two world wars, is actually a very pertinent reaction to those catastrophes, often experienced at first hand by the authors. It is not so much a retreat from modernism as an alternative response to the forces in society that produced the hitherto more (or indeed exclusively) critically acclaimed movement. The influence of the war on Tolkien has been explored in some detail, notably by John Garth. However, the interest of this volume is that although the longer first section deals with the Inkings, including Lewis and Barfield, there is also a second section that brings in G.K. Chesterton, Lord Dunsany, Sylvia Townsend Warner, E.R. Eddison and T.H. White, as well as a more general contribution on post-war alternate history.

One danger of looking for the influence of a major historical event like the Great War is the temptation to apply the principle *post hoc ergo propter hoc*: anyone writing about the topic of a widespread phenomenon like war after 1918 is assumed to have been influenced, however unconsciously, by that particular war, and by extension must be demonstrating a response to it. This is an outlook that one or two writers in the present collection exploit.

Another danger, which is understandable in the interests of keeping the articles reasonably short, is to over-simplify the contrast between before the war (comfortable consensus of tradition) and after the war (disorientation, disillusionment, modernism), forgetting the iconoclastic influence of cultural movements such as cubism, futurism and vorticism in the years before 1914. Considering popular perceptions, when I was growing up, nearly everybody's father had fought in World War II and many of the grandfathers had fought in World War I, and had their stories to tell. Needless to say, these were the lucky survivors who might have been deployed far from the front, but at least this was a reminder that the war had not traumatised everyone and changed their outlooks. Cultural historians nowadays necessarily gain their knowledge from written sources, of which there are plenty available, although it was striking here just how many of the authors based their characterisation of post-war changes on selective quotations from Paul Fussell. Fussell's main aim was of course to show the mediated nature of people's perceptions of the war, both at the time and later. It is ironical that his book is now one of the major channels of mediation.

That said, by and large these articles are perceptive and thought-provoking. Because of the sheer number of them it is possible to devote only a short paragraph to each contribution, although several of them would repay a much closer analysis.

Michael Livingston reviews what is known about Tolkien's experiences on the Somme and concludes that his portrayal of Frodo's condition after the destruction of the Ring corresponds closely to the symptoms of Post-Traumatic Stress Disorder, known at the time as shell-shock.

S. Brett Carter focuses on Faramir as a new kind of hero for the post-World War I age. Like the soldier poets he is well-read, and he thinks deeply about his responsibility as a leader of men. His covert operation in camouflage is one that would have been unlikely before the advent of trench warfare, when front-al clashes were doomed to failure. Unfortunately Carter's depiction of the classical hero-type like Aragorn that he opposes him to is too generic to be convincing. He makes a valid point, but its effectiveness is weakened by the rather undifferentiated presentation.

Margaret Sinex gives a clear and concise presentation of characters in the Túrin story who reflect men so mentally and physically damaged in war that they cannot function normally. Of these, Túrin is "shell-shocked" by his accidental killing of Beleg. The other three are physically mutilated, and therefore perceived by their society as something less than full adult males, as was the fate of so many young men of Tolkien's generation: Sador/Labadal, Flinding/Gwindor, and Tamar Lamefoot/Brandir, although in fact two of these receive their disabilities not as a direct result of fighting. Additionally, Gwindor and Brandir both lose the woman they love to the at least physically undamaged male, Túrin.

E.J. Christie's article ranges from the British Official Secrets Act via psychological theories about the individuation of the subject and Tolkien's dislike of the machine to Old English gnomic literature in order to present Sméagol and Déagol as symbols of the complementary, partly interpenetrating ideas of secrecy and discovery. The fact that so much ground is covered, mostly in an abstract and allusive manner to fit it all into the space available, while the actual First World War is mentioned only obliquely, could easily leave the reader with an impression of smoke and mirrors. This would be unfortunate, since it contains a great deal of erudition which deserves a more leisurely exposition.

Nora Alfaiz, whose article mentions the real war even less than the previous one, deals with the topic of how events pass into popular memory and become history, which was undoubtedly important to Tolkien as a reader of historical texts. However, her arguments are less than convincing because she starts with theories about the manipulation of memory in the modern nation state and attempts to force the completely different world of Tolkien into this mould. Thorin and his companions can hardly be seen as a nation; the dwarves are undoubtedly aware of their identity as a race, but they function more as a clan or extended family. Their song at Bag End is certainly evocative, but it is not "history" because a number of those singing it were present at the events it describes. Similarly, the fact that no-one in Gondor knows that Isildur wrongly kept the Ring is unlikely to be deliberate suppression of a guilty national secret; few people knew in the first place, and none of his companions survived to tell how it betrayed him at the Gladden Fields. In any case, three thousand years have passed since then, so to make a connection with the Gondor of Denethor would be like attributing the problems of the modern Greek state to mistakes made at the siege of Troy!

Peter Grybauskas takes real-world theories about the way in which wars enter the cultural memory and applies them with a fascinating new twist to the representation of the defeat of Sauron at the end of the Second Age. He traces the contexts in which different characters refer to that war, suggesting that Gollum, who seems to be familiar with the story and recounts parts of it to Frodo and Sam, might even identify himself with the hero Isildur as he bites off Frodo's finger with the Ring, just as Isildur cut off Sauron's finger.

Shandi Stevenson attempts to identify why Tolkien and Lewis were not affected by the reaction against the traditional certainties experienced by so many of their generation, which led directly to the existential doubt of modernism. She sees the reason in their Christian belief in divine providence, which allows them to hope for a final positive resolution of the events in history, even if the outcome cannot be seen by the characters caught up in them. In this way they were able to steer a middle path between the rationalistic over-optimism of the pre-war years on the one hand and the nihilistic tendencies of some of their contemporaries on the other. It is perhaps not a completely new insight, but she states the case clearly and concisely, albeit at the expense of a certain over-simplification, particularly when she sees the whole period from the Enlightenment to 1914 as permeated by uninterrupted belief in progress.

Andrew Krokstrom's article is of a piece with other articles in this collection which deal with post-traumatic stress disorder. He sets out to demonstrate that Lewis was a great deal more troubled by his wartime experiences than he would usually admit, and concludes that, like many of his contemporaries, he was silenced by the general opinion in society that any reference to one's hardship and suffering was an unacceptable proof of weakness. (Is the spelling "Maudlin College" in the footnote to page 133 really just an unconscious typo?)

Brian Melton covers a lot of the same ground, collating Lewis's few references to his war experiences, but starts from a different premiss: since Lewis seems to have had the ability to separate his objective observations from his feelings, in the absence of further evidence it would be unwarranted to assume that he must have suffered from some trauma. Therefore he concentrates on an analysis of the descriptions of battle in the Narnia stories, concluding that the gritty accounts of pain and wounds are derived from realistic memories of what he saw in the trenches, but the absence of dead bodies is a reflection of his own abhorrence of corpses.

The article on Owen Barfield's early fiction by Tiffany Brooke Martin demonstrates his sympathy for the plight of the traumatised ex-soldier, even though he joined up too late in the war to see any action himself. Starting from short stories using techniques typical of the early modernism of the immediate post-war period, he turned to fantasy with the fairy tale *The Silver Trumpet* published in 1925. Martin gives a fairly detailed summary interspersed with interpretation, which is unfortunately not altogether clear for anyone who has not read it.

The second half of the volume begins with an examination by Nick Milne of alternat(iv)e[1] histories in the aftermath of the war. Several works in more recent times have explored the possibilities of how the world might have been different if the series of events leading up to the outbreak of war had not happened, since this is what exercises the minds of people today far more than the actual conduct of the war. However, the most significant alternate history to appear within a dozen years of 1918, *The Cavalry Went Through* by Bernard Newman, involved a radically different approach to strategy and tactics. Ironically it was used for training purposes by the German army but ignored in Britain.

Philip Irving Mitchell's contribution on a little-known piece of blatant war propaganda masquerading as history by Chesterton, *The Crimes of England*, is ambitious but not always easy to follow. In a volume of this kind, anyone writing on Tolkien or Lewis can assume that readers have a considerable amount of background knowledge. Not so with Chesterton. Mitchell struggles to explain the contents of the book and its relationship to Chesterton's thoughts about fantasy, but even then the reader is left with a feeling of lacking context. As a result, the professed topic, the symbolism of desire, to be examined in a theoretical framework provided by Paul Ricoeur, receives short measure as the article falls between an analysis of the text and a psychoanalysis of the author. Perhaps the topic calls for a lengthier treatment, since I would like to understand how an author so admired by Tolkien and Lewis could have produced something which, based on the lengthy extracts, appears to be a luridly rhetorical concoction of cultural prejudices, traditional heroic ideals and religion which would not appear out of place in the mouth of an IS terrorist.

---

1   AmE alternate, BrE alternative (in this meaning), although the economic dominance of
     the USA means that the American form is found increasingly in British publications.

David J. Carlson presents Lord Dunsany's *Don Rodriguez*, published in 1922, as an attempt to reclaim ground for heroic fantasy after the disillusionment of the war. Its mixture of high chivalry well leavened with irony, together with the designation as "magic history" is intended to break down resistance to what could have been seen as an outdated genre. The assumption is *post hoc ergo propter hoc*, since no actual evidence is produced to suggest what Dunsany had in mind, or to show that his ploy was motivated specifically by the war rather than general expectations of scepticism, but the concept is at least plausible.

Sylvia Townsend Warner's two fantasy novels, *Lolly Willowes* and *Kingdoms of Elfin*, from the beginning and end of her writing career respectively, are analysed by Meyrav Koren-Kuik as parables showing the author's perception of how gender roles had changed as a result of the war. Her first novel is particularly striking; the protagonist is a middle-aged spinster whose old self seems to die just as the armistice is declared, and she is re-born as a witch who is able to shake off her previous dependency on her brother and establish her own independence.

It is gratifying to see two articles on E.R. Eddison, one by Jon Garrad and the other by Joe Young, since this author has been largely ignored by serious criticism up to now. Both of them try to defend Eddison against charges by Tolkien and de Camp that his novels portray vainglory and contempt for human life. For Young, this is the main point of his argument. The evidence he presents for *The Worm Ouroboros* is pretty tenuous, but he manages to demonstrate convincingly that *A Fish Dinner in Memison*, written a good 15 years later round about the start of World War II, presents a sharp critique of war and aggression which gains poignancy from the device of making Lessingham, the character who articulates it, both an insider and an outsider, since he lives on earth and has experienced historical 20th century conflicts, but he actually comes from the more culturally advanced Zimiamvia. Garrad uses most of his article in an attempt to show that although Eddison is not a modernist, he has features in common with the modernists. Unfortunately his analysis seldom dips far below the surface; since archaising language alone hardly meets the criterion of difficulty, he is left saying simply that both Eddison and the modernists had to find an adequate response to the Great War, and his was different from theirs.

The final item in the collection, by Ashley Pfeiffer, traces the anti-war message in T.H. White's five novel Arthurian series *The Once and Future King*. Probably on the assumption that this work is not widely known, Pfeiffer limits herself to the format of plot summary plus commentary, which gives the necessary information but does not allow her to argue a more searching thesis.

Allan Turner

Janet Brennan Croft & Leslie A. Donovan (Eds.):
Perilous and Fair: Women in the Works and Life of J.R.R. Tolkien.
Altadena: Mythopoeic Press, 2015, 349 pp.

Brennan Croft and Donovan bring together 14 articles, including seven classics and seven new ones, on women in the works and life of J.R.R. Tolkien. The book is divided into five sections: Historical Perspectives, Power of Gender, Specific Characters, Earlier Literary Contexts, Women Readers. The introduction gives an overview of criticism on Tolkien's female characters, from the 'classic' view that they are either absent or set on a pedestal to newer criticism that has a more nuanced approach: for example recognising that his women are very powerful—in fact more so than in many more recent fantasy novels.

Starting off the Historical Perspectives, Robin Anne Reid has collected an anthology of scholarship on the subject from the 1970s to today. She does not shy away from moving beyond peer-reviewed journals to fanzines—which however only consist of *Mallorn* and *Mythlore*. The only non-Anglo-Saxon perspectives that make the cut are those published (in English) by *Walking Tree Publishers*, based in Zurich. She includes works with both a positive and negative outlook on Tolkien's use of female characters, which makes the article one of the more balanced one in the collection in that regard.

John D. Rateliff then gives a fascinating overview of women in academia in Tolkien's life. He notes that while many Oxford dons were dismissive of women at the university, Tolkien tutored many and became affiliated with women's colleges. In the otherwise informative article, his observations on Helen Gardner and C.S. Lewis seem a bit long-winded for their relevance to the topic. The comments and question raised on Éowyn by Rateliff's wife in the envoy perfectly capture the essence of the issue.

Sharin Schroeder takes a look at the initial reception of *The Lord of the Rings*, which saw the work in the tradition of Victorian books for boys. She points out the parallels between Galadriel and Henri Rider Haggard's *She*—which Tolkien named as an influence. While Haggard said he wrote specifically for boys, Schroeder writes that Tolkien never made that restriction—though at least *The Hobbit* started as a story written for very specific boys: his own sons!

In the Power of Gender section, Melanie Rawls points out that feminine and masculine principles need to be in balance to keep the world in order in

Tolkien's work. While setting aside characters' gender in her analysis was probably highly innovative in the 1980s when the article was written, it now seems dated (e.g. the list of concepts and adjectives connected to a specific gender) as more recent feminism has been striving to transcend such rigid gender concepts. That does, of course, not detract from the validity of the analysis as the historical context is relevant to Tolkien's time. While she gives some very good examples, e.g. Faramir as a well-balanced character due to his mother's influence in his upbringing, or the failure of whole races due to a lack of the feminine principle (orcs, ents, dwarves), she sometimes ignores those examples that would contradict her thesis. Thus she omits all the great male singers to make a point on 'female' creativity.

Nancy Enright picks up a similar thread, noting that the typically masculine hero does usually not fare very well in Tolkien's world. She explores the religious depths and the spiritual power of his female characters, also using historical gender stereotypes and linking them to religious themes (e.g. Marian submission).

Edith Crowe notes that Tolkien certainly was no feminist but that he covers a lot of themes that are central to feminism: the main one being power, and how it is distributed and used. She points out his strong female characters, chiefly among the Valar and elves, and describes the 'higher cultures' as fairly gender-balanced. She identifies Lúthien's story, for example, as a feminist retelling of Rapunzel.

The articles in the next section focus on specific female characters. Romuald Lakowski traces the development of Galadriel's role, especially concerning her involvement in the Kinslaying at Alqualondë, within the textual history of Tolkien's legendarium. That role ranges from taking an active part in the atrocities to not being involved at all, as Tolkien kept returning to the character and her motivation until shortly before his death. Cami Agan identifies Lúthien as a highly-powerful female character at the heart of *The Silmarillion*, and as a character with a healthy relationship to her body and sexuality at that. Kristine Larsen takes a close look at Nienna, compiling a textual history and tracing her character development from *The Lost Tales* to Tolkien's later writings. With pity and mercy as central themes in the legendarium, her role as its god-like embodiment in later versions are revealing another integral female character, which has been overlooked in previous criticism.

Melissa Smith's examination of Éowyn as a two-fold war bride (as the one left behind by Aragorn and the one brought home by Faramir) draws fascinating parallels with the issues such brides were facing in the real world in and after World War I and II. The only difficulty with the comparison is that Éowyn's traditional role is a very different one from that of the women before and during the two World Wars.

Leslie Donovan's well-known "Valkyrie Reflex" starts with an overview of positive and negative reception of Tolkien's female characters, then goes on to analyse Galadriel, Shelob, Éowyn and Arwen against a backdrop of Germanic and Old Norse traditions. She points out, for example, that Éowyn is not left behind as a lowly female but as a leader of her people. Phoebe Linton takes a more in-depth look at Éowyn, tracing her character development from silent court lady, via acting lord and female knight to wife and healer, and explores medieval romance as a genre for her story arc. She names Sir Thomas Malory as the defining influence on Tolkien but omits intermediary William Morris, who already put strong female characters into his romances.

Maureen Thum points out that Tolkien and Shakespeare are using similar strategies to present strong female characters. She uses *Twelfth Night* as an example for a carnivalised world, in which traditional gender roles are subverted, e.g. through masquerade or men with traditionally female attributes. While Thum points out that Éowyn has a legitimate and official claim to power in contrast to Viola in *Twelfth Night*, she writes that Éowyn disguises herself as Dernhelm because a woman warrior is "unacceptable to Théoden and his advisers" (p. 299)—a statement that doesn't ring true in light of her training as a shieldmaiden. She also describes Galadriel, at first glance, as an "expected heroine of romance… confined to a garden-like realm." (p. 300) She makes her out as a court lady from medieval romances—with masked powers that are only revealed later on. This misses the clear hints, even before the adventurers meet Galadriel in Lothlórien, that she is a Fairy-Queen-like character, and thus a perilous and very powerful figure right from the beginning.

The last article in the collection looks at women's reception of Tolkien's works. Una McCormack points out women's engagement in fanfiction as a strategy to repair representational gaps in the fantasy world, and mentions several examples. She raises excellent points on world-building flaws and male transmission of (hi)story. A nuance that could have been added on reader representation is the fact that Tolkien used ordinary people (the hobbits) as a focal point of the story rather the big heroes.

Overall, Brennan Croft and Donovan's collection provides a good overview of Anglo-Saxon scholarship on women in Tolkien's work. While some articles seem a bit 'fannish'—and often apologetic of Tolkien's treatment of women in his works—all of them offer valuable insights and approaches to the topic. Adding a few international sources, and more on negative criticism as well as on women in Tolkien's life and within the context of readers' reception, would have helped to even better balance the collection.

Marie-Noëlle Biemer

Lembas Extra:
Unexplored Aspects of Tolkien and Arda.
Soest: Bookscout.nl, 2015, 298 pp.

*L*embas Extra* is the periodical research journal of Unquendor, the Dutch Tolkien Society. According to the Preface, this is the second number to be devoted to a specific topic, the first having been *Tolkien in Poetry and Song*, reviewed in *Hither Shore 7*. In terms of production the present edition shows a considerable step forward, since instead of coming in a ring binding it is a smart paperback with large, uncluttered type and on the cover a neatly reproduced drawing of a flying dragon by Cécile van Zon. However, it is less unified in theme than its predecessor, since the only ostensible link between the articles is that they are on aspects of Tolkien which have not often been considered in the past.

The big problem for publications of a society of enthusiasts is to decide on the particular readership that it is aimed at. *Hither Shore* is overtly academic in its presentation, while the journal of the British Tolkien Society, *Mallorn*, caters more for the broad non-specialist spectrum of its membership. Academics generally expect a succinct, tightly focused argument, while fans often prefer more circumstantial detail about the books they enjoy, "filled with things that they already kn[o]w, set out fair and square with no contradictions", including excessively long quotations. Some articles in this collection have fallen between the two stools, concentrating on inessential details and losing focus in the process. In such cases the editors would have been justified in making more use of the blue pencil (or whatever its electronic equivalent may be). The other way in which the book leans towards the non-specialist is its concentration on aspects of the invented world and their relation to the real world rather than specifically literary questions. In fact none of the articles could be called literary criticism in the strict sense.

Although there is no clear thread linking the articles, nevertheless certain groupings can be distinguished. Therefore I propose to treat the articles in these groupings rather than in their order within the volume.

Three of them belong to the category of establishing connections between the Secondary World and modern science or scholarship. "The bill for Bill the pony" by D.J. Rout uses a knowledge of historical economics to elaborate by analogy a possible economy of the Shire. A more complex analysis is given by Jan van Breda, who works as a judge, of concepts of justice in *The Lord of the Rings* in the light of Tolkien's professed hankering after anarchy or "unconstitutional" monarchy. His argument about the rightness of Aragorn's merciful judgement of Beregond is undoubtedly correct, although to be accurate Beregond is not simply "allowed to serve in the Guard of Faramir" (165) as a concession, but is positively rewarded by being made its captain. In playing down the contrast of the two halves of the judgement in this way, van Breda (perhaps deliberately) disregards the literary effect of eucatastrophe that is achieved by it. In evaluating Tolkien's views on the status of laws within a polity he acknowledges the danger of basing too much on an opinion expressed at a particular moment and in a particular mood (and indeed all critics should be extremely careful in their use of the published letters), but does not completely avoid falling into the trap with his eyes wide open.

Kristine Larsen is already known for her articles on Tolkien and science, particularly astronomy. Here she evaluates his knowledge of contemporary research into palaeontology and the hypothetical reconstruction of fossil remains through his depiction of two prehistoric creatures, the pterodactyl-like steed of the Nazgûl and the mûmakil of Harad. She also touches on his reference to cave paintings in the Father Christmas letters and debates about human origins in the first and second typescripts of *The Hobbit*, although unfortunately she completely misses the playful pun in the "Notion Club Papers", where Frankley's book, clearly a collection of poems rather than a palaeontological textbook, is entitled *Experiments in Pterodactylics*, dactylics being a poetic metre. In a second article, Larsen explores the interface between popular science and theology. She traces the history of opinions about whether God could have created other worlds, and if so, whether Christ's coming could also have secured the salvation of extraterrestrials. Lewis confronted the question in his space trilogy, whereas Tolkien seems to have done his best to side-step it.

In another pair of articles, Antje vom Lehn deals with animals in Tolkien and Elise McKenna with plants. The first of these two relies to a large extent on a statistical listing of all the animals mentioned in *The Hobbit* and *The Lord of the Rings*, with incidental comments on the role they play either in the story or the narrative technique. For example, oliphaunts appear at the battle of the Pelennor Fields, they are dangerous in spite of the humorous poem about them, they help to spotlight the oral tradition of the Shire, and they help to broaden Sam's horizon. The writer correctly notes that crows and wolves are used to make distances more concrete, but she overlooks the fact that this is all a word-play on the idiomatic expression *as the crow flies* meaning "in a straight line", "in der Luftlinie". Similarly she forgets that the "wildgoose chase" on which Wormtongue sends the Rohirrim is not an actual hunt for birds but a phrase meaning a futile expedition. However, she suggests the possibility of more detailed research in the future.

The second article also begins with a rather encyclopedic survey of the colour green in Tolkien, but soon develops into a more detailed analysis of his feelings towards trees as reflected in the task that Yavanna gives to the Ents.

Nancy Bunting presents the evidence that both Tolkien and his brother were active members of the Boy Scouts, and suggests three possible connections between this and his later life. Firstly, *The Book of Foxrook*, containing his earliest invented alphabet or code, was elaborated from signs used by scouts. The other two connections are more speculative: the extra activity of scouting gave him the increased appetite that had to be satisfied with food provided by Edith Bratt, so introducing him to his future wife; and the character of Bard embodies the ideal scout.

In an article which complements a similar one by Michael Cunningham, Tommy Kuusela traces the growth of Tolkien's influence on "black metal" music. He comes to the conclusion that most of the initial impetus for this inter-generic impulse originated in Scandinavia.

The final contribution, "The Complexity of Tolkien's Attitude towards the Second World War" by Franco Manni and Simone Bonechi, which appears first in the book, I have left until last because it is by far the longest, the one closest to current fields of research into Tolkien as an author of his time, but also in some ways the most problematic. To do justice to all the issues raised by it would require a review of its own no shorter than that of the whole book, but obviously that is impracticable.

Their basic thesis is that in the writing of *The Lord of the Rings* Tolkien was profoundly influenced by the world crisis unfolding around him, but tried to deny it afterwards, primarily because of his mental confusion about the conflict and his own contribution to the fight between good and evil. In fact the two halves of this thesis call for completely separate arguments based on different kinds of criteria, so that two articles, each with its own focus, would have been much more effective. As it is, the contribution appears rambling and unfocused, the more so because it is written in an academic discourse more typical of the Romance languages, which accepts more circumstantial detail.

However, its chief defects are a) that the authors do not question their assumptions closely enough, and b) that many of its claims are simply not susceptible to the standards of normal academic proof. As an example of the first category, Manni and Bonechi forget that civilians' experience of the war in England was vastly different from that in Italy: no fascist government to polarise opinions, no invading army, no resistance movements, no divided loyalties. In spite of the terror of bombing, and even though the famous "Keep calm and carry on" poster was never issued, for the majority of the population there was a feeling of struggling to maintain everyday life rather than a sense of good versus evil. And in any case, the authors should have thought that Tolkien had already spent 20 years writing about the conflict between a good (though not entirely innocent) side and elemental evil.

The second defect is more serious. A substantial part of the article is based on assertion rather than proof; pages 25-33 consist entirely of long quotations presenting opinions without either commentary or any indication of why the opinions of these particular people are more valid than any others. The amateurish psychologising of Tolkien is pure speculation; but perhaps the authors recognised this and attempted to counter it by quoting a remark by Patrick Curry on "the English prejudice against psychology/psychoanalysis" (67). In short, the topic is a valuable one but it deserves a different treatment.

Regarding technical details, the book contains a large number of typographical errors, and ideally the articles would have been checked by a native speaker of English for language inaccuracies. So overall, congratulations to Unquendor for producing this mixed but never uninteresting collection, but a plea to the editors to exercise stricter control in future over both the focus of articles and the accuracy of language.

Allan Turner

J.R.R. Tolkien:
A Secret Vice: Tolkien on Invented Languages
Eds. Dimitra Fimi & Andrew Higgins
London: HarperCollins, 2016, lxv + 157 pp.

First of all, the facts about this new edition of Tolkien's article, originally a talk to a college society, which was first published in 1983 in *The Monsters and the Critics*, a collection of seven essays edited by Christopher Tolkien. The present volume consists of five main sections: an introduction running to 54 pages; the text of the article with notes by the editors; the previously unpublished, incomplete "Essay on Phonetic Symbolism" with notes; the text of notes and drafts from several manuscripts held in the Bodleian Library, Oxford, again with notes; and finally as a "coda", a short account of the reception of Tolkien's invented languages and their legacy in the works of later writers of fantasy fiction. The big question is: who was this book intended for?

The introduction and coda are undoubtedly of great interest for the general reader who has read Tolkien's novels and has discovered the fascination of the invented languages. The introduction provides a brief summary of "A Secret Vice" and attempts to place it within the context of Tolkien's professional and personal interest in language. There is a lengthy history of the development of his languages from the earliest Qenya of 1915 through to their maturity in *The Lord of the Rings*, concentrating on their relationship to his mythology rather than the linguistic details. In keeping with the current trend in Tolkien criticism, his creations are placed in the context of contemporary developments: on the one hand, the widespread interest in artificial languages such as Esperanto to facilitate international communication, and on the other the more narrowly academic attempts to establish a universal connection between the sounds of human speech and particular meanings, such as the possible relationship between the "narrow" vowel sound of /i/ and words expressing smallness, such as *little*, a phenomenon for which Tolkien used the term "sound symbolism", the subject of his fragmentary essay.

So far, so good. However, the remaining sections of the book are highly specialised. The editions of all the texts are "diplomatic"; that is, they attempt to give the impression of the documents as they exist, complete with all the crossings out, revisions, incomplete sentences and lacking punctuation. Even with the benefit of rigorous training in both general and historical linguistics, I find myself challenged to work out the big picture of Tolkien's meaning in the "Essay on Phonetic Symbolism" because it is in the form of a draft full of short, oblique references to ideas which were clearly in the front of his mind and needed no more than a brief reminder, but which have to be reconstructed by anyone else. The editors' notes give excellent information about incidental details such as contemporary references or the meaning of words not current in modern English, but there is no attempt at the broader interpretation which would be necessary to make the essay and the manuscript sheets meaningful for the non-specialist reader.

The even greater danger is that without some interpretation the real heart, in my opinion, of the new material will go unnoticed. This is Tolkien's aesthetic view that language as pure sound can be an artistic achievement on the same level as music. However, it is impossible to disconnect sound from sense in one's first language, and possible only to a limited extent in a "learned" language, that is another modern foreign language or a classical one such as Latin. The invention of a phonology can create a satisfying music, to which meaning need be added as only as far as required. This concept can lead to a new evaluation of the poems in Quenya and Sindarin included in "A Secret Vice". Unlike his contemporary poems in English, which are either narrative or else portray a specific situation or event, these have a much more tenuous connection to the details of the mythology. "Oilima Markirya", for example, consists of a series of vaguely evocative, impressionistic phrases which could be linked to Elvish ships seeking Valinor, but do not have to be. We can now be sure that this was a deliberate aesthetic effect and not the result either of uncertainty about the mythology itself or lack of skill in handling the language. It could be argued that the same allusive vagueness persists right through to the Elvish verses in *The Lord of the Rings*, and particularly Galadriel's lament.

However, if this were a purely scholarly book, more precise details about the editorial methods might have been expected. The text of "A Secret Vice" is not so different from Christopher Tolkien's version except for the inclusion of discarded words, plus a whole section on the "Fonwegian" language, but it would have been useful to have the differences highlighted, since presumably *The Monsters and the Critics* has not been superseded. There are some slight changes of detail in the Quenya poems, so readers could expect to have these pointed out and to be told if they were improved readings of the manuscripts, so as to avoid the impression that either this edition or the original one contains typographical errors.

This is not meant as criticism of the editors, who have clearly done their work with great care, but of the concept of the book, which was presumably influenced by the publishers. A large commercial publisher like HarperCollins does not launch a new Tolkien volume without an eye to sales. If the introduction and coda had been published separately under the names of its authors as a work of criticism and exegesis, this would have been a thoroughly justified addition to the secondary literature. The texts could then have appeared in the much more appropriate framework of *Parma Eldalamberon*, where they would have found their specialised readership.

But this book appears on the shelves of local bookshops in an attractive format which makes it indistinguishable from the popular stories by Tolkien which surround it, and indeed has his name in black letters two centimetres high on the dust jacket, while the names of Fimi and Higgins are relegated to the bottom half of the page, with letters a quarter of the size in light brown ink. Perhaps the publishers are even relying on the slightly risqué title to help sales—some sex in Tolkien at last! There are going to be some big surprises when well-meaning uncles and aunts buy it as a present for their Tolkien-crazy family members.

Allan Turner

Journal of Tolkien Research

Available online at:

http://scholar.valpo.edu/journaloftolkienresearch

It is unusual to find a review of a website in *Hither Shore*, since such Tolkien-related sites usually serve the interests of commercialism or fans rather than serious research. However, the *Journal of Tolkien Research* is devoted to precisely that. The best known and most highly respected scholarly journal in its field for several years now has been *Tolkien Studies*. However, even though that is now produced on a print to order basis and appears in a paperback format that contrasts poorly with its original handsome hardback presence, its price of $70 for delivery to Europe puts it outside the price range of most private individuals, while the libraries that stock it are few and far between. Therefore an internet competitor will be welcome to many people if it manages to match it in quality.

The *Journal of Tolkien Research* is an open access journal which can be read and downloaded free of charge. According to its Aims and Scope page, in addition to Tolkien's own work it will publish articles on "transformative and derivative texts", focusing on "multi- and inter-disciplinary approaches to Tolkien studies, including gaming, media and literary adaptations, fan productions, and audience reception". This distances it from *Tolkien Studies*, which so far has by and large restricted itself to a traditional literary critical approach.

It appears under the aegis of Valparaiso University, Indiana, and its editor is Bradford Lee Eden, who is Dean of Library Studies at that university and also the editor of a volume of articles on Tolkien and music, while its editorial board includes such well-known Tolkien scholars as Douglas Anderson and Dimitra Fimi. Crucial for assurance of academic quality which puts it on the same level as *Tolkien Studies* is its claim that articles are peer-reviewed. However, Volume 3 has included some which are differentiated as conference papers, which rather calls the policy into question, even though the authors concerned are respected Tolkien scholars.

The articles are published individually as they are peer-reviewed and accepted, but bundled annually into volumes for ease of reference. The current one, Volume 3, is divided into three issues, which no doubt reflects the increasing number of articles and book reviews being submitted. This method of publication is quick and convenient, but it has the disadvantage that it lacks the copy-editing facilities of a conventional publisher, so that each contributor bears the responsibility for his or her own proofreading. As a result there is some inconsistency in the format of citations, and in the sigla used to refer to works by Tolkien (it would be to everyone's advantage if the usage could conform to that of *Tolkien Studies*), while some typographical errors and mis-spellings have been allowed to remain. For example, the first article in Volume 1 twice mis-spells *precede* as *preceede*, and makes mistakes in names, turning Thomas Honegger into *Honneger*, Bryn Dunsire into *Brian*, and Laodameia (the form used in the article cited, although the Latin *Laodamia* would also be correct) into *Laodemia*. However, the flexibility of online publishing means that such errors can be corrected retrospectively, so it may be that by the time this review appears, there is no longer anything to quibble about.

The second article in Volume 1 shows up a weakness that is less easy to put right. Quite apart from the fact that the wording seems to suggest that an article from 1966 quotes words that Tolkien wrote in 1972, the author also claims that according to Tom Shippey Tolkien showed "disapproval of etymological reconstruction for its own sake (even when the reconstruction is valid)". Needless to say, Shippey did not say that, nor is it likely that Tolkien, who had worked as a lexicographer, would have held such a view. The whole point is that Tolkien might have been worried that philology, in which he believed strongly, had become bogged down with minutiae. Such relatively minor points are unlikely to be commented on in a peer review, which has to decide whether the article overall is suitable for publication, but they might be queried by a vigilant editor, which would make for stronger and more convincing arguments. However, in return for the speed of online publishing, authors must be prepared to take the flak themselves.

There is no need here to introduce and comment on each of the articles as there would be in the case of a printed volume, since it costs no money and little time to skim through the abstracts of the 17 articles currently available at. However, it is worth mentioning that Volume 3, Issue 3 is a special issue with guest editors, devoted to "Authorizing Tolkien: Control, Adaptation, and Dissemination of J.R.R. Tolkien's Works". In line with the journal's Aims and Scope mentioned above, the four articles, together with an introduction to the concepts by the guest editors, examine issues in the reception of Tolkien's works and their use as material for further, sub-sub-creation.

The word "authorizing" is used in an unusual sense, not connected with the legal powers of the holders of the copyright and the film rights to grant or withhold permission, which is a hurdle that Tolkien scholars may well encounter, but signifying the groups of people, whether critics or various groups of fans (devoted to books, films, games, etc.), who take it upon themselves to voice opinions and exert influence over what they consider it legitimate to do with his works. "'Tolkien' the cultural phenomenon is far bigger than J.R.R.

Tolkien the author, or even J.R.R. Tolkien the author-and-*oeuvre*", *claims one of the authors.* Anyone who can stomach the reduction of Tolkien to 'Tolkien' is recommended to take a look at these articles.

Overall, then, this is a new departure to be welcomed. An ongoing project of this kind will inevitably have teething problems, and no doubt some of the niggles I have mentioned will already have been taken in hand. Another possible improvement would be the provision of page numbers on the discrete pages for ease of reference. Watch this space!

Allan Turner

Our Authors

Annie Birks, Ph.D., teaches English language, literature and translation at the Université Catholique de l'Ouest, Angers, France. Her long-lasting interest in J.R.R. Tolkien and C.S. Lewis, together with her doctorate on *La Rétribution dans l'oeuvre de J.R.R. Tolkien* (Université Paris-Sorbonne), have led to articles and lectures on these two authors.   annie.birks@uco.fr

Tobias Escher, M.A. studied Musicology and British Studies at the University of Mainz/Germany and is currently working on his Dissertation about world-building through music in adaptations of J.R.R. Tolkien's works. He holds a diploma in Music for the Media and Cinematic Orchestration as well as a C-Degree in Church Music. He works as a composer, organist and choir conductor, runs a consulting service for media composers and works as a QA Lead, translator and technical writer for music software. He is a member of the German Tolkien Society and has spoken at conferences about Music in Tolkien's works.
www. middle-earth-music.info

Thomas Fornet-Ponse, Dr. theol. Dr. phil., studied Catholic Theology, Philosophy, and Ancient History at Bonn and Jerusalem. He received his PhD in Fundamental Theology and Ecumenics from the University of Salzburg and his PhD in Philosophy from the University of Bonn. He was a committee member of the German Tolkien Society and has been charged with conceptually coordinating the DTG Tolkien Seminars as well as *Hither Shore*.
thomas.fornet-ponse@tolkiengesellschaft.de

David A. Graziano received his first state exam accreditation for studying German and English Philology for a federal grammar school teaching position at the University of Saarland and at the University of California, San Diego. He received his second state exam accreditation at the teacher training college in Aachen. His research work covered the subject of "The Evolution Of World Building In Contemporary Fantasy Fiction." At present, he teaches the subjects of English and German at the Leibniz-Gymnasium in Pirmasens.
mail.davidgraziano@gmail.com

Wilhelm Kuehs, Mag. Dr., studied German Philology and General and Comparative Literature in Klagenfurt. He works as lecturer at the Institut für Kulturanalyse at the AAU Klagenfurt. He has written several novels and non-fictional books.   w.kuehs@gmx.at

Jonathan Nauman, Secretary of the Vaughan Association (USA), often visits England and Wales to read papers on seventeenth-century poetry. His chapter on "'The truth and light of things': Henry Vaughan and Nature" recently appeared in *Henry Vaughan and the Usk Valley* (Hereford: Logaston Press, 2016).

jonnauman@hotmail.com

Łukasz Neubauer, Dr. phil., studied English Philology at the Nicolaus Copernicus University in Toruń (Poland) and Scandinavian Literature at the University of Bergen (Norway). He received his PhD in English Philology from the University of Łódź (Poland). He is a member of the British branch of the International Arthurian Society and a conceptual coordinator of the annual Medieval Fantasy Symposium in Unieście (Poland).   lukasz_neubauer@poczta.onet.pl

Helmut W. Pesch, Dr. phil., studied English Philology, History of Art and Classical Archaeology in Cologne and Glasgow/UK. His doctoral dissertation, published in 1981, was the first scholarly study of fantasy as a literary genre in Germany. After several years as a research associate in English Language Didactics at Cologne University, and more than three decades as a full-time editor and editorial director with a major German publisher, he is now in retirement. He is also known as an author and translator—including works by and about J.R.R. Tolkien—and an expert on Tolkien's invented languages. He lives in Cologne.   mail@helmutwpesch.de

Patrick Schmitz studied English and History at RWTH Aachen University. After working in Cologne and Aachen, he currently works as a teacher at a school in Nideggen. He is a member of the German Tolkien Society and has given presentations on topics such as violence in fantasy literature. His current area of work is focused on literary world-building.

patrick.schmitz1@rwth-aachen.de

Ross Smith is the author of *Inside Language: Linguistic and Aesthetic Theory in Tolkien* (Walking Tree Publishers 2011). His articles on J.R.R. Tolkien's ideas about phonosemantics are acknowledged as a landmark in the field and he has also published extensively on World English, translation theory and machine translation.   rosstranslations@gmail.com

Friedhelm Schneidewind studied Biology and some terms Computer Science. He is currently working as a free-lance teacher especially for media design and in commercial and economical subjects, as journalist, editor, publisher, musician, and as author of several lexicons and several books on mythology, fantastic literature and Tolkien.   www.friedhelm-schneidewind.de

Allan Turner, Ph.D., was until recently Lecturer in English at the Friedrich-Schiller-Universität, Jena. He now lives in retirement in north-eastern England, trying to find his way in a post-Brexit world. His main interests within Tolkien studies lie in the fields of stylistics and translation.

allangturner@aol.com

Unsere Autorinnen & Autoren

Annie Birks unterrichtet Englische Sprache, Literatur und Übersetzung an der Université Catholique de l'Ouest, Angers (Frankreich). Ihr lang anhaltendes Interesse an J.R.R. Tolkien und C.S. Lewis führte mit ihrer Dissertation *Vergeltung in den Werken J.R.R. Tolkiens* (Universität Paris-Sorbonne) zu Vorträgen und Aufsätzen über beide Autoren.   annie.birks@uco.fr

Tobias Escher, M.A., studierte Musikwissenschaft und Britisches Englisch an der Johannes-Gutenberg-Universität Mainz und arbeitet derzeit an seiner Dissertation *Welten-Erschaffung durch Musik in Adaptionen von J.R.R. Tolkiens Werken*. Er hält ein Diploma in Music for the Media und Cinematic Orchestration und ist C-Kirchenmusiker. Er arbeitet u.a. als Komponist, Organist und Chorleiter, als Consultant für Medienkomponisten sowie als Übersetzer und technischer Autor für Musiksoftware-Unternehmen. Er ist Mitglied der Deutschen Tolkien Gesellschaft und spricht auf Konferenzen über Musik in Tolkiens Werken.
                                                www.middle-earth-music.info

Thomas Fornet-Ponse, Dr. theol. Dr. phil., studierte Katholische Theologie, Philosophie und Alte Geschichte in Bonn und Jerusalem. Er wurde in Fundamentaltheologie und Ökumenischer Theologie in Salzburg und in Philosopie in Bonn promoviert. Er war Vorstandsmitglied der Deutschen Tolkien Gesellschaft und ist der inhaltliche Koordinater der Tolkien Seminare wie von *Hither Shore*.
                                thomas.fornet-ponse@tolkiengesellschaft.de

David A. Graziano studierte im Rahmen des ersten Staatsexamens für das gymnasiale Lehramt Anglistik sowie Germanistik in Saarbrücken und an der University of California, San Diego. Das zweite Staatsexamen erhielt er am Studienseminar Aachen. Seine Examensarbeit trägt den Titel *The Evolution Of World Building In Contemporary Fantasy Fiction*. Derzeit unterrichtet er am Leibniz-Gymnasium Pirmasens die Fächer Deutsch und Englisch.
                                        mail.davidgraziano@gmail.com

Wilhelm Kuehs, Mag. Dr., hat Germanistik und Komparatistik in Klagenfurt studiert. Derzeit arbeitet er als Lehrbeauftragter am Institut für Kulturanalyse an der AAU Klagenfurt. Autor mehrerer Romane und Sachbücher. Zuletzt: *Mythenweber – Mythos und soziales Handeln*, Springer, Wiesbaden, 2015: *Der* *letzte Rock hat keine Taschen*, Krimi, Haymon, Innsbruck/Wien 2015; *Wer zuletzt lacht*, Krimi, Haymon, Innsbruck/Wien 2015.   w.kuehs@gmx.at

Jonathan Nauman, PhD, wurde von der Duke University promoviert und veröffentliche über den York Zyklus der Mysterienspiele, Macbeth, T.S. Eliot und W.B. Yeats sowie besonders über die metaphysischen Dichter George Herbert und Henry Vaughan. Er lebt in Beverly, Massachusetts, und arbeitet als Ingenieur.

jonnauman@hotmail.com

Łukasz Neubauer, Dr. phil., studierte Englische Philologie an der Nikolaus-Kopernikus-Universität in Toruń (Polen) und Skandinavische Literatur an der Universität Bergen (Norwegen). Er wurde in Englischer Philologie von der Universität Łódź (Polen) promoviert und ist Mitglied des britischen Zweigs der International Arthurian Society sowie Koordinator des jährlichen Symposiums mittelalterliche Fantasy in Unieście (Polen).

lukasz_neubauer@poczta.onet.pl

Helmut W. Pesch, Dr. phil., studierte Anglistik, Kunstgeschichte und klassische Archäologie in Köln und Glasgow/UK. Promotion 1981 mit der ersten deutschsprachigen Dissertation über Fantasy als literarisches Genre. Nach einer Tätigkeit als wissenschaftlicher Mitarbeiter an der Universität Köln und über dreißig Jahren als Redakteur, Lektor und Programmleiter bei *Bastei Lübbe* ist er heute im Ruhestand. Zu seinen Werken zählen mehrere Fantasy-Romane sowie *Das große Elbisch-Buch*; außerdem hat er Bücher von und über J.R.R. Tolkien und zahlreiche Romane übersetzt. Er lebt in Köln.

mail@helmutwpesch.de

Patrick Schmitz studierte Anglistik und Geschichte an der Rheinisch-Westfälischen Technischen Hochschule in Aachen. Nach Stationen in Köln und Aachen arbeitet er derzeit als Lehrer an einer Schule in Nideggen. Er ist Mitglied der Deutschen Tolkien Gesellschaft. Sein derzeitiger Forschungsbereich betrifft literarische Weltenschöpfungen in der Fantasyliteratur.

patrick.schmitz1@rwth-aachen.de

Friedhelm Schneidewind studierte Biologie und einige Semester Informatik. Er ist tätig als freier Dozent im Medien- und kaufmännisch-betriebswirtschaftlichen Bereich, als Autor, u.a. mehrerer Lexika und Sachbücher zu Mythologie, zur phantastischen Literatur und zu Tolkien, als Journalist, Herausgeber, Verleger und Musiker. 2016 erschien von ihm *Das neue große Tolkien-Lexikon*.

www.friedhelm-schneidewind.de

Ross Smith ist der Autor von *Inside Language: Linguistic and Aesthetic Theory in Tolkien* (2011, *Walking Tree Publishers*). Seine Artikel über J.R.R. Tolkiens Ideen über Phonosemantik sind anerkannte Meilensteine in diesem Forschungsfeld. Darüber hinaus hat er zahlreiche Publikationen über Weltenglisch, Übersetzungstheorie und maschinelle Übersetzung vorzuweisen.

rosstranslations@gmail.com

Allan Turner, PhD, ist kürzlich von seinen Tätigkeiten als Dozent in Englischer Sprache, zuletzt an der Friedrich-Schiller-Universität Jena, in den Ruhestand gewechselt und hofft, mehr Zeit für seine Forschung in Übersetzungsstudien und Stil, insbesondere mit Bezug zu Tolkien, zu finden.

allangturner@aol.com

Siglenverzeichnis

D ie Schriften von J.R.R. Tolkien werden im Text jeweils ohne Angabe des Verfassernamens mit den folgenden Siglen zitiert. Die jeweils benutzte Ausgabe findet sich im Literaturverzeichnis.

AI:	The Lay of Aotrou and Itroun
ATB:	The Adventures of Tom Bombadil and other Verses from the Red Book / Die Abenteuer des Tom Bombadil und andere Gedichte aus dem Roten Buch
AW:	Ancrene Wisse and Hali Meiðhad
B:	Die Briefe von J.R.R. Tolkien
BA:	Bilbos Abschiedslied
BB:	Baum und Blatt
BGH:	Bauer Giles von Ham
BL:	Beren and Lúthien / Beren und Lúthien
BLS:	Bilbo's Last Song
BMC:	Beowulf: The Monster and the Critics
BT:	Blatt von Tüftler
BUK:	Beowulf: Die Ungeheuer und ihre Kritiker
BW:	Die Briefe vom Weihnachtsmann
CH:	The Children of Húrin
CP:	Chaucer as a Philologist
EA:	The End of the Third Age (History of Middle-earth 9). Auszug
EW:	English and Welsh / Englisch und Walisisch
FA:	The Fall of Arthur
FC:	Letters from Father Christmas
FGH:	Farmer Giles of Ham
FH:	Finn and Hengest
FS:	On Fairy-stories
GD:	Gute Drachen sind rar
GN:	Guide to the Names in the Lord of the Rings
GPO:	Sir Gawain and the Green Knight, Pearl, and Sir Orfeo
H:	The Hobbit / Der Hobbit / Der kleine Hobbit
HB:	The Homecoming of Beorhtnoth Beorhthelm's Son
HdR:	Der Herr der Ringe
HdR I:	Der Herr der Ringe. Bd. 1. Die Gefährten
HdR II:	Der Herr der Ringe. Bd. 2. Die Zwei Türme
HdR III:	Der Herr der Ringe. Bd. 3. Die Rückkehr des Königs / Die Wiederkehr des Königs
HdR A:	Der Herr der Ringe. Anhänge
HG:	Herr Glück
HH I/II:	The History of the Hobbit
HL:	Ein heimliches Laster
KH:	Die Kinder Húrins
L:	The Letters of J.R.R. Tolkien
LB:	The Lays of Beleriand (History of Middle-earth 3)

LN:	Leaf by Niggle
LotR:	The Lord of the Rings
LotR I:	The Fellowship of the Ring. Being the first part of The Lord of the Rings
LotR II:	The Two Towers. Being the second part of The Lord of the Rings
LotR III:	The Return of the King. Being the third part of The Lord of the Rings
LotR A:	The Lord of the Rings. Appendices
LR:	The Lost Road and other Writings (History of Middle-earth 5)
LSG:	The Legend of Sigurd and Gudrún
LT 1:	The Book of Lost Tales 1 (History of Middle-earth 1)
LT 2:	The Book of Lost Tales 2 (History of Middle-earth 2)
MB:	Mr. Bliss
MC:	The Monsters and the Critics and Other Essays
ME:	A Middle English Vocabulary
MR:	Morgoth's Ring (History of Middle-earth 10)
My:	Mythopoeia
NM:	Nachrichten aus Mittelerde
OE:	The Old English Exodus
OK:	Ósanwe-Kenta
P:	Pictures by J.R.R. Tolkien
PM:	The Peoples of Middle-earth (History of Middle-earth 12)
R:	Roverandom
RBG:	The Rivers and Beacon-hills of Gondor
RGEO:	The Road Goes Ever On (with Donald Swann)
RS:	The Return of the Shadow (History of Middle-earth 6)
S:	Silmarillion
SD:	The Sauron Defeated (History of Middle-earth 9)
SG:	Der Schmied von Großholzingen
SGG:	Sir Gawain and the Green Knight / Sir Gawain und der Grüne Ritter (Essay)
SK:	The Story of Kullervo
SM:	The Shaping of Middle-earth (History of Middle-earth 4)
SP:	Songs for the Philologists
SV:	A Secret Vice
SWM:	Smith of Wootton Major
SWME:	Smith of Wootton Major Essay
TB:	On Translating Beowulf
TI:	The Treason of Isengard (History of Middle-earth 7)
TL:	Tree and Leaf
ÜB:	Zur Übersetzung des Beowulf
ÜM:	Über Märchen
UK:	Die Ungeheuer und ihre Kritiker. Gesammelte Aufsätze
UT:	Unfinished Tales
VA:	Valedictory Address
VG 1:	Das Buch der Verschollenen Geschichten 1
VG 2:	Das Buch der Verschollenen Geschichten 2
WJ:	The War of the Jewels (History of Middle-earth 11)
WR:	The War of the Ring (History of Middle-earth 8)

Index